Issues in teaching numeracy in primary schools

Second edition

Edited by
Ian Thompson

Open University Press

Open University Press
McGraw-Hill Education
McGraw-Hill House
Shoppenhangers Road
Maidenhead
Berkshire
England
SL6 2QL

email: enquiries@openup.co.uk
world wide web: www.openup.co.uk

and Two Penn Plaza, New York, NY 10121-2289, USA

First edition published 1999

Reprinted 2011

A catalogue record of this book is available from the British Library

ISBN-13: 978-0-33-524153-8 (pb)
ISBN-10: 0335241530 (pb)

Library of Congress Cataloging-in-Publication Data
CIP data applied for

Typeset by RefineCatch Limited, Bungay, Suffolk
Printed in the UK by CPI Antony Rowe, Chippenham and Eastbourne

Fictitious names of companies, products, people, characters and/or data that may be used herein (in case studies or in examples) are not intended to represent any real individual, company, product or event.

The **McGraw·Hill** Companies

Contents

To my wife, Barbara, and our two children, John and Anna, my mathematical guinea pigs.

Notes on contributors

Mike Askew is Professor of Mathematics Education, King's College London and is widely regarded as one of the country's leading experts on primary mathematics education. Mike has directed many research projects including the influential 'Effective Teachers of Numeracy in Primary Schools' (Teacher Training Agency), 'Raising Attainment in Numeracy' and 'Mental Calculations: Interpretations and Implementation' (both funded by the Nuffield Foundation). He was deputy director of the five-year Leverhulme Numeracy Research Programme that examined teaching, learning and progression in number from age 5 to age 11. The findings from these and other research have influenced policy both in England and abroad.

Patrick Barmby is a lecturer in mathematics education at Durham University. His main research interests are the notion of mathematical understanding, both for children and for teachers, and the use of representations of mathematical concepts in the classroom. Prior to working in Durham, Patrick was working in a rural secondary school in Kenya, teaching mathematics, physics and chemistry. It was there that his interest in educational research was stimulated, trying to find out about the difficulties that his students were having with mathematics and science subjects.

Meindert Beishuizen was a senior lecturer in the Department of Education at Leiden University. After his studies in psychology he worked on instructional technology in the Netherlands Navy, where he did his PhD research. After his move to Leiden, the cognitive shift in psychology changed his interest towards the study of learning processes. Research into mental arithmetic strategies brought him into contact with the Freudenthal Institute. In cooperation with Adri Treffers a study on the empty number line was carried out in ten Dutch second grade classrooms. In England he stayed as a visiting scholar at Homerton College, Cambridge. Later he was involved with Laurie Rousham in the Suffolk 2003–07 Empty Number Line publication for Years 1, 2 and 3 in English schools. Unfortunately, Meindert died in December 2009 shortly before the publication of this book.

Margaret Brown is Professor of Mathematics Education at King's College London. After teaching in primary and secondary schools and teacher training, Margaret directed over 25 research projects in the teaching, learning and assessment of mathematics, including the Leverhulme Numeracy Research Programme. These have concerned all age groups. She was a member of the Numeracy Task Force, and has also been Chair of the Joint Mathematical Council of the UK, President of the Mathematical Association, President of the British Educational Research Association and a member of the Advisory Committee on Mathematics Education.

Kev Delaney worked in 'normal' primary schools for five years before joining John Dichmont at Lynncroft Primary School in Nottingham. Here, under John's inspired guidance, he discovered what working with primary age children could really be like when a creative and thoughtful staff dared each other to do useful and interesting things. In 1986 he joined Nottingham Trent University, where he has coordinated and taught on various primary mathematics courses. From 1990 until 1998 he co-edited *Strategies: Maths and Problem Solving 3–13*. He is excited by Islamic patterns and his own and other people's 'Aha!' moments during the teaching and learning of mathematics.

Nick Dowrick is the Head of Every Child Counts Programmes at Edge Hill University and leads the Numbers Count intervention and the professional development programmes that are provided for Teacher Leaders and Numbers Count Teachers. He has taught in nursery and primary schools and was previously the Head of Primary and Early Years Education at Edge Hill University.

Sylvia Dunn is the Professional Development Coordinator for Every Child Counts at Edge Hill University and leads the MA programme studied by all Every Child Counts Teacher Leaders as part of their training. She has taught in both primary and secondary schools and has been working in the Faculty of Education at Edge Hill University for more than 20 years.

Richard English taught in Hull schools before spending three years as a mathematics advisory teacher for Humberside. For the past 17 years he has been involved with primary initial teacher training programmes at the University of Hull and has responsibility for both mathematics and information and communication technology (ICT). He has written a number of mathematics books aimed at primary teachers and has also done some consultancy work for the National Strategies.

Sue Gifford is a Principal Lecturer in mathematics education at Roehampton University, where she works with Postgraduate Certificate of Education (PGCE) students and teachers involved in action research in primary mathematics. Previously she taught in London primary schools and worked as an Inner London Education Authority (ILEA) mathematics consultant. Her research and publications have focused on children's own recording and early years mathematics and she was a founder of the Association of Teachers of Mathematics (ATM) Early Childhood Mathematics Group. Publications include *Mathematics in Primary Schools: A Sense of Progression* (third edition with C. Hopkins and S. Pepperell, London: Fulton), *Teaching Mathematics 3–5* (Open University Press) and a report on dyscalculia for the Qualifications and Curriculum Authority (QCA). Recent research interests include dyscalculia and the prevention of mathematics difficulties.

Tony Harries is a senior lecturer in Mathematics Education at Durham University. He has worked in the primary and secondary sectors of the education system both here and abroad. Following a period of time as Head of Mathematics at a Bristol comprehensive school and at Bath Spa University, he joined the School of Education, Durham, in 1999. His particular interest is in the way in which mathematical ideas can be represented and the way in which the learner moves between different representations of the same idea in order to solve problems.

Steve Higgins is Professor of Education at Durham University. His research interests are in the areas of effective teaching and learning with a particular focus on mathematics in primary schools and the use of information and communication technologies in the classroom. As a former primary teacher he is interested in the pragmatic application of research knowledge in classrooms and the work of John Dewey and C.S. Peirce.

Jeremy Hodgen is Senior Lecturer in Mathematics Education at King's College London. He previously taught mathematics in primary and secondary schools in London. His research interests include mathematics teaching and learning, assessment and teacher education. He is currently directing the Economic and Social Research Council (ESRC)-funded study Improving Competence and Confidence in Algebra and Multiplicative Structures (ICCAMS) which is investigating how teachers can implement classroom assessment in mathematics.

Louise Matthews is a National Trainer for Every Child Counts at Edge Hill University and has been involved in the development of the Numbers Count programme and the professional development of teachers and teacher leaders. She also works as a School Improvement Partner and has 20 years' experience in primary education.

Frank Monaghan is a Senior Lecturer in the Faculty of Education and Language Studies at the Open University (OU) and Vice-Chair of NALDIC, the UK's professional association for those working with learners of English as an additional language. Before joining the OU he spent 20 years teaching in a large, multilingual comprehensive school in London. He was a member of the

Thinking Together research group led by Neil Mercer, and his research and publications focus on the role of language in the teaching and learning of mathematics in school.

Mike Ollerton. As a child who 'failed' the 11+ because I was too frightened to 'turn over to the next page' I have some insights into how children fail. As a young teacher in the early 1970s I was inspired by a head of department, Eric Love, who encouraged me to use investigative, problem-solving approaches to enable those I taught to have greater opportunities to 'shine'. Forty years on, as an 'old lag', I am driven, pedagogically speaking, by the exact same educational principles that problem solving supports: access to knowledge, differentiation by outcome and enabling learners' greater opportunities to enjoy learning the most complex and abstract of disciplines.

Julie Ryan is a teacher, lecturer and education researcher. She has worked in schools and universities in Australia and England and is now a senior lecturer in mathematics education at Manchester Metropolitan University. Her current research interests include discussion in the mathematics classroom, teacher subject knowledge, teacher education and mathematical identity.

Ian Thompson taught for 19 years before moving into teacher education. During his time working on secondary and primary PGCE courses at Newcastle University he began researching children's mental and written calculation strategies and their understanding of place value. He has edited two other books for Open University Press: *Enriching Primary Mathematics Teaching* (2003) and *Teaching and Learning Early Number*, second edition (2008). He was seconded to the National Numeracy Strategy for two years as a Regional Director for Initial Teacher Training, and in 2002 became an independent mathematics consultant and researcher. He is currently Visiting Professor at Northumbria University and at Edge Hill University.

John Threlfall is the Senior Lecturer in Primary Mathematics Education at the School of Education, University of Leeds. He teaches on PGCE and Masters courses in primary mathematics and on assessment. As a member of the Assessment and Evaluation Unit within the school, John was a writer of items for the World Class Tests in mathematics, and contributed to the development of the related Maths Insight resources for gifted and talented pupils, published by the QCA and NFER Nelson.

Julian Williams is Professor of Mathematics Education and Director of postgraduate research studies at the University of Manchester. After a career in mathematics teaching, he spent a decade in curriculum development and mathematics teacher education, and then another decade in teaching about research, research design and methodology for Masters and Doctoral students. His current interests span sociocultural and cultural-historical activity theory, educational measurement, and mathematics education.

Jan Winter is a senior lecturer at the University of Bristol where she coordinates the secondary mathematics PGCE programme and works with pre-service and in-service teachers. Her research interests include assessment of mathematics and the professional development of teachers. She was a member of the team of researchers working on the Home School Knowledge Exchange project, funded by the ESRC. She has published many articles in professional journals for mathematics teachers, and co-authored a book: *Assessment: What's in It for Schools?* Most recently she co-authored *Improving Primary Mathematics – Linking Home and School*, which reports on the project and its findings.

Editor's preface

The 16 chapters included in the first edition of this edited collection were written in 1998 – a year before the introduction of the National Numeracy Strategy (see Brown, Chapter 1). The book was, to a certain extent, a sequel to the first edition of *Teaching and Learning Early Number* (Open University Press 1997), which looked at research findings concerning children's early number acquisition and the implications of these findings for classroom practice.

The original aim of the first edition of this book, *Issues in Teaching Numeracy in Primary Schools*, was to address the many issues, government publications and research findings that had influenced the development of the National Numeracy Strategy (NNS). Because of the rapid developments that have taken place in mathematics education since the first edition was written, only four of the original chapters have been retained and updated, with a further 14 new, more relevant chapters added.

The planning of this second edition has involved several interesting decisions: one concerning the title of the book and the other regarding the structure of the various sections. Initially the title was to be changed to *Issues in Teaching Mathematics in Primary School*, given the argument that primary school children are taught more than what is accepted as being included in the word 'numeracy', and also because some of the chapters focus slightly more widely than just on numeracy. However, it was felt that changing the title might suggest that specific chapters on shape and space, measures and handling data had been included – which is not the case.

Given the fact that the important and influential Williams Review was published at the time the various chapters were being written for this edition, it was inevitable that one of the sections of the book would focus on issues emerging from this review. As all 18 chapters in the book have some connection with the issues raised in the report, in that they are concerned with the teaching and learning of mathematics in – and out of – primary school, deciding what to place where in the book was not straightforward. For example, one of the ten recommendations of the Williams Review is that there should be a renewed focus on mental mathematics, and yet it was decided to include the chapter on mental calculation along with four others concerned with calculation. Similarly, although the Every Child Counts initiative has a chapter to itself in the Williams Review, it was decided to include the chapter on the new numeracy intervention, Numbers Count – the outcome of the Every

Child Counts team's research and Williams's recommendations – in a short section dealing with special needs issues.

The result is that this second edition is loosely structured into five sections: an historical overview followed by issues relating to the Williams Review, assessment, calculation and special needs. Many chapters contain cross-references to other parts of the book where particular ideas are dealt with differently or in more detail. Each chapter, however, is self-contained, and is written to be read as a free-standing unit.

The information in the table gives details of the ages of children starting school in England and in the Netherlands. The information is included to help readers check the ages of children referred to by the contributors to this book.

School year England	The Netherlands	Age on entry
Early Years Foundation Stage		Birth to end of Reception
Reception	Groep 1	4
Year 1 (Yl)	Groep 2	5
Year 2 (Y2)	Groep 3	6
Year 3 (Y3)	Groep 4	7
Year 4 (Y4)	Groep 5	8
Year 5 (Y5)	Groep 6	9
Year 6 (Y6)	Groep 7	10

SECTION 1
Setting the context

The late 1980s and the whole of the 1990s proved to be a period of substantial change in the teaching of mathematics, culminating in the launch of the National Numeracy Strategy and the adoption by primary schools of the 'daily mathematics lesson' in 1999. As a key participant in very many of the developments that took place in the teaching of numeracy during this time, and afterwards, Margaret Brown gives a detailed historical overview of these and earlier developments in relation to the prevailing social and political contexts and the key people involved. In the initial chapter of the book she provides the necessary background to enable the reader to make sense of the current situation.

She provides a detailed analysis of the background to, and implementation of, the National Numeracy Project (NNP) and its development into the National Numeracy Strategy (NNS), discussing the role of international comparisons in stimulating developments; the in-service training that was provided by the NNS; and the effects that this training had on teachers, schools and children. She discusses some of the findings of the Leverhulme Project – of which she was a principal researcher – specifically in relation to those children that were expected to gain from the NNS and those who, in fact, did gain.

She suggests reasons why a new framework was produced in 2006 by the Primary National Strategy, and asks why, despite the fact that it was a more complex web-based resource, less training for its introduction was provided for teachers. Her chapter finishes with a brief discussion of the Rose and Alexander reports.

1 Swings and roundabouts

Margaret Brown

Introduction

Ever since the practical use of numbers and number operations has been part of the curriculum for a significant proportion of the population in England, there has been a tension between accurate use of calculating procedures and the possession of the number sense which underlies the ability to apply such procedures sensibly. These two positions can be broadly characterized as *procedural* and *conceptual*, respectively.

Alongside this has been a different type of tension between individualistic *progressive* philosophies emphasizing the importance of autonomy of both pupils and teachers in order to lead to personal development and empowerment, and *public education* philosophies emphasizing a greater degree of state intervention in the curriculum and in teaching methods in order both to protect the equal entitlement of pupils and to meet the skilled person power requirements of the state (Ernest 1991).

Over the years the pendulum has swung back and forth in both of these dimensions as the primary mathematics roundabout has turned, depending on both the social and economic contexts. In prosperous times progressive and conceptual approaches have had the edge, whereas high unemployment and internationally uncompetitive industries have tended to fix the state's attention on public education and the uniform teaching of procedural number skills. The political context has been important since it determined whose were the most powerful voices.

As with the inescapable tensions between the fundamental notions of cultural norms and individual rationality, and of freedom and equality, which respectively underlie the two dimensions, it is probably both proper and necessary that the emphases should shift from time to time to adapt to prevailing philosophies or circumstances.

In the sections which follow, these swings will be described, together with the people who have supported them. There is, however, one constant theme, which is that of poor standards in number skills. By quoting hand-wringing sentiments spanning over 100 years, McIntosh (1981) demonstrated that there has never been a time when those who speak for the nation have been satisfied with the level of what is now generally known as 'numeracy' achieved by primary children. This has always provided a reason for yet another swing of the pendulum.

Pre-1950: the rise and fall of the first national curriculum

In the first half of the nineteenth century, the state had taken a relatively laissez-faire attitude to education, looking on while different private and charitable systems developed. However, by the end of the century concern over both increasing international industrial competition and the threats of insurrection among the uncivilized poor drove the state into action. The Newcastle Commission, set up to enquire into primary education in 1858, found that the majority of the pupils who did attend elementary schools were taught no arithmetic at all, and even when taught, the provision was judged to be generally ineffective.

This report formed the basis for state intervention to ensure in the 1870 Act each child's entitlement to primary education, following a national curriculum introduced in the Revised Code of 1862, concentrating on the three Rs of reading, (w)riting and 'rithmetic.

In the original version the curriculum for the first three standards (intended respectively for pupils aged 7–8, 8–10 and 10+) stated:

> Standard I   Form on blackboard or slate, from dictation, figures up to 20; name at sight figures up to 20; add and subtract figures up to 10, orally, from examples on blackboard.
>
> Standard II   A sum in simple addition or subtraction, and the multiplication table.
>
> Standard III   A sum in any simple rule as far as short division.

This looks not unfamiliar, in relation to Levels 1 to 4 of the national curriculum introduced over 100 years later, and most primary teachers still refer to these objectives as the major targets for their own pupils.

As with the more recent 1988 national curriculum, it is interesting to note that there were two major changes made to the Revised Code within the first ten years, with the aim of raising standards. As with levels in the 1989 curriculum, the standards were not necessarily tied to age, recognizing that children progressed at different rates. The difference then was that each class was focused on and identified with one standard, so that classes were of mixed age; slower children remained in the same class (for example, Standard II) until they had achieved that standard.

However, there were some authoritative sources even in the 1850s which considered that some form of number sense was at least as important as mechanical arithmetic. Thomas Tate, a mathematician and educationist, advised:

> Teachers of elementary schools . . . would confer a great benefit on society, by teaching the simple and fundamental principles of estimation, rather than waste the time of their pupils in giving sums . . . those investigations which have the greatest practical bearing invariably form the most healthful and instructive exercise to the intellectual powers.
>
> (Quoted in Howson 1982: 120)

He added that 'a good teacher will vary his methods of instruction', and attacked the blind unreasoning attachment to any particular system of teaching, believing that a teacher's judgement must be exercised in selecting those methods which are most suited to the existing conditions of his school.

Matthew Arnold, the most senior of Her Majesty's Inspectors (HMI), also took a progressive line denouncing this system. He wrote in his 1869–70 report that however brilliant the committee who drew up the curriculum, 'the teacher will in the end beat us by [getting] children through the examination without their really knowing of these matters'. He noted that although the children 'sedulously practised all the year round', the failure rate in arithmetic was considerable since the system gives 'a mechanical turn to the school teaching' and must be 'trying to the intellectual life of the school' (quoted in Howson 1982: 121).

For financial and educational reasons the Revised Code was abandoned in 1898, but in spite of the removal of curriculum constraints, it would appear that there was gradual evolution rather than radical change in the teaching of arithmetic in primary schools during the first half of the twentieth century (Pinner 1981). Generally, classes became smaller and teachers better trained, which led to more humane classrooms and less punishing arithmetic. Influences of continental thinkers such as Montessori and Froebel on teacher training colleges encouraged more practical activities to be introduced for younger children.

In primary education more generally, the 1931 Hadow Report foreshadowed the later Plowden Report in taking a firmly progressive line backing themes rather than subjects, recommending that: 'the curriculum of the primary school is to be thought of in terms of activity and experience rather than knowledge to be acquired and facts to be stored' (Board of Education 1931: 93). A broader curriculum in mathematics was recommended with more emphasis on geometric form and practical measurement. The fact that too much time is given to arithmetic was attributed to the influence of the examinations at 11+ which were then enabling increasing numbers of pupils from elementary schools to enter fee-paying grammar schools. Nevertheless a firmly traditional line was taken in relation to arithmetical skills: 'it is however essential that adequate drill be provided in arithmetic'. Moreover it was not reasonable 'to expect a child to justify the process he employs, say in subtraction or division; this is too hard an exercise of his reasoning powers'. The compromise was achieved by asserting that higher procedural arithmetic standards could be attained in less time, thus allowing the newer broader and more conceptual content.

1950–85: towards a progressive paradise (Piaget, Plowden, Nuffield and Cockcroft)

In 1955 the Mathematical Association finally produced the long-awaited report, *The Teaching of Mathematics in Primary Schools*, on which work had started 17 years earlier. The Second World War caused an interruption, but the greatest delay was because the new post-war committee changed the brief, since it 'did not share the belief of its predecessor that a curriculum should be drawn up prescribing the mathematics to be taught at each stage of the primary years'.

After disagreements had required yet more membership changes, the eventual report set a radical tone for the second half of the century. It adopted an unequivocal child-centred position which merged the Piagetian view of learning, as the result of an individual child's interaction with the physical environment, with the activity-oriented British primary tradition endorsed by the Hadow Report and to be further developed in the Plowden Report. A key member of the committee throughout was Elizabeth Williams, who, while at King's College London in the 1930s and later as lecturer and principal at other teacher training colleges, was instrumental in introducing Piagetian ideas (Howson 1982). Older teachers will know her best through the classic text *Primary Mathematics Today*, published in collaboration with Hilary Shuard (Williams and Shuard 1970).

The key belief of the 1955 report was that:

> Children developing at their own individual rates learn through their active response to the experiences which come to them; through constructive play, experiment and discussion children become aware of relationships and develop mental structures which are mathematical in form and are the only sound basis for mathematical techniques.
>
> (Mathematical Association 1955: v)

The broader curriculum recommended by Hadow was thus opened even wider, with no one admitting that this might allow less time for number skills. Teachers were required, through their own reading and listening to children, to come to understand better how children learn, in much the same way as children were expected to come to understand mathematical concepts.

It is, of course, a long way from writing a report to seeing it implemented throughout England, but there were many allies in this task. Support from teacher trainers was significant, but there were also meetings with teachers all over the country. An energetic and inspiring travelling HMI, Edith Biggs, ran courses on the activity and investigation approach over more than 20 years (estimated by the Plowden Report (CACE 1967) to have directly involved more than 15 per cent of teachers).

An even more Piagetian line was followed by the Nuffield Mathematics Teaching Project (1964–71), led by Geoffrey Matthews, who became the first Professor of Mathematics Education at Chelsea College, part of London University, which later merged into King's College. Using a *conceptual* progression based broadly on Piagetian research, a sequence of *Teachers Guides* were produced on a variety of mathematical topics, including, for the first time, logic, graphs leading to algebra, and probability. These explained the underlying mathematics with ideas for different approaches and activities, attractively illustrated with pupils' work. The approach reflected the more structural ideas of modern mathematics like sets, number bases and properties of number operations (for example, commutativity), to help form a conceptual basis for calculation.

There was much debate about whether the project should have produced a set of pupil textbooks, but the philosophy was to treat the teachers in the same way as it was hoped that they would treat pupils; as one of the Nuffield team said later, '*I do and I understand* was the unofficial motto of the Project; well, it applied to teachers as well as children'. Teachers were encouraged to work together in local groups in each authority. An important and enduring innovation of the Nuffield Project was the creation of mathematics teachers' centres where teachers could meet with advisers; many of these later became the first general purpose professional centres.

The end of the selection examinations at 11+ in most areas, following the change from selective to comprehensive schooling, provided additional freedom to enable teachers to work in new ways. There is no doubt that large numbers of teachers were inspired by the new approaches of Nuffield and Edith Biggs, but with considerable staff turnover it is not clear that there was a great deal of change in what most teachers did in their classrooms. This probably only really took place on a large scale after new pupil materials became available after 1970, the first scheme being written by Harold Fletcher, one of the Nuffield team. These published schemes, including eventually an official Nuffield scheme, permeated most schools. Translated to text, some of the practical and investigatory spirit was inevitably lost.

The major effects on classroom teaching of the various texts were a broadening of the curriculum and many activities attempting to build understanding through different diagrams and representations. This meant a much slower approach to calculation algorithms, with often a variety of different methods of recording calculations presented to children. Thus there was less time for practice, the belief being that better understanding avoided the need for constant mechanical drill.

Many teachers chose to stick closely to the books, and often to let children work through them on their own. There were several reasons for this. First, the lack of confidence of teachers in their own mathematics, and especially in modem mathematics, discouraged them from departing from well-written and apparently authoritative sets of texts with many attractive activities that pupils seemed to enjoy. There was also, especially following the 1967 Plowden Report, increasing emphasis on pupil autonomy; children were expected to be able to work on their own or in small groups and to organize themselves, with the teacher being seen as a resource to call upon rather than a classroom expositor.

However, a backlash against excessive freedom given to primary teachers and children gathered momentum during the 1970s. The well-publicized curricular anarchy at William Tyndale Junior School in London drew attention to the fact that with the demise of the 11+ there was no longer any control over what primary teachers taught. The Assessment of Performance Unit was launched in 1974 to monitor national standards at ages 11 and 15, and the idea of a common core curriculum began to be discussed. Certainly the texts like Nuffield which were published at the end of the 1970s tended to be less radical than those Fletcher and his colleagues published earlier.

Although there were occasional tirades against this 'new' mathematics in the primary schools, it was the perceived lack of numeracy of young employees, in a speech by Prime Minister James Callaghan at Ruskin College in 1976, which was used to justify a significant change in government policy towards exerting tighter control over the curriculum.

However, the Labour government was keen not to upset its allies in schools and local education authorities (LEAs), and started by asking LEAs to work with teachers to produce local curriculum guidelines. Mathematics advisers were appointed by LEAs which did not already have them, creating a national network for disseminating innovation. Advisers were able to draw on the expertise of a pool of teachers who had been appointed as mathematics coordinators in primary schools and had acquired a Diploma of the Mathematical Association, run mainly by teacher training colleges and universities. Guidelines were informed by the publication by DES/HMI of *Mathematics 5–11: A Handbook of Suggestions* (DES 1979); although progressive in tone, this detailed list of aims and objectives marked a much firmer line in steering the contents of the primary curriculum for the purposes of more uniform public education.

One of the final acts of the Labour government was to set up a Committee of Inquiry into the Teaching of Mathematics in Schools, chaired by Sir Wilfred Cockcroft, previously associated with the Nuffield Project. While the bulk of the report was aimed at secondary schools, the presence on the committee of Hilary Shuard, a forceful teacher trainer and Elizabeth Williams's collaborator, ensured that primary interests were not forgotten.

In fact it found much less concern from employers about standards of arithmetic than had been expected, but the surveys undertaken revealed an adult population which was fearful of mathematics, suffering from both lack of confidence and an inability to apply what they had been taught at school. In regard to primary mathematics, this tended to reassure the committee, whose membership was in any case mainly drawn from the progressive-minded leaders within the professional bodies, that the previous more formal styles of teaching were to blame. The more practical and investigative style which had long been recommended for, but not necessarily implemented by, primary schools would encourage confidence and self-expression, and the ability to understand, and hence apply, knowledge; it was this which should be supported and extended into secondary schools.

Thus the findings led the Cockcroft Report, *Mathematics Counts*, published in 1982, to endorse the wide curriculum: 'We believe that this broadening of the curriculum has had a beneficial effect both in improving children's attitudes to mathematics and also in laying the foundations of better under-standing' (DES 1982: 83). There was, however, a new utilitarian emphasis, removing some of the last vestiges of the more esoteric structural content brought in by the original Nuffield Project.

The report contained a whole section emphasizing the importance of mental mathematics, including:

> young children should not be allowed to move too quickly to written work in mathematics. It follows that, in the early stages, mental and oral work should form a major part of the mathematics which is done. As a child grows older, he needs to begin to develop the methods of mental calculation which he will use throughout his life.
>
> (DES 1982: 92)

Two aspects of contemporary research informed the recommendations: first that both children and adults tended to apply idiosyncratic methods of calculation rather than standard school methods; second, that there was a seven-year gap between ages when the higher- and lower-attaining children grasped a mathematical concept, even though they might be in the same class. This result led to an emphasis on curricular differentiation, later also stressed by inspectors, which encouraged schools to continue many of the progressive organizational practices which they were already using, either allowing pupils to work individually at their own pace through a scheme, or grouping children by attainment to do different work.

> Even though an individual learning system may be in use the teacher will often assemble a small group to begin a new topic or to draw together common strands in work which is going on. On such occasions mental mathematics is easily and naturally introduced, both in the form of mental calculation and of questions which develop new ideas . . .
>
> (DES 1982: 93)

Some whole-class teaching is recommended, but with an eye on the range of attainment:

> there are some skills, puzzles and problems which are appropriate for every child no matter what stage of learning he may have reached and short class sessions can be arranged for work of this kind . . . some problems should be posed with general discussion in mind. Both children and their teachers learn from different strategies and methods which other members of the class use . . . it is valuable experience for children to explain the approach which has been used . . .
>
> (DES 1982: 92)

In order to enable the Cockcroft recommendations to be put into effect in classrooms, advisory teachers (known as 'Cockcroft missionaries') were appointed by LEAs. Those appointed succeeded in enthusing other teachers about mathematical investigation in the same way as Edith Biggs had started to do 20 years earlier.

Hilary Shuard, emerging as the main champion of the progressive movement in primary mathematics, succeeded in 1985 in attracting funding for a major project, Primary Initiatives in Mathematics Education (PrIME). Although this had many foci, with groups of teachers working in different LEAs, the major innovation was in the Calculator Aware Number Curriculum Project (CAN). The basic principle of CAN was to put into effect the firm endorsement of sensible calculator use in primary schools made by the Cockcroft Report, and to fulfil the recommendation that research be undertaken to find how the use of calculators might change the primary mathematics curriculum. Children were given unrestricted access to calculators from the beginning, and there was a specific emphasis on mental calculation and investigational work with number. Teachers were asked not to teach pencil and paper algorithms at all.

The CAN project excited much national and international attention. Such results as are available suggest that pupils from the project developed better mental facility and more positive attitudes, and performed better even in non-calculator written tests. However, it is not clear whether the effect was due to the increased emphasis on mental calculation, the in-service support, the investigative ethos or the calculator use. But the full effect was never to be found as it came to an abrupt end in 1989, due to other changes which are reported in the next section.

It is clear that the changes which took place in primary mathematics between 1950 and 1985 were significant, marking a shift in attention from the teacher to the learner. They were led by a set of inspired individuals with broadly similar views, all with strong mathematical backgrounds and earlier experience of teaching in secondary schools, who occupied high-status roles in the educational establishment. It was clear that by the end of the period most teachers had come to espouse the principles underlying the changes, even if they had not always fully implemented the principles in their practice.

1985–95: the second national curriculum and the national tests

The primary mathematics results in the international surveys carried out in 1990 by the International Assessment of Educational Progress (IAEP) and in 1994 as part of the Third International Mathematics and Science Study (TIMSS) demonstrated that many of the Cockcroft objectives were achieved. British pupils were comparatively confident, unusually including those pupils whose attainments were modest, and they generally enjoyed mathematics. There was some evidence that many children seemed to enjoy the greater control they had over their own pace of work. More importantly, British pupils did very well in tests in applying mathematics to solve practical problems, in both mathematics and science. The successful implementation of a wide curriculum was demonstrated by the fact that, in 1994, English primary children were top of the international table in geometry and, in 1990, were second in statistics.

However, comparatively low English results in the number category in both surveys suggested that these successes had been achieved at a cost. Concern about such international comparisons in secondary schools in the mid-1980s coincided with a continuing movement under the post-1979 Conservative government following that initiated under James Callaghan towards clearer curriculum specification and greater central control. In the White Paper *Better Schools* (DES 1985a) came the first announcement of the intention to formulate both national objectives, to be known as attainment targets, for age 11 in mathematics, and an associated system of assessment. Formative assessment for diagnostic and planning purposes was espoused as a key aspect of assessment (see Hodgen and Askew, Chapter 10), but it was also pointed out that assessment results should also allow schools to evaluate their own practices against national standards.

The focus on targets and assessment at primary level reflected the national criteria for the new General Certificate of Secondary Education (GCSE) examinations which had been recently announced, to start in 1988. At primary level, also, many LEAs were already developing local assessment systems to match their new local curriculum guidelines, although these took a variety of forms ranging from written tests to practical tasks and included informal profiling. In many cases they were influenced by assessments developed by the Assessment of Performance Unit.

Related to the focus on clear targets to be found in *Better Schools*, a series of DES/HMI publications was being issued which contained objectives and assessment advice for each subject. *Mathematics from 5 to 16* (DES 1985b) was, at primary level, an amalgamation of the 1979 DES/HMI publication *Mathematics 5–11* with selected recommendations from the Cockcroft Report. Thus the 24 objectives were listed under the headings of facts, skills, conceptual structures, general strategies and personal qualities, and were themselves unspecific (for example, remembering notation, sensible use of a calculator, trial and error methods, a positive attitude to mathematics). However, a detailed list of what most 11-year-olds should know, under the content objectives only, was contained in the appendix. The list contained few surprises and reflected the contents of the more recent textbook series, emphasizing concepts rather than procedures, for example, including equivalence of fractions rather than the four rules for fractions. Pencil and paper multiplication and division was by single digits only, using calculators for more complex cases. While underlining the progressive credentials of HMI, it was nevertheless seen as a further step towards state prescription.

Deciding that mathematics would be an easier subject than English to tackle, the Secretary of State, Sir Keith Joseph, initiated a one-year feasibility study to start in September 1986, which would define a three- to four-year programme for research, development and implementation of national attainment targets at age 11 and corresponding assessment. The contract went to Brenda Denvir and myself, colleagues of Geoffrey Matthews at Chelsea College, then in the course of merging into King's College London. Hilary Shuard was on the Steering Committee.

But the feasibility study was soon overtaken by events. A new Secretary of State, Kenneth Baker, swept in during the autumn of 1986, determined to make his mark. Persuaded by recent reports that low mathematical standards compared with our competitors were responsible for national industrial failure, he announced in January 1987 his decision to implement swiftly a full national curriculum determining what pupils should be taught in primary and secondary schools. This went considerably beyond the aim of his predecessor who supported attainment targets but had no desire otherwise to control the detail of the curriculum.

Ignoring the feasibility study, Baker announced at Easter that there would be national testing at ages 7, 9 (later abandoned), 11 and 14, as well as GCSE at 16. The consultative document *The National Curriculum 5–16* (DES 1987) was rushed out in July in order to form the core of a new and radical Education Reform Bill that autumn. At the same time National Curriculum Working Groups in mathematics and science were set up, as well as a Task Group on Assessment and Testing (TGAT).

The brief was for the subject groups to draw up attainment targets for ages 7, 11, 14 and 16, with each target differentiated for three levels of attainment, to frame a programme of study for each key stage (KS) of education covering the two to four years prior to the tests, and to advise on teacher assessment and national testing. In the case of the mathematics group, among those with knowledge at primary level were Hilary Shuard (co-opted after initial objections from the Department for Education and Science (DfES)), a primary mathematics adviser, two primary heads and myself. Significantly Anita Straker, then developing new primary guidelines for the Inner London Education Authority as an inspector, and writing innovative computer programs to teach mathematics, was also drafted in as an adviser.

As with the Steering Committee for the mathematics feasibility project, and not surprisingly in view of the shared membership, the group demanded a revision of the brief so that attainment targets were written, not separately for four key stages, but in the form of hierarchical strands, made up of statements of attainment describing the important steps of progression in each target. The statements of attainment could then be assigned to broad levels, each of which could be described as being attained by average pupils of a specific age. This would both ensure continuity through the 5–16 age range and cater for the documented wide range of attainment among pupils of any specific age. The result would be progressive and child centred to the extent that it would take the progression in the learning of the child as the core of the system rather than fixing a syllabus for each key stage and measuring each child's attainment of it.

The TGAT group also favoured this solution, and persuaded Kenneth Baker to adopt it. Experience of the graded assessment movement at secondary level suggested that in order to characterize the progress in a wide span of students from age 5 to 16, giving each child a reasonable chance of progressing one level each year, then 20 levels would be needed. The TGAT group felt that ten levels were enough, which gave an average progression rate of one level every two years for students of average attainment. They defined level 2 as that which could be achieved by the broad average group of students at age 7, level 3 at age 9, level 4 at age 11, level 5 at age 13, and level 6 at age 15. Other levels would be defined around this. The working groups for each subject were then asked to define these ten levels by attainment criteria in their subject. The

TGAT group also set a national system of labelling of year groups, from Year 1 to Year 11, and key stages, from KS1 to KS4, for the first time.

The TGAT group was also radical in proposing an assessment system which depended on ongoing teacher assessment. For moderation of teacher assessment only, there would be theme-based standard assessment tasks (SATs) at the end of Key Stages 1 and 2 which would sample the attainment targets across all the core subjects of English, mathematics and science. For example, a SAT on the topic of 'pets' might include questions on knowledge of essential functions of animals, a story about a school or home pet, and some work on measurement and growth of pets. It was also proposed that this might be accompanied by separate tests in English and mathematics at KS2, but again that since these would be only for moderation of teacher assessment, they would be short and would only need to lightly sample the curriculum.

The national curriculum proposed by the Mathematics Working Group was – not unexpectedly – strongly influenced by the Cockcroft ethos, with a broad curriculum including investigation and problem solving. Hilary Shuard also fought to maintain the principles of the Calculator Aware Number curriculum (CAN) with its strong emphasis on mental arithmetic, estimation and calculators. The eventual outcome mainly reflected this, but a compromise was negotiated with the DES to include some written arithmetic (for example, multiplication of a three-digit by a two-digit number), but avoiding specification of any particular standard method. To an extent the strands were research based, at primary level using studies like that of Denvir and Brown (1986), although in some areas of the primary curriculum there was little research to guide the progression and, especially in number, some political compromises were made. Generally the placing of statements had to be at slightly lower ages than research suggested in order to show positive expectations of improvement. So the conceptual spirit of primary mathematics remained largely intact, even if the progressive aspect was significantly dented by the first step in state control of both curriculum and assessment.

The proposals, both from TGAT and from the Mathematics Working Group, received a guarded welcome by teachers as being better than they had feared, and although cosmetic changes (for example, the organization of attainment targets, the degree of specificity, and references to ICT) were made to the format of the Order specifying the National Curriculum for Mathematics in 1991, 1995, 2000 and 2010, the content has remained substantially constant between 1989 and the present day.

The immediate effect in 1989 was for teachers to check that their textbooks matched the attainment targets fairly closely, which was generally the case for those bought within the previous decade. These generally emphasized concepts rather than procedures, although many teachers supplemented them with practice on tables and written computation exercises. Schemes brought out supplements and new editions to fill a few gaps like probability, which was now included in the curriculum, foreshadowed in the 1960s by one of the Nuffield Teachers' Guides.

The fact that the curriculum framework for attainment targets was structured by levels, rather than year groups, encouraged a continuing emphasis on differentiation. This meant that the many schools which had, with the aim of pupil autonomy, individualized their mathematics teaching, saw no need to change. However, other teachers and schools, now wanting greater control over pace and coverage, started revising the curriculum into modules, using the national curriculum attainment targets as a basis. All the pupils would then work on, say, multiplication or measurement at the same time, although children in different attainment groups would be likely to be working on different activities within that topic, usually selected from different books in their scheme. These teachers thus moved from being what Johnson and Millett (1996) call *scheme driven planners* to *scheme assisted planners*, with the national curriculum framework liberating them from the framework imposed by the published scheme itself.

Although the 'Using and Applying Mathematics' attainment target was supposed to incorporate problem-solving and investigation skills, reasoning and communication into the teaching of content, in practice teachers felt they were fulfilling the requirements by either using practical work with structural apparatus like Unifix cubes, and/or real-world examples, often artificial ones of shopping and cutting up fractions of cakes (Johnson and Millett 1996). At KS2, the occasional investigations, introduced following the work of the Cockcroft advisory teachers, were generally continued. Few had the resources, the confidence or the insight to introduce a fully investigatory style to the teaching of content, although some teachers used activities or games which incorporated such principles, without always being able to justify them.

There were, however, changes during this period which did affect the nature of primary mathematics teaching. The first was as a consequence of national assessment. In the late 1980s and early 1990s, teachers, led initially by LEAs, had put much effort into devising assessment and recording systems as a result of the TGAT emphasis on ongoing teacher assessment. While these assessment sheets relating to statements of attainment became denigrated as bureaucratic 'ticklists', many teachers still found that focusing on assessing pupils' attainment of particular ideas and skills was helpful in monitoring progress and in curriculum planning. The combination of teacher assessment and the first national rounds of practical SATs at Key Stage 1 in 1991 and 1992 revealed that pupils' attainment sometimes differed from teacher expectations (Gipps et al. 1995).

However, the role of national assessment was evolving; rather than topic-based tasks sampling the curriculum, to moderate teacher assessment as envisaged by TGAT, the new minister, Kenneth Clarke, and the DES had taken a further step towards central control by now requiring tests in each core subject at each key stage with as far as possible a full coverage of the curriculum. This was closer to the original concept of Margaret Thatcher, which was of a national curriculum as a list of basic skills in literacy and numeracy and corresponding tests. By the time national assessment was finally introduced at Key Stage 2 in 1995, a national teacher boycott of all national assessment in 1993–94 had ensured that there was no longer any requirement for continuous assessment, and the tasks had become externally marked class tests. The next step in centralization was, against teacher opinion, to implement published league tables of performance. Although teachers were still expected to make a judgement on the basis of their views of the child's attainment, this was no longer regarded as of importance and many teachers waited for the external test results before making their assessment.

This led in many schools to the tests slowly beginning to drive the curriculum, at least in Years 2 and 6. However, the style of written questions in the early years of the national tests had little effect on the curriculum, since they were similar to the style of work in most of the commonly used schemes. Before 1998 there were hardly any straightforward numerical calculations. Almost all items took the form of a word problem set in a real-world context or a puzzle, and thus required some degree of conceptual knowledge, including interpretation of the problem and selection of a strategy.

While assessment against specific criteria was confirming the range of attainment of different children in each class, it also made it clear to teachers that individualization of teaching was not necessarily delivering basic skills in number. Perhaps this was not surprising given that children did not have to react orally or quickly to mental calculations while working through books, and had very little opportunity to talk about the methods they had used, which were often primitive and slow.

Problems about pupil autonomy and progressive methods more generally were featured in research studies in Leicester, Inner London and Leeds; a report commissioned by the Secretary of State (known as the Three Wise Men report) (Alexander et al. 1992), brought these together, proposing more whole-class teaching in primary schools. However, momentum was lost due to a worsening of relations between the government and the teachers during the teacher boycott of national tests. Appeasement followed, led by Sir Ron Dearing, who negotiated a pause in innovation, which turned out to be rather briefer than expected.

1996–2010: the National Numeracy Strategy and the Primary National Strategy

Concern about low standards of number skills, and about teaching methods, surfaced again in 1996. First, unfavourable international comparisons were highlighted both by leaked new TIMSS results for primary schools in 1995 and by a report reviewing earlier results which was co-authored by David Reynolds, later the chairman of the Numeracy Task Force. In June 1996 there was an announcement that mental arithmetic tests and non-calculator papers would be included in all the end of key stage national tests, persuading many more teachers to include whole-class sessions of mental arithmetic in their lessons, often guided by the mental mathematics pupil books written by Anita Straker.

This was followed by Ofsted reviews of weak literacy, and rather less weak numeracy, standards in inner city LEAs, initiated by the Chief Inspector, Chris Woodhead, a co-author of the 'Three Wise Men report'. Press reports also highlighted an apparently successful introduction of Swiss-style number teaching into Barking and Dagenham schools, led by Professor Sig Prais, an economist and right-wing member of the National Curriculum Mathematic Working Group. Influenced by both of these, Gillian Shephard, the Tory Secretary of State, announced the launch of parallel National Numeracy and Literacy Projects involving schools in poorly performing LEAs. The aim was to raise standards in basic skills by a prescribed programme for each year, reducing differentiation and including a high proportion of whole-class teaching. Support would be offered by numeracy consultants, a revival of the Cockcroft advisory teachers, long since lost due to continual LEA cutbacks. Anita Straker was appointed as director of the National Numeracy Project, and worked with enormous energy to get the project started in autumn 1996.

Numeracy was being slowly redefined; where previously it had referred, first, broadly to scientific literacy and later to the ability to apply number ideas and skills in employment and everyday life, it now was taken to mean mainly abstract number skills, both written and mental, together with solving routine artificial word problems. The Numeracy Project relegated those parts of mathematics which dealt with anything other than pure number work, that is, measurement, space and shape, and data handling, introduced into most schools in the 1960s, to the margins, by producing, as well as new teaching methods for number, a framework specifying in detail a number curriculum which was to occupy most of the teaching time available.

Even before the Labour Party came into power in May 1997, it had already appointed a Literacy Task Force in 1996 and a Numeracy Task Force in April 1997, thus taking over the Conservatives' growing focus on raising standards in basic skills in literacy and numeracy. David Reynolds, the chair of the Numeracy Task Force, had been a member of the Literacy Task Force and was not a mathematics educator but a researcher in international school improvement; his research and, as noted earlier, his comparison with other countries, had led him to suggest that there was significant room for improvement in English mathematical standards. Anita Straker was also a member; I was the only member who had previously been on the National Curriculum Working Group.

Almost the first move of the new Labour government in office was to announce the start of the National Literacy Strategy in September 1998; the National Numeracy Strategy would start the following year. Alongside this it set ambitious targets for the number of pupils who would reach the 'age expectations' in the national tests, in particular within five years 75 per cent should reach Level 4 of the national curriculum at the end of Key Stage 2 (age 11). So what had started as a set of levels devised in order to report each child's attainment, with Level 4 defined as what could reasonably be attained by the broad average group of children at age 11, had now become the definition of a requirement that almost all children should reach.

Differentiated progress and differentiated teaching would no longer be tolerated as they were at odds with social justice and human rights; schools were now under pressure to meet externally set norms in national tests, whatever the nature of their intakes. If schools could not meet these norms, then they were not likely to be judged by Office for Standards in Education (Ofsted) inspectors as delivering a satisfactory education, and would be threatened first with shame, having their names publicly listed as a 'failing school', and finally, if insufficient improvement was made, with closure.

So the pendulum had swung back finally for the first time in over 100 years from a progressive system which valued autonomy in teachers and pupils, encouraging sensitivity to difference, towards a public education emphasis which decreed equal treatment for all students and all teachers. Perhaps the differentiation had for too long favoured the middle-class child and the middle-class school, and the weaker performance of other children – of whom less was expected – was not sufficiently serving either their own occupational ambitions or the raised standards of national economic performance, the latter being uppermost in the agenda of the new government.

As with the Literacy Task Force, the Numeracy Task Force was pressured into recommending the universal adoption of the National Numeracy Project to form the National Numeracy Strategy and to prepare appropriate plans and estimates for its universal implementation in September 1999. Although early evaluation reports did suggest the Numeracy Project was having a favourable effect on basic skill standards, the extension was required to go ahead before full evaluation results were available.

The National Numeracy Strategy issued *The National Numeracy Strategy Framework for Teaching Mathematics from Reception to Year 6* (DfEE 1999), piloted by the earlier project, which prescribed an extremely detailed curriculum, year by year, for primary mathematics. This was a large document and each teacher was provided with a personal copy. Each group of between three and ten lessons, on a schedule which went through each year, had a specified set of objectives with sets of examples to illustrate the type of work intended. Thus in any given week every class in the country in a particular year group would be engaged on the same objectives on the same topic. This was a level of curricular prescription which had never before happened in English primary schools.

In 2000 the national curriculum was altered to correspond to this framework, although as before this only contained broader outlines of what should be taught during each key stage. While only this national curriculum was technically statutory, there were very strong pressures to implement the week-by-week detail in the framework, since schools were inspected regularly by Ofsted inspectors who were briefed that schools should be following the precise recommendations of the National Numeracy Strategy. Unless a school had exceptionally good test results, failure to comply would be regarded as the cause of lower standards.

Not only was there prescription of the curriculum, but also of the shape of each lesson, including the type of activity which should take place, and for how long. The lessons should commence with a mental/oral starter to revise mental arithmetic skills (5 to 10 minutes), then involve a presentation of new work by the teacher to the whole class using interactive questioning, followed by pupils working in groups to practise exercises, during which time the teacher would teach one group at a time, and finally a whole class plenary (10 to 15 minutes) to overview the topic and lead forward. The whole lesson would take 45 minutes or more with younger age groups increasing up to 60 minutes with Years 5 and 6. After initial guidance in the national project that no differentiation at all would be allowed, finally a degree of differentiation during the group work time was reluctantly approved, provided all groups worked on the same objectives and not more than three levels of differentiation occurred in any class.

The research base for this focus on whole class teaching and specification of pedagogic structure was fragile (Brown et al. 1998). The Numeracy Task Force commissioned a detailed review of the English 1994 TIMSS data to see whether more whole-class teaching was significantly associated with higher standards in numeracy. The results were not referred to in the final report or ever published since it was found that in Year 5 the opposite was the case; in Year 4 the results were inconclusive.

This was supported by a nationally financed research project aimed at determining characteristics of effective teachers of numeracy, which had noted that there was no particular pattern in the way effective teachers organized their classes or lessons (Askew et al. 1997). While some favoured individualized working through textbooks, others favoured only group working, and others taught whole classes. What seemed to differentiate effective teachers (here measuring effectiveness by the gains made across the year in average class performance) was not their pedagogic strategies but their well-developed personal philosophies of mathematics teaching and teaching methods. These emphasized connections, between different mathematical ideas, between mathematics and the real world, and between their knowledge of children and mathematics (see Askew, Chapter 2).

However, there were aspects of the National Numeracy Strategy which did reflect research findings. The opportunity was taken by English researchers like Ian Thompson, Julia Anghileri and Mike Askew to include research-validated didactic methods, some first used in the Netherlands. These included different forms of early counting, new mental calculation methods with an emphasis on working with complete numbers rather than splitting into separate digits, the greater use of hundred squares and the empty number line for addition and subtraction. Counting sticks were also encouraged for practice in multiplication, although with rather less research support or success, as these favoured a narrow concept of multiplication which was based on repeated addition only (see Delaney, Chapter 5).

So led by Anita Straker, who became the first National Numeracy Strategy director, the curriculum emphasis was very much on mental methods and on moving only slowly to written methods, and then to those like the grid method for multiplication and 'chunking' for division, which were likely to make conceptual sense to the child (see Thompson, Chapters 15 and 16). Teachers were recommended in their class teaching phases of lessons to ask children to explain their own methods and strategies for calculating, so that children would discuss different methods and learn from others. Nevertheless there was some inconsistency here, for in many cases the lesson objective selected from the framework was to introduce a certain specific procedure, often for mental calculation. This meant that teachers often started teaching by asking children what methods they chose to use and then had to ignore this information to require them all to practise the designated procedure. It might be expected that at least children would thus extend their repertoire of possible procedures on which to draw. However, many teachers came to feel that having too many possible strategies was confusing and chose to restrict the choice. Thus a generally conceptual orientation adopted by the strategy sometimes was interpreted as more procedural than intended (see Thompson, Chapter 12).

The implementation of the National Numeracy Strategy, like that of the National Literacy Strategy a year earlier, was undertaken with military precision; little expense was spared. Under the national director were regional directors who trained consultants appointed to each LEA. These consultants trained the teacher coordinator responsible for mathematics in each school, on three-day sessions, with head teachers and school governors attending for some sessions. The training was centrally designed, including the exact timetable to be followed, the training videos to be shown and the PowerPoint slides to be used. Where awkward questions were asked, consultants simply responded that 'research had shown' the strategy methods to be more effective than alternatives. In order to ensure every teacher in every school received exactly the same messages, coordinators were also issued with similar packages to be used on each of three national training days. The Canadian team evaluating the implementation of both strategies noted that this was probably the largest national project implementation ever attempted, and were impressed by the thoroughness of the exercise (Earl et al. 2002).

With all this prescription it might have been expected that there would be significant teacher opposition, but in fact the strategy was widely welcomed by teachers. It benefited from lessons learnt from the introduction of the National Literacy Strategy and was perceived as a little less tightly controlled. Anita Straker was widely trusted by teachers and had assembled an able team. The project received support from most quarters, with the exception of higher education which had been left out of the strategy implementation plans. An additional factor may well have been that few primary teachers were confident about their mathematics expertise, especially since with primary training increasingly being cut from three- or four-year BEds to a one-year PGCE, the average amount of training in understanding and teaching primary mathematics received was rapidly declining. This meant that authoritative prescription delivered by friendly faces was widely welcomed.

Teachers were, however, generally exhausted by having to replan all their lessons, first in literacy and then in numeracy/mathematics over the period of two years. Tight timescales meant that no revised textbooks or other supportive materials were available, and in any case the use of these was generally frowned upon by the strategy which felt that teachers had more than enough support from its own productions, and other sources were only likely to be off-message. An interesting but unplanned consequence was that some schools introduced setting, especially where teachers were worried about teaching a uniform curriculum across the wide attainment spectrum, and/or where national test results were low and heads felt that they had to take radical action of some sort.

But however successful the implementation, the changes in national test results were disappointing. Strangely, the percentage of students achieving Level 4 at age 11 had increased significantly in the summer of 1999, just before the strategy was officially introduced, but the rise in the following few years was very small, and the national targets for increased performance were not met. Although the government explained the 1999 rise by the action of premature adopters, evidence suggests that this is unlikely to have been a significant factor. The fact that the trends in mathematics national test results were almost identical to those in English and science, although the National Literacy Strategy was introduced a year earlier and there was no national strategy for science, suggest that other factors were responsible for the 1999 increase, including a combination of increased pressure on teachers to coach Year 6 students for the tests, and a slippage in the test standards which evidence suggests took place between 1995 and 2000.

There was corroboration from other sources that the introduction of the National Numeracy Strategy, which was costing more than £50 million per year, had only a small effect on test results. A five-year longitudinal study of primary numeracy financed by the Leverhulme Trust suggested a very small effect on Year 4 results, with declining performance in more than a third of schools in the sample (Brown et al. 2003). More worryingly for the Labour government was the finding from this study that the range of attainment had widened, not narrowed, as a result of more uniform teaching. It was the lowest achievers who had benefited least from the strategy, whereas the greatest gains were in the middle of the range. From the same source came some evidence also that while pupils' knowledge of the number system and addition was enhanced, some areas like problem solving and multiplication seemed not to have improved. This suggested that improvements had been due more to improved teaching methods (didactics) in some areas than to the changes in lesson format and whole-class pedagogy.

There was some panic in the new Department for Education and Skills (DfES) when it became clear that national test results were still failing to rise significantly. The strategy director was called in to explain the failure and to take urgent action to address it. The blame was eventually laid rather unfairly at the hand of teachers, whom it was suggested were not implementing the guidance faithfully, when in fact there is substantial evidence that they were.

Thus a further turn of the centralization screw was made. Since teachers could not be trusted to interpret the guidance, they would be issued with lesson plans for every lesson, specifying exactly how it would be taught – little was missing other than some sets of examples for practice. This was all to be done quickly, with these 'unit plans' for lessons put on the Internet, starting in 2001–02 at least in some areas and for some year groups, and spreading more widely in 2002–03 and 2003–04. Although these had been trialled, clearly they were not always suitable for all classes in all schools, and there is some evidence that teachers sometimes misunderstood the point of activities that they were asked to deliver. Teachers who had recently bought and got used to new published schemes relating to the strategy, some at least as sound in quality as the unit plans, were forced to abandon them for the new orthodoxy.

But even after unit plans had been widely implemented, still only minor improvements were observed in national test results. Although teachers had broadly welcomed the unit plans at the start, as they discovered they did not always work well with their classes there was more scepticism. With new ministers and new strategy personnel, new regimes were also introduced for children with lower attainment who had appeared to suffer most in the early days of implementation, with more customized work in Wave 2 (for groups) and Wave 3 (for individuals with special needs).

So within the previous 50 years there had been enormous changes in primary mathematics. First, from a broad and conceptually based curriculum in which investigation and problem solving were encouraged, a curriculum was now in place which emphasized abstract number knowledge and procedures and which downplayed applications and problem solving. While the overt advice of the strategy remained broadly conceptual, the pressure on teachers to move quickly through a tightly specified curriculum and to coach children to achieve high scores in national tests, led in many classes to a more procedural style of teaching. Children were focused on what has to be done to achieve high test scores rather than on learning to enjoy, explore and use mathematics. Nevertheless, England has still generally avoided the most mindless styles of teaching of formal written algorithms which pertain in many countries.

Perhaps more radical have been the changes in control of the curriculum and the possibility of adapting to the motivation and needs of individual children. From broadly progressive teaching methods, where well-trained teachers were trusted to find ways of exciting and communicating with their individual children, we had moved to a situation where each lesson in most year groups was centrally prescribed, in order to achieve a public education system which adopted methods previously used only in totalitarian countries to equalize experiences and outcomes for each child.

The reality, of course, is that change is never so extreme as it may seem from an abstract description of the system. Even in apparently progressive times, most schools, most of the time, have been dependent on published schemes to set their curriculum as well as their teaching activities. These schemes have generally covered a wide curriculum, but have always had a major emphasis on number work. Most schools have continued throughout to teach and test number bonds and multiplication tables, and calculators have been used sparingly, if at all, to teach number sense rather than as a substitute for traditional calculation methods. Thus the combined good sense and inertia of the teaching profession has substantially damped the pendulum swings recommended in the past, and no doubt will do so again.

Postscript: releasing the stranglehold post-2006

By 2006, with still no significant rise in national test results, it was decided that further changes were needed; since there was little potential left for greater control of the system, a new framework was issued which was distinctly lower key in its specification than its predecessor. Most teachers were expected to use it online; while this provided more flexible planning tools, it proved quite complex to access all the many different components, with much less of the training and implementation systems which had been used in 1999. The yearly schedules were now intended to be organized in slightly larger units of equal length to ensure less fragmentation in teaching, but since many units contained sections from different areas of mathematics, the effect was scarcely noticeable. While it is difficult to get a clear overall picture of what is happening currently, it is clear that more decisions are being taken at school level than was the case in 2005.

National tests at age 7 have been abandoned in favour of teacher assessment with support from classroom tests, which leaves more freedom for Key Stage 1, and among considerable national opposition it is very possible that tests at age 11 will be replaced by single level tests and/or moderated teacher assessment in Key Stage 2. Single level tests may well lead to more domination of the curriculum by test preparation which could permeate the whole of KS2, but since different children will be practising for different tests the uniform curriculum may not hold for long.

Further, an official review by Sir Jim Rose (DCSF 2009) and an independent report by Professor Robin Alexander and colleagues from schools, local authorities and universities (Alexander 2009), became available in 2009. Both men were, perhaps ironically, co-authors of the Three Wise Men report in 1991 which launched the swing towards greater control of teaching. Both these recommended a new more progressive and less specified curriculum with wider aims, and the Rose Review led to a new version of the national curriculum to be implemented in 2011 which has less specified content and more emphasis on process.

So again the pendulum is swinging back; after concerns at much less improvement in standards than expected we move on in the only way possible, towards more progressive and greater conceptual emphasis once again. Maybe such swings are inevitable since standards will never be as high as we would wish, and there will always be someone with a new vision ready to keep the roundabout turning!

References

Alexander, R., Rose, J. and Woodhead, C. (1992) *Curriculum Organisation and Classroom Practice in Primary Schools*. London: DES.

Alexander, R. (ed.) (2009) *Children, their World, their Education: Final Report and Recommendations of the Cambridge Primary Review*. London: Routledge.

Askew, M., Brown, M., Rhodes, V., Wiliam, D. and Johnson, D. (1997) *Effective Teachers of Numeracy*. London: King's College London, for the Teacher Training Agency.

Board of Education (1931) *Report of the Consultative Committee on the Primary School* (Hadow Report). London: HMSO.

Brown, M., Askew, M., Baker, D., Denvir, B. and Millett, A. (1998) Is the National Numeracy Strategy research-based? *British Journal of Educational Studies*, 46(4): 362–85.

Brown, M., Askew, M., Millett, A. and Rhodes, V. (2003) The key role of educational research in the development and evaluation of the National Numeracy Strategy, *British Educational Research Journal*, 29(5): 655–72.

CACE (Central Advisory Council for Education) (1967) *Children and their Primary Schools* (Plowden Report). London: HMSO.

DCSF (Department for Children, Schools and Families) (2009) *Independent Review of the Primary Curriculum: Final Report* (Rose Review). Nottingham: DCSF. http://publications.teachernet.gov.uk/eOrderingDownload/Primary_curriculum_Report.pdf (accessed March 2010).

Denvir, B. and Brown, M. (1986) Understanding of number concepts in low attaining 7–9 year olds, *Educational Studies in Mathematics*, 17: 15–36 and 143–64.

DES (Department of Education and Science) (1979) *Mathematics 5–11: A Handbook of Suggestions* (HMI Matters for Discussion 9). London: HMSO.

DES (Department of Education and Science) (1982) *Mathematics Counts: Report of the Committee of Inquiry into the Teaching of Mathematics in Schools* (Cockcroft Report). London: HMSO. http://www.dg.dial.pipex.com/documents/docs1/cockcroft.shtml (accessed March 2010).

DES (Department of Education and Science) (1985a) *Better Schools*. London: HMSO.

DES (Department of Education and Science) (1985b) *Mathematics from 5 to 16* (HMI Curriculum Matters 3). London: HMSO.

DES (Department of Education and Science) (1987) *The National Curriculum 5–16: A Consultation Document*. London: HMSO.

DfEE (Department for Education and Employment) (1999) *The National Numeracy Strategy Framework for Teaching Mathematics from Reception to Year 6*. London: DfEE.

Earl, L., Levin, B., Leithwood, K., Fullan, M. and Watson, N. (2002) *Watching and Learning 3: OISE/UT Evaluation of the Implementation of the National Literacy and Numeracy Strategies, Third and Final Report*. Toronto: OISE/University of Toronto.

Ernest, P. (1991) *The Philosophy of Mathematics Education*. Basingstoke: Falmer Press.

Gipps, C., Brown, M., McCallum, B. and McAlister, S. (1995) *Intuition or Evidence? Teachers and National Assessment of Seven-year-olds*. Buckingham: Open University Press.

Howson, A.G. (1982) *A History of Mathematics Education in England*. Cambridge: Cambridge University Press.

Johnson, D. and Millett, A. (eds) (1996) *Implementing the Mathematics National Curriculum: Policy, Politics and Practice*. London: Paul Chapman.

Mathematical Association (1955) *The Teaching of Mathematics in Primary Schools*. London: Bell.

McIntosh, A. (1981) When will they ever learn? (article reprinted from *Forum*, 19(3)), in A. Floyd (ed.) *Developing Mathematical Thinking*. London: Addison-Wesley, for the Open University.

Pinner, M.T. Sr (1981) Mathematics: its challenge to primary school teachers from 1930–1980, in A. Floyd (ed.) *Developing Mathematical Thinking*. London: Addison-Wesley, for the Open University.

Williams, E.M. and Shuard, H.B. (1970) *Primary Mathematics Today*. London: Longman.

SECTION 2
Post-Williams issues

As mentioned in the Editor's Preface, the decision as to what to put in a post-Williams section was a difficult one. For example, the chapter by Julie Ryan and Julian Williams (Chapter 11) on errors and misconceptions could quite easily have been situated in this section. However, because of the formative assessment aspect of the topic, it was decided to put this chapter in the assessment section along with Jeremy Hodgen and Mike Askew's chapter on Assessment for Learning (AfL) and Assessing Pupils' Progress (APP). Similar arguments could be made for other chapters, given that the whole book is concerned with issues relevant to the teaching and learning of primary number.

Chapter 2 has been deliberately retained in the form in which it was originally written. The author, Mike Askew, was principal investigator for the study Effective Teachers of Numeracy which was carried out by King's College in 1995–96 for the Teacher Training Agency. The aims of the study were to explore the key factors that made teachers into effective teachers of numeracy. To do this the researchers explored the knowledge, beliefs and practices of a sample of effective teachers of numeracy, where 'effectiveness' was defined on the basis of learning gains. Several of the project's findings were surprising in that they challenged some popularly held beliefs about what it is that makes a teacher effective. The chapter includes illustrative examples of effective teachers in action; describes three different orientations to the teaching of numeracy; and discusses the relationship between these orientations and effectiveness. In Chapter 3, Patrick Barmby, Tony Harries and Steve Higgins ask what we mean by 'understanding' in mathematics and how we teach in order to develop it in children. They also examine the understanding required by teachers of mathematics, thereby making links with the content of the previous chapter.

Chapter 4, by Frank Monaghan, provides a brief introduction to the role of discussion in the mathematics classroom and more specifically to the approach known as Thinking Together, initially developed by Neil Mercer and colleagues at the Open University. The chapter describes the outcomes of a research and professional development project aimed at encouraging exploratory talk in primary mathematics lessons. These lessons involve the explicit teaching of talking skills; the development of an agreed set of ground rules for talk in the classroom; and the skilled intervention of the teacher to ensure that talk becomes an effective tool for learning.

After a brief historical overview of the place of practical equipment in the teaching of primary mathematics, Kev Delaney argues in Chapter 5 that although official publications in England recommend a range of practical resources, they fail to include a rationale for their use. By analysing 'official' video material he attempts to ascertain what this rationale might be, and proceeds to offer an alternative approach to the use of what are known in the USA as 'manipulatives'.

The usual approach to teaching mathematics in primary schools is to teach various skills, understandings or techniques and then 'use and apply' them in problem-solving situations. In Chapter 6 Mike Ollerton turns this practice on its head, arguing for the use of problem solving as a vehicle for supporting children's learning of mathematics. He links the teaching and learning of mathematics through problem-solving approaches to the broader qualities that he believes are desirable for children to develop in order to support their learning. He illustrates his point by leading us through a variety of 'rich' tasks, before challenging some of the prescribed orthodoxies such as the recommended lesson structure and the notion of differentiation occurring at three different levels in classrooms.

Chapter 7 deals with information and communications technology (ICT). In the first part of this chapter Richard English argues the case for making use of ICT in teaching and learning mathematics, concluding that many things can be done better with ICT than without it. He then proceeds to consider three particular issues identified in the Williams Review – using and applying mathematics, oral and mental work, high-quality discussion – and explores the role that ICT can play in addressing these issues.

Sue Gifford begins Chapter 8 by making the important point that educators in England are in the rare position of having a mathematics curriculum for children from birth to 5. She argues that the Early Years Foundation Stage succeeds in setting out principles for early years education that could go some way towards preventing inappropriate mathematics teaching. However, as she outlines the recommendations contained in those documents dealing with the teaching of mathematics in the early years, she offers many insightful suggestions as to how these recommendations might have been improved. Key Stage 1 and 2 teachers will no doubt benefit from being made aware of the strengths and limitations of these various documents.

In Chapter 9, the final chapter in this section, Jan Winter discusses the numeracy strand of the Home–School Knowledge Exchange project (2001–05)

– a project based on the assumption that both parents and teachers are in possession of knowledge that is relevant to the enhancement of children's learning. She describes and evaluates the activities that the project team developed for taking knowledge from school to home as well as from *home* to *school*.

2 It ain't (just) what you do: effective teachers of numeracy

Mike Askew

Introduction

I met John a few years ago when he was a Year 4 pupil. Sitting alone, he was working on a scheme page which asked what had to be added to several three-digit numbers to make each up to 500. He had done the first and what was written in his book is shown in Figure 2.1.

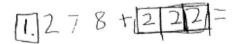

Figure 2.1 John's calculation.

As I sat down, John slipped a piece of paper under the desk. I asked him to read what he had written in his book.

'278 plus 222 makes 500.'

When I asked him how he had found the answer, John replied, 'I just worked it out.'

'Did you do it in your head?'

'No, I used a bit of paper.'

'Is that the paper that you used?' (indicating the piece under the desk)

'No, it's in the bin, that's my working for the next one.'

When John reluctantly showed me the paper it became clear why, 20 minutes into the lesson, he had only done one question. Counting on from 278 to 500 in single tally marks and then recounting them is a slow process (especially if you want to get it right. I, of course, had interrupted the counting for the second question, so was not too popular) (see Figure 2.2).

Before reading on you might like to consider for a moment what your response would be to John's strategy. What would you do to help him?

Figure 2.2   John's tally marks.

I have been posing this question to many teachers at workshops and lectures. Usually there is a range of responses, including:

- work on building up his confidence. John got the right answer, so to try and show him a different method might demotivate him;
- ask him if he can think of a quicker method;
- work with much smaller numbers – he needs to be able to deal with those efficiently before working with greater numbers;
- work with much larger numbers – by asking how many more, say, 5000 is than 2780, John might realize the inefficiency of his method;
- refine his method – say, getting him to organize his tallies in tens and ones;
- show a practical method – get out tens and ones blocks and demonstrate how to model the situation;
- persuade him that the calculation is actually a subtraction and can be answered using a standard algorithm;
- show a more efficient method, say, shopkeeper arithmetic (rounding up to the nearest 10 then 100) or counting up using an empty number line.

I want to suggest the following simple model of the challenge that John's work poses. At one end of a continuum you have the child's methods and understanding, and at the other end the teacher's methods and understanding. The challenge is to bridge this gap.

Child's method(s) _____ Teacher's methods

So where do you focus your attention on this continuum? Do you start 'near' to where the child is (or further back than that) or do you leap in at the other end? The strength of the first option is that you build on what children can do, but a weakness is that it may take some time to move them on. On the other hand, showing a different method may increase efficiency in the short term but at the cost of longer-term understanding and the ability to apply the skill in different situations.

Any decision will rest on some theory or beliefs, however informal or unarticulated, about the relationship between teaching and learning. Exploring teachers' beliefs about this relationship was one aspect of the Effective Teachers of Numeracy project carried out at King's College by myself and colleagues Margaret Brown, David Johnson, Valerie Rhodes and Dylan Wiliam and funded by the Teacher Training Agency.[1]

The beliefs of the teachers in the project appeared to be significant not only in terms of what they did in the classroom, but also in terms of children's learning outcomes. This chapter explores some of these issues. Anyone wishing to read more about the project should see Askew et al. (1997).

Effective teachers of numeracy

The principal aim of the Effective Teachers of Numeracy project was:

- to identify key factors which enable teachers to put effective teaching of numeracy into practice in the primary phase.

Realizing this aim posed three initial problems for us:

- What is meant by numeracy?
- How do we identify effective teaching of numeracy?
- How do we find effective teachers of numeracy?

Only when we had resolved these could we begin to identify the factors that enabled teachers to put effective teaching into practice.

Defining numeracy

Starting the project we could find no agreed definition of numeracy. We therefore decided to adopt a definition that was broad enough to encompass the ability to calculate accurately but also go beyond that to include a 'feel for number', and the ability to apply arithmetic:

> Numeracy is the ability to process, communicate and interpret numerical information in a variety of contexts.

Identifying effective teaching of numeracy

Identifying teachers believed to be effective in teaching numeracy was crucial to the project. But before we could identify such teachers we had to decide what we meant by effective teaching of numeracy. Our starting point was to build on our definition of numeracy, and this enabled us to be more specific about our expected outcomes of effective teaching. We defined effective teaching of numeracy as teaching that helps children:

- acquire knowledge of and facility with numbers, number relations and number operations based on an integrated network of understanding, techniques, strategies and application skills;
- learn how to apply this knowledge of and facility with numbers, number relations and number operations in a variety of contexts.

Although this definition gave some sense of the outcomes of the teaching, it moved us no nearer to identifying what the actual teaching might look like.

Many people in mathematics education – researchers, inspectors, teachers – would claim to know what 'good' practice in primary mathematics should look like. However, evidence about teaching practices that are effective in terms of bringing about learning of numeracy is limited. At the time of the study, research in mathematics education in the UK largely separated findings on children's learning from those on teaching.

It seemed sensible therefore to base our identification of effective teaching on some measure of children's actual learning gains, rather than presumptions of 'good practice'. If we could find classes whose average gains were higher than others, then we could go about exploring what practices appeared to be most effective in promoting this learning.

We measured children's learning by looking at the gains for individual classes over part of a school year. Specially designed tests of numeracy were administered to whole classes from Year 1 to Year 6, first towards the beginning of the autumn term 1995, and again at the end of the spring term 1996 (Year 1 being assessed only on this second occasion). The tests related as far as possible to the definition of numeracy and outcomes of effective teaching given above. Aspects of numeracy covered in the tests included:

- Understanding of the number system, including place value, decimals and fractions. For example, given the numbers 30, 76 and 174, Year 2 children were asked to write down the number one less than each.
- Methods of computation, including both known number facts and efficient and accurate methods of calculating. For example, 'share 76 equally among 4' was on the Year 5 test.

- Solving numerical problems, including complex contextualized word problems and abstract mathematical problems concerning the relationships between operations. For example, given that $86 + 57 = 143$ could Year 3 children quickly figure out answers to $86 + 56$, $57 + 6$, $860 + 570$, $85 + 57$, $143 - 86$? Or, asked how many different sandwiches can be made from six different fillings and three types of bread, could Year 4 children identify an appropriate calculation?

Average gains were calculated for each class providing an indicator of 'teacher effectiveness' for the teachers in our project.

Finding effective teachers of numeracy

In ideal circumstances, we might have chosen some teachers; judged their effectiveness through class scores on our tests; and then gone back to look at what the teachers did in their lessons.

However, the project was only funded for just over a year. By the time we had the data on children's gains there was not going to be time to go back and work with the teachers. We had to study classroom processes in the time between the two test administrations. This meant we somehow had to maximize our chances of working with teachers who were already effective.

Selecting potentially effective teachers was done through a progressive 'filtering' from local authority (LA) to school to class. We approached three local authorities (Berkshire, Croydon and Wandsworth) as we knew each held considerable school-level data on standards in numeracy in relation to other school variables. On the basis of these data, each LA agreed to assist in identifying one or two *focus schools*: a total group of four schools identified as performing well above expectations in relation to numeracy. We also made sure that the sample contained schools with different socio-economic intakes in different environments (inner city, suburban, rural).

We also considered it important to include teachers in independent schools. The Incorporated Association of Preparatory Schools assisted us in identifying two further focus schools in the independent sector which were acknowledged to be effective in teaching numeracy. Our main data on teachers were gathered from these focus schools. In order to check out these findings, a further set of five validation schools was also identified. These schools represented a range of levels of performance in mathematics.

So, from an initial sample of all the primary schools in three LAs (some 587 schools), together with independent schools, we had selected 11 schools – six focus schools and five validation schools – to study in detail, giving an overall sample of 90 teachers (Figure 2.3).

From the six focus schools, we worked closely with 18 teachers, three in

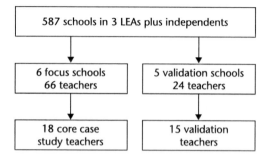

Figure 2.3   The sample of teachers.

each school. This group of 18 teachers formed our sample of *case study teachers*, providing data on classroom practices, together with data on teacher beliefs about, and knowledge of, mathematics, pupils and teaching. Three teachers in each school were identified as those most likely to prove effective, selected through discussion with head teachers and, where appropriate, with advice from the LA inspectors and advisers. While the emphasis was on identifying effective teachers, the 18 were chosen so that teachers were reasonably evenly distributed across year groups 1–6.

Exploring teachers' beliefs and practices

An understanding of the teachers' beliefs and practices was built up from data from four sources:

- questionnaire data from the full sample of 90 teachers (66 in focus schools, 24 in validation schools);
- observations of 54 mathematics lessons with the 18 case study teachers (three for each teacher) and 30 lessons with the 15 validation teachers (two for each teacher);
- three interviews with each of the 18 case study teachers: a general interview on classroom practices, teaching intentions and experiences; a structured task to explore their mathematical understandings; an interview focused on children and the similarities and difference between them;
- two interviews with each of the 15 validation teachers.

Children test data on our tests of numeracy were gathered for all 90 classes in both core and validation schools. All the classes demonstrated gains on our test over the year. Putting the classes in order of their gains provided the range of 'teacher effectiveness'.

Some findings

Some of our findings were surprising in that they challenge some popularly held beliefs about what makes a teacher effective. For example, style of organization for mathematics teaching was not a predictor of how effective teachers were. Whole-class 'question-and-answer' teaching styles were used by both highly effective and comparatively less effective teachers. Similarly, individualized work and small-group work were used by teachers across the range of effectiveness.

At the school level, setting across an age group was used in schools with both high and low proportions of highly effective teachers. The same published mathematics schemes were used by highly effective and comparatively much less effective teachers. Our findings also raised questions about the sort of mathematical knowledge teachers need in order to be effective. Despite what might be expected, being highly effective was not positively associated with higher levels of qualifications in mathematics. The amount of continuing professional development in mathematics education that teachers had undertaken was a better predictor of their effectiveness than the level to which they had formally studied mathematics.

Levels of effectiveness

So, if styles of classroom organization and levels of mathematical qualification did not determine effectiveness, what did? On the basis of the average gains made by each class the teachers were put into three groups: highly effective, effective and moderately effective (Table 2.1). In order to try and answer this question we looked at how our focus case study teachers were distributed across these categories.

The initials of the pseudonyms chosen for the teachers are the same for teachers from the same school, so, for example, Anne, Alan and Alice all

Table 2.1 The case study teachers and levels of effectiveness

Highly effective	Effective	Moderately effective
Anne	Danielle	Beth
Alan	Dorothy	Brian
Alice	Eva	Cath
Barbara	Fay	David
Carole		Elizabeth
Faith		Erica

taught in School A. Year 1 teachers (Claire and Frances) are not included in Table 2.1 since they could not be readily identified according to effectiveness on the basis of the testing of their classes on one occasion only.

By looking at the data for each group of teachers, and in particular those identified as highly effective, we noticed that some patterns began to emerge. Before discussing these, a couple of examples might provide some flavour of what the highly effective teachers did in practice. The first example is adapted from the field notes of Claire's lesson. As indicated it was not possible to determine which of the three categories Claire would be in, but her beliefs and practices were very similar to those of the group of highly effective teachers and the children's responses in class suggested that it was likely that she was a highly effective teacher.

Example 1: Place value

A Year 1 whole-class lesson: There is a large 0–99 hundred square on the board with some numbers filled in. Claire shows the children how looking at the left-hand numbers gives the name of the numbers in that row and how the top row gives the second number (that is, row headed 20 intersects with column headed 4 at 24). She identifies an empty space (say 37) on the hundred square. The children have to work out what the missing number is and someone is invited to the board to fill it in.

On a table are a blue hoop and a yellow hoop and some interlocking cubes. Two children put three cubes into the yellow hoop and seven into the blue hoop. Claire asks each child in turn how many their cubes represent to which they respond 'ten, twenty, thirty and seven'. Under the hundred square are drawn a yellow circle and a blue circle (labelled 'tens' and 'ones' respectively). A pair of children draw squares in the circle for the appropriate number of tens and ones and, in a similar fashion to the pair with the cubes, read out the numbers.

After several numbers have been filled in, the teacher asks what the biggest number on the square is and which number would come next. The children identify 100 and a lively discussion follows on where the box for 100 should be drawn: next to 99 or under 90. They agree to under 90. A child comes and writes it in. Claire adds another hoop to the table and a third circle on the board. While the children can represent 100 using these, 102 causes difficulty and there is much discussion about recording and the order of the digits.

Example 2: Fractions, decimal fractions, percentages and ratios

A Year 6 class: Alan, the teacher, has put a chart on the whiteboard which has columns for fractions, decimal fractions, percentages and ratios. One value has been entered in each row and the children are working in pairs to convert from one form of representation to another. They are using a variety of methods but working mainly in their heads and most are checking their results using a different method.

As they begin to complete the task Alan brings the class together. Individuals are invited to provide answers and explain methods of calculation. The class is attentive to these explanations. More efficient methods are offered and errors dealt with in a supportive manner either by the teacher or other pupils. Finally they discuss the sort of contexts where the different representations would be used.

A connectionist orientation towards teaching numeracy

From our analysis what seemed to distinguish some highly effective teachers from the others was a consistent and coherent set of beliefs about how best to teach mathematics while taking into account children's learning. In particular, the theme of 'connections' was one that particularly struck us. Several of our highly effective teachers seemed to pay attention to:

- connections between different aspects of mathematics, for example, addition and subtraction or fractions, decimals and percentages;
- connections between different representations of mathematics: moving between symbols, words, diagrams and objects;
- connections with children's methods – valuing these and being interested in children's thinking but also sharing other methods.

We came to refer to such teachers as having a *connectionist* orientation to teaching and learning numeracy. This connectionist orientation includes the belief that being numerate involves being both efficient and effective. For example while 2016–1999 can be effectively calculated using a paper and pencil algorithm, it is more efficient to work it out mentally. Being numerate, for the connectionist orientated teacher, requires an awareness of different methods of calculation and the ability to choose an *appropriate* method. As Anne put it: 'I have tried to provide them with a whole range of different ways of going about adding numbers, or taking them away, so that they will be able to become comfortable with the strategies that they like best' (Anne Y2/3/4).

Further to this is the belief that children come to lessons already in possession of some strategies for calculating but that the teacher has responsibility for intervening, working with the children on becoming more efficient. Misunderstandings that children may display are seen as important parts of lessons, needing to be explicitly identified and worked with in order to improve understanding (see Ryan and Williams, Chapter 11).

As indicated, a connectionist orientation emphasizes the links between different aspects of the mathematics curriculum.

> I think you've got to know that they are inverse operations those two (addition and subtraction), and that those two (multiplication and division) are linked, because when you are solving problems mentally you are all the time making links between multiplication, division, addition and subtraction . . . I think mental agility depends on you seeing relationships between numbers and being aware of links.
>
> (Barbara Y6)

The application of number to new situations is important to the connectionist orientation, with children drawing on their mathematical understandings to solve realistic problems. The connectionist orientation also places a strong emphasis on developing reasoning and justification, leading to the children developing early ideas of proof. Reasoning about number is as important as its application, and so working with 'pure' mathematics is as important as applying it to real-life situations.

Associated with the connectionist orientation is a belief that most children are able to learn mathematics given appropriate teaching that explicitly introduces the links between different aspects of mathematics.

> But I have the same expectations for the children, I always think about it as not so much what the children are doing as what they have the potential to do. So even if I have children like Mary in the classroom who are tremendously able, I am really just as excited with the children who are having that nice slow start, because, who knows, tomorrow they may fly – you just don't know.
>
> (Anne Y2/3/4)

Within a constructivist orientation a fundamental belief is that teaching mathematics is based on dialogue between teacher and children, so that teachers better understand the children's thinking and children gain access to the teacher's mathematical knowledge.

> If I am honest with myself I probably spend more time talking with them than doing exercises and things like that . . . because I want them to be able not to just give an answer, I want them to explain the process and what they are doing, to be looking for these links again, and to be able to be adventurous as well.
>
> (Alan Y5/6)

Other orientations towards teaching numeracy

Two other orientations were also identified: one where the teacher's beliefs were more focused upon the role of the teacher (a transmission orientation) and one of beliefs focused upon the children learning mathematics independently (discovery orientation).

The *transmission* orientation means placing more emphasis on teaching than learning. The transmission orientation entails a belief in the importance of a collection of procedures or routines, particularly with regard to paper and pencil methods, one for doing each particular type of calculation regardless of whether or not a different method would be more efficient in a particular case. This emphasis on a set of routines and methods to be learned leads to the presentation of mathematics in discrete packages, for example, fractions taught separately from division.

Teaching is believed to be most effective when it consists of clear verbal explanations of routines. Interactions between teachers and children tend to be question and answer exchanges in order to check whether or not children can reproduce the routine or method being introduced to them. What children already know is of less importance, unless it forms part of a new procedure.

Linked to this is a view of 'using and applying' as the application of mathematics to word problems (basic calculations set in a real-world context). These word problems can be tackled after learning to do calculations or procedures in an abstract form. The numeracy emphasis is on the ability to perform set routines, so the reasoning, logic and proof aspects of mathematical thinking are not seen as particularly relevant.

Children are believed to vary in their ability to become numerate. If the teacher has explained a method clearly and logically, then any failure to learn must be the result of the children's inability rather than a consequence of the teaching. Any misunderstandings that children may display are seen as the result of the children's failure to 'grasp' what was being taught; misunderstandings are remedied by further reinforcement of the 'correct' method and more practice to help children remember.

In the *discovery* orientation learning takes precedence over teaching and the pace of learning is largely determined by the children. Children's own strategies are the most important: understanding is based on working things out for themselves. Children are seen as needing to be 'ready' before they can learn certain mathematical ideas. This results in a view that children vary in their ability to become numerate. Children's misunderstandings are the result of pupils not being 'ready' to learn the ideas.

Teaching children requires extensive use of practical experiences that are seen as embodying mathematical ideas so that they discover methods for themselves. Learning about mathematical concepts precedes the ability to apply these concepts and application is introduced through practical problems.

The discovery-orientated teacher tends to treat all methods of calculation as equally acceptable. As long as an answer is obtained, whether or not the method is particularly effective or efficient is not perceived as important. Children's creation of their own methods is a valued process, and is based upon building up their confidence and ability in practical methods. Calculation methods are selected primarily on the basis of practically representing the operation. The mathematics curriculum is seen as being made up of mostly separate elements.

Orientation and effectiveness

The orientations of connectionist, transmission and discovery are ideal types: no single teacher is likely to hold a set of beliefs that precisely matches those set out within each orientation. However, analysis of our data revealed that some teachers were more predisposed to talk and behave in ways that fitted with one orientation over the others. In particular, Anne, Alan, Barbara, Carole and Faith, all displayed characteristics indicating a high level of orientation towards the connectionist view. On the other hand, Brian and David both displayed strong discovery orientations, while Beth, Elizabeth and Cath were characterized as transmission-orientated teachers (Table 2.2).

Other case study teachers displayed less distinct allegiance to one or other of the three orientations. They held sets of beliefs that drew in part from one or more of the orientations. For example, one teacher had strong connectionist beliefs about the nature of being a numerate pupil but in practice displayed a transmission orientation towards beliefs about how best to teach pupils to become numerate.

The connection between these three orientations and the classification of the teachers into having relatively high, medium or low mean class gain scores suggests that there may be a relationship between pupil learning outcomes and teacher orientations.

Implications of orientations

I suggest that examining orientations towards teaching mathematics can help us understand why practices that have surface similarities may result in different learner outcomes. For example, while all the teachers in the study employed some whole-class question and answer sessions, the nature of the interaction with children within such sessions varied according to orientation. Our highly effective teachers demonstrated a range of classroom

Table 2.2 The relation between orientation and effectiveness

	Highly effective	*Effective*	*Moderately effective*
Strongly connectionist	Anne Alan Barbara Carole Faith		
Strongly transmission			Beth Cath Elizabeth
Strongly discovery			Brian David
No strong orientation	Alice	Danielle Dorothy Eva Fay	Erica

organization styles including whole-class teaching, individual and group work. On such measures their practices were indistinguishable from those of the teachers who were only moderately effective. While the interplay between beliefs and practices is complex, these orientations provide some insight into the mathematical and pedagogical purposes behind particular classroom practices and may be more important than the practices themselves in determining effectiveness.

Exhortations for teachers to adopt new practices may result either in the practices being adapted to fit with existing beliefs or in limited take-up of the practices themselves. As other research on developing teaching has demonstrated, expecting teachers to adopt particular practices without helping them develop a deep understanding of the principles behind these practices does not in itself lead to raised standards (Alexander 1992).

Teachers may find it helpful to examine their belief systems and think about where they stand in relation to these three orientations. In a sense the connectionist approach is not a complete contrast to the other two but embodies the best of both of them in its acknowledgement of the role of both the teacher and the pupils in lessons. Teachers may therefore need to address different issues according to their beliefs: the transmission-orientated teacher may want to consider the attention given to pupil understandings, while the discovery-orientated teacher may need to examine beliefs about the role of the teacher.

Just in case anyone is left wondering what I did with John, I showed him how to find the difference using shopkeeper arithmetic. I hoped we were on to a winner when he said, 'Oh, that's a lot quicker isn't it!' But of course, whether I had any long-term impact is another question.

Note

1   The views expressed here are those of the author and should not be interpreted as representing the views of the Teacher Training Agency.

References

Alexander, R. (1992) *Policy and Practice in Primary Education*. London: Routledge.
Askew, M., Brown, M., Rhodes, V., Wiliam, D. and Johnson, D. (1997) *Effective Teachers of Numeracy: Report of a Study Carried Out for the Teacher Training Agency*. London: King's College, University of London.

3 Teaching for understanding/ understanding for teaching

Patrick Barmby, Tony Harries and Steve Higgins

Introduction: the context for understanding

The issue of understanding in mathematics has been a particular focus for educational policy in England and Wales in recent years. A report published by Ofsted (2008: 5) highlighted the lack of development of mathematical understanding in the classroom:

> The fundamental issue for teachers is how better to develop pupils' mathematical understanding. Too often, pupils are expected to remember methods, rules and facts without grasping the underpinning concepts, making connections with earlier learning and other topics, and making sense of the mathematics so that they can use it independently.

The *Independent Review of the Primary Curriculum: Final Report* (the Rose Review) (DCSF 2009) recommended that one of the proposed strands of learning should be 'mathematical understanding'. It highlighted the need to develop children's thinking and discussion in mathematics, and opportunities to use and apply mathematics – areas that perhaps are being neglected in the classroom through a conception of 'numeracy' that is too narrow. The *Independent Review of Mathematics Teaching in the Early Years and Primary Schools* (the Williams Review) (DCSF 2008: 7) specifically recommended the provision of mathematics specialist teachers 'with deep mathematical subject and pedagogical knowledge', with a focus on impacting on standards and attainment in mathematics. A Nuffield review of mathematical learning (Nuñes et al. 2009: 3) aimed 'to identify the issues that are fundamental to understanding children's mathematics learning' and focused throughout on 'key understandings in mathematics'.

However, although the importance of understanding is agreed upon, a vital issue is what we mean by understanding in mathematics and how we teach in order to develop it in children. We have already seen that it draws on ideas and terms such as 'discussion' (see Monaghan, Chapter 4), 'using and applying' (see Ollerton, Chapter 6) and 'deep subject and pedagogical knowledge'. But what is this deep knowledge? Why are discussion and using and applying important? In this chapter, we set out to clarify exactly what we mean by understanding in mathematics. In doing so, we look at the implications of our definition on teaching for understanding and the understanding that teachers need to bring to the classroom. We hope that this discussion of understanding will help teachers and prospective teachers of mathematics to be clear about why they are doing what they are doing in the classroom, and also help them to develop their practice in the future.

Defining understanding

An important characteristic of understanding is that it involves connections between different ideas or concepts. More specifically, Hiebert and Carpenter (1992: 67) defined mathematical understanding as involving the building up of a conceptual 'network':

> The mathematics is understood if its mental representation is part of a network of representations. The degree of understanding is determined by the number and strength of its connections. A mathematical idea, procedure, or fact is understood thoroughly if it is linked to existing networks with stronger or more numerous connections.

The mental representations that make up this network are defined by Davis (1984: 203) as follows: 'Any mathematical concept, or technique, or strategy – or anything else mathematical that involves either information or some means of processing information – if it is to be present in the mind at all, must be represented in some way.'

Goldin (1998) highlighted the fact that we have a variety of internal representations, including verbal, imagistic, symbolic, planning (for example, problem-solving approaches) and affective (that is, attitudes about maths) representations. Therefore, we have this picture of understanding as being this variety of internal or mental representations associated with mathematical concepts, being connected together to form a complex network. This view of mathematical understanding is closely related to the 'connectionist' view of mathematics teaching (see Askew, Chapter 2). The question then is how are these mental representations connected together?

Sierpinska (1994) identified the 'processes of understanding' as involving connections being made between mental concepts through reasoning

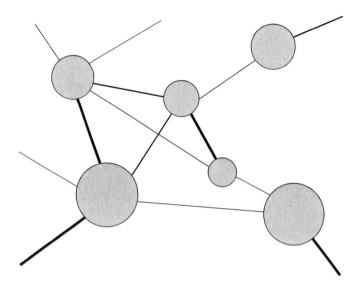

Figure 3.1 Representational–reasoning model of understanding.

processes. For example, in our minds, the concepts of 'addition' and 'multiplication' may be connected because we can show that multiplication can be the same as 'repeated addition' – perhaps because calculations give the same answer, or perhaps through pictures such as the number line (we will say a little more about the 'quality' of this reasoning later). Therefore, the overall picture or model of understanding that we have adopted is a 'representational–reasoning' model of understanding, as shown in Figure 3.1. The model shows the different representations (the circles) connected together by different levels of reasoning (the lines).

It has to be emphasized here that this is not meant to be a picture of what is actually happening inside our minds. Rather, we emphasize that this is a 'model' of understanding: a picture that helps us to make sense of this concept. However, because we have this picture to work with, we can start to look at what such a model means for what teachers do in the mathematics classroom. In the next section, we examine the implications of the model for teaching for understanding.

Implications of the model: teaching for understanding

The first issue that we can note from the model of understanding is that there is no limit to the connections we can make – there is no 'boundary' to our understanding:

> Understanding is not a dichotomous state, but a continuum ...
> Everyone understands to some degree anything that they know
> about. It also follows that understanding is never complete; for we
> can always add more knowledge, another episode, say, or refine an
> image, or see new links between things we know already.
>
> (White and Gunstone 1992: 6)

Understanding of a mathematical topic is not something that we suddenly
attain at the end of some programme of learning. Rather, it is a continuously
evolving process – a process rather different from the often conveyed perception of mathematics as being about 'right' and 'wrong' answers. The latter
issue of 'wrong' answers is also challenged by the idea that 'everyone understands to some degree anything that they know about'. Certainly, we all have
'misconceptions', but to simply label them as 'wrong' fails to recognize that
there are often good reasons for us to possess these misconceptions (see Ryan
and Williams, Chapter 11). For example, a child that states that we cannot do
$2 \div 5$ because '5 into 2 doesn't go', is basing their reasoning on a conception
of division as repeated subtraction. Within this limited understanding, their
misconception is entirely reasonable. In order to tackle this misconception, we
need to build upon their conception of division (that is, increase the variety of
mental representations) and to develop their subsequent reasoning.

In examining the issue of misconceptions, we have touched upon the issue
of how we develop understanding in the mathematics classroom. And because
our model of understanding has two components – the representations and
the reasoning – this provides us with two areas to explore with regards to how
we teach for understanding. Let us examine first the issue of representations.
In order to develop the range of mental representations available to a person,
we can provide them with a variety of external representations (for example,
concrete manipulatives, pictures, symbolic representations, procedures). Let us
give an example of this from some work that we have been carrying out with a
group of experienced primary mathematics teachers. We were working
with the array representation for multiplication (Figure 3.2). One of the
strengths of the array is that we can easily show the distributive properties of
multiplication. For example, from the diagram, we can see that 8×6 is the
same as $(5 + 3) \times (5 + 1)$, which in turn is $(5 \times 5) + (5 \times 1) + (3 \times 5) + (3 \times 1)$. Now,
let us look at another representation for multiplication, that of the grid
method (Figure 3.3).

Figure 3.3 shows the grid method to calculate 18×16. By comparing the
two representations of the grid method and the array, we can see why we can
split the numbers in the grid method as we do. But one of the teachers we were
working with went further, with the realization that the grid method did not
have to be based on units, tens, and so on. For example, the grid could be split
into multiples of 5 (see Figure 3.4).

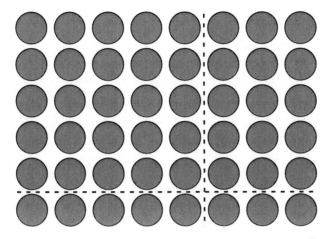

Figure 3.2 Array representation for multiplication.

The teacher felt that this modified grid method might be better for lower-attaining pupils as they could change more difficult times tables such as the 8 times tables into the 5 and 3 times tables. By increasing the range of representations available to the teacher, this led to the development of their understanding in multiplication.

One aspect of teaching for understanding can be seen to be this development of the range of mental representations of mathematical concepts. However, this in itself is not sufficient. This has been highlighted by Sowell (1989) who concluded that the long-term use of concrete materials led to

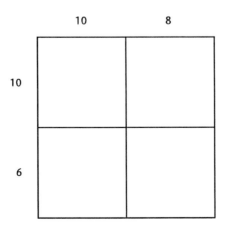

Figure 3.3 Grid method for multiplication.

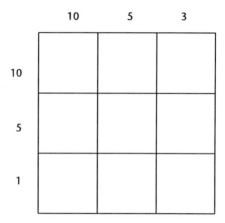

Figure 3.4 Modified grid method.

benefits for children. The emphasis was on *long-term* use, and significant benefits were not observed for pictorial representations. In fact, we have emphasized in our model of understanding that we need to develop our reasoning between representations as well.

The process of trying to make connections between our existing understanding of a concept and alternative representations for that concept is what brings about the processes of assimilation of the new representation (if our existing understanding is compatible) or accommodation of the new representation (through restructuring of our understanding) that was highlighted by Piaget (1968). Therefore, an additional implication for teaching for understanding in the classroom is to provide opportunities for children to develop their 'reasonings' – for example, explaining why they do a calculation in a certain way (Nuñes et al. 2009: 10–11). Now this reasoning may not necessarily be formal mathematical reasoning – for example, a child might split up a multiplication calculation according to the distributive law simply because their teacher had told them that they could do this. Nevertheless, this is the reasoning that is used by the child. We can now bring in here the issue of discussion that we highlighted at the beginning of the chapter. Hoyles (1985) suggested three aspects to pupil–pupil discussion:

- articulating ideas brings about reflection on those ideas;
- discussion involves framing ideas in a way that will be accepted by others;
- listening to others modifies your own thoughts.

All three of these aspects of discussion bring about an examination of one's own reasonings. Discussion and explanation of methods by children can be used in our teaching for understanding so that children can reflect upon the quality of their reasoning, and thereby strengthen or change their connections (see Monaghan, Chapter 4).

The representational–reasoning model of understanding provides us with a basis for how we can approach teaching for understanding in the mathematics classroom. Interestingly, both 'representing' and 'reasoning' appears in the five themes within 'using and applying' identified by guidance notes provided by the Department for Education and Skills (DfES 2006: 4):

- Solving problems;
- Representing – analyse, record, do, check, confirm;
- Enquiring – plan, decide, organize, interpret, reason, justify;
- Reasoning – create, deduce, apply, explore, predict, hypothesize, test;
- Communicating – explain methods and solutions, choices, decisions, reasoning.

However, based on the explanation of the themes provided by the DfES, where aspects of representation and reasoning seem to appear in different themes, we could simplify the picture of using and applying mathematics in terms of the two aspects of understanding that we have already identified. Let us draw on some example problems from the guidance paper to illustrate this. First, we have a word problem such as 'How much will seven oranges cost if four oranges cost £1?' Based on our existing understanding, we could represent this problem in a variety of ways (Figure 3.5).

We can then examine each alternative representation to see which is most useful for providing an answer. Perhaps multiplying by 1¾, and therefore multiplying £1 to £1.75, provides the most direct answer. The important issue here is that the act of representing the problem in alternative ways provides us with a solution. Also, the act of solving the problem results in different representations of the concept being linked (for example, multiplication by fractions with ratios). The sharing of problem-solving approaches in the classroom through discussion will hopefully result in new connections being made

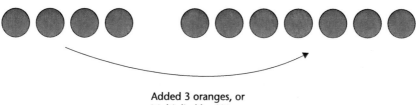

Added 3 oranges, or
Multiplied by 1¾, or
Ratio of 4 : 7

Figure 3.5   Representing a problem in a variety of ways.

within children's understanding. Taking a broader view of mental representations as well, this will also result in new 'planning' representations (for example, what to do when faced with a ratio problem) within this understanding.

Let us look at one more problem – this time a sequence problem. What is the 51st number in the sequence 2, 7, 12 . . .? We can start by representing the problem in a different way again (Figure 3.6).

Figure 3.6   Representing a sequence.

We could keep adding 5 until we reach the 51st number. However, this is rather laborious – let us use another representation. The first number is 2 with no fives added; the second number is 2 with 1 five added; the third number is 2 with 2 fives added, and so on. From this pattern, we can reason that the 51st number would be 2 with 50 fives added, or 252. However, this is not the end of the problem. We can also examine the reasoning we have used. Are we correct in reasoning that 'adding 5' is the only way in which the sequence 2, 7, 12 can be obtained? Are there other representations that we could have used? Likewise, in the previous problem, are there other ways of approaching this problem? Calling into question our reasoning in a problem, as well as using a variety of representations, can lead to a development in our understanding either through strengthening connections or developing new ones. We can therefore start to see the role of using and applying in developing our understanding of mathematical concepts.

Let us examine one last implication of the earlier model on teaching for understanding – this time a particular difficulty that the model implies. The complex network that makes up our model means that if we are to assess a child's understanding of a mathematical concept, then we need to try and assess the variety of representations and reasonings associated with that concept in a child's mind. This is no simple task: 'Understanding usually cannot be inferred from a single response on a single task; any individual task can be performed correctly without understanding. A variety of tasks, then, are needed to generate a profile of behavioural evidence' (Hiebert and Carpenter 1992: 89).

A broader approach to assessment then, rather than one simply based on an examination of procedural calculations, is required. Perhaps we can use problem-solving tasks where we have greater access to the representations that the child can draw upon or greater access to their reasoning. Davis (1984) advocates the use of task-based interviews where children are questioned while they tackle mathematical tasks about the approach they are using, the reasons for their approach, the possibility of other approaches, and so on. Alternatively, we could use other approaches such as mind maps to access the variety of representations that a child associates with a concept.

This need for a broader approach to assessment is seen in intervention situations where it is important to access a child's understanding so that gaps in understanding and misconceptions can be identified. In the Every Child Counts intervention (see Dunn, Matthews and Dowrick, Chapter 17), teachers spend an initial period of around two weeks carrying out a broad assessment of a child in order to identify particular difficulties in numeracy. This assessment involves traditional tests, classroom observations and task-based diagnostic work with the child. In the broader context of teaching for understanding, we need to be aware of the limitations of our traditional forms of assessment, and look for opportunities within our teaching where a broader assessment of children's understanding can be gained. This approach is very much part of the introduction of APP or 'Assessing Pupils' Progress' by the National Strategies in England and Wales (see Hodgen and Askew, Chapter 10).

Implications of the model: understanding for teaching

Through the model of understanding that we have adopted, we have been able to highlight some implications for how we can approach 'teaching for under-standing' in the mathematics classroom. Another area that we would like to explore is the understanding that is required by teachers themselves – what the Williams Review (DCSF 2008: 3) referred to as 'deep mathematical subject and pedagogical knowledge'. We can use the picture of understanding that we have, alongside existing research in this area, to gain further insight into this 'deep knowledge'.

Previous research by Shulman (1986) has been very influential in provid-ing a theoretical view for the categories of knowledge possessed by teachers. With regard to subject-specific knowledge (for example, mathematics), these categories are:

- subject-matter content knowledge;
- pedagogical content knowledge;
- curricular knowledge.

Subject-matter content knowledge includes not only the organized factual content of the subject, but also how the subject functions as a discipline in terms of establishing the validity of ideas. In mathematics, this is the need for proof and deductive reasoning in order to establish as strongly as possible the connections between ideas. This view of subject-matter content knowledge is mirrored by what constitutes our understanding and also how we improve the quality of our reasonings that we touched upon before. Pedagogical knowledge is the content knowledge required to teach the subject. Shulman proposed the following components to this area of content knowledge: how we represent ideas, including the most powerful representations (models, illustrations, analogies, examples, and so on) for teaching, and also an understanding of how pupils generally learn the subject (including what makes topics easy or hard, typical conceptions and misconceptions, and how to tackle typical misconceptions). Curricular knowledge, then, is knowledge about the teaching programmes and teaching materials used in the subject.

Although Shulman's work is best remembered for these categories of teacher knowledge, he also strongly emphasized the importance of 'understanding', that is teachers' understanding, in the teaching of a subject: 'With Aristotle we declare that the ultimate test of understanding rests with the ability to transform one's knowledge into teaching. Those who can, do. Those who understand, teach' (Shulman 1986: 14).

Returning to pedagogical content knowledge, this emphasis on understanding is also highlighted by the need for a variety of representations required to teach a subject: 'Since there are no single most powerful forms of representations, the teacher must have at hand a veritable armamentarium of alternative forms of representation, some of which derive from research whereas other originate through practice' (Shulman 1986: 9).

This last quote also emphasizes the 'forms' or sources of knowledge for teachers. Shulman emphasized *propositional* knowledge in the form of principles that are taught to teachers, which is introduced to them through research on teaching (this chapter is mainly propositional!). We also have *case* knowledge which is more detailed reporting of specific events or sequences of events which are presented to the teacher (for example, through research, through courses, through colleagues, and so on). Then we have *strategic* knowledge where the teachers experience particular events themselves, drawing on propositional and case knowledge but developing these in light of practice.

The understanding of mathematics that a teacher has is based then on their subject-matter content knowledge and pedagogical content knowledge, where concepts and ideas are connected, not just through mathematical reasoning, but also reasoning based on principles, examples of specific cases and personal experience in the classroom. In fact, research has shown that for more experienced teachers, their subject-matter content knowledge and their pedagogical content knowledge are indeed more connected (see, for example, Krauss et al. 2008). To illustrate these connections, let us provide an example from our own experience in the classroom.

We argued earlier that the array representation is a useful representation for multiplication, as it clearly shows the distributive properties of multiplication. However, when we have introduced this representation to children in the classroom, we have found that younger children (for example, Year 2) are very unlikely to recognize the array as a representation of multiplication. This is despite the fact that according to the framework for teaching used in schools in England and Wales, it is suggested that the array is introduced to them in Year 2 for multiplication. Even in Year 4, only about half of the children will have this recognition. In Year 6, however, almost all the children recognize the array as a representation of multiplication. Therefore, despite our mathematical understanding that the array is a powerful representation for multiplication, and despite our knowledge of the curriculum, our pedagogical knowledge based on classroom experience suggests that we have to be careful about how we use the array in the classroom. Perhaps we need to introduce it alongside less abstract representations of multiplication (Figure 3.7). We can, in turn, examine this reasoning in the future through further work in the classroom to see whether this does help children to recognize the array as a representation of multiplication.

What we are emphasizing here is that although the understanding of mathematics subject matter that a teacher brings to the classroom is important, the understanding required for teaching is broader than that. In this understanding for teaching, the constituent representations and reasoning go beyond that of mathematical concepts alone, but include pedagogical principles, examples and experiences, informing our reasoning in building up our understanding.

Conclusion

In conclusion, what we have tried to do in this chapter is to look in detail at this concept of 'understanding' that seems to be of central importance for how we teach children in the mathematics classroom. What we hope is helpful for teachers and student teachers is that, by trying to clarify exactly what we mean by this idea, there are clear implications for how we should be approaching the teaching of the subject in the classroom. Of course, it is not as if the recommendations for using, for example, discussion or using and applying in the classroom are not already there. However, what we feel to be important

Figure 3.7   Array alongside less abstract representation (plate of strawberries).

about this examination of understanding is that it makes clear why there are these recommendations. We also hope that it provides a model with which we can examine our own understanding of the subject.

We have further emphasized that the understanding required for teaching is more than that. Of course, we all accept that there is pedagogical knowledge that we need in order to teach the subject. However, our understanding is more integrated than separate bodies of subject and pedagogical knowledge. Our subject knowledge informs our pedagogy but, in turn, our pedagogical knowledge causes us to reflect on our subject knowledge. This then has implications for teachers' professional development and the training of teachers too. In developing their skills in teaching mathematics, we need to develop teachers' understanding; we need them to know how they can develop pupils' understanding; and we need to provide opportunities to reflect upon both of these so that they can further develop as teachers. We can illustrate this with two comments from student teachers of primary mathematics that we work with:

> Although I know I have the subject knowledge to be able to teach to the children, I feel as if sometimes, although I have learnt so much on the course, I have not learnt things like, how to teach it, how to do the addition and the subtraction and how they are doing it in schools.

> When it came to teaching it, I found it quite difficult to explain what I knew. I accept rules and . . . I apply it and it works. Trying to explain that to children, I found it at first a bit like, 'how am I going to break down what I just accept?' . . . But by the end of my placement this year, I felt much more confident in doing that. I would start to go back over what I knew and figure out how I had learnt it and how I had come to the point to be just doing it, which helped when it came to teaching it.

Both comments emphasize the importance of developing understanding in teaching mathematics. And this development will be an ongoing process, where, as we have seen from the model of understanding, it is a process without any end point, where we are continually developing as teachers of mathematics.

References

Davis, R.B. (1984) *Learning Mathematics: The Cognitive Approach to Mathematics Education*. London: Croom Helm.

DCSF (Department for Children, Schools and Families) (2008) *Independent Review of Mathematics Teaching in Early Years Settings and Primary Schools* (Williams Review). Nottingham: DCSF. http://publications.teachernet.gov.uk/ eOrderingDownload/Williams%20Mathematics.pdf (accessed March2010).

DCSF (Department for Children, Schools and Families) (2009) *Independent Review of the Primary Curriculum: Final Report* (Rose Review). Nottingham: DCSF. http://publications.teachernet.gov.uk/eOrderingDownload/Primary_ curriculum_ Report.pdf (accessed March 2010).

DfES (Department for Education and Skills) (2006) *Primary Framework for Literacy and Mathematics – Guidance Paper – Using and Applying Mathematics.* http:// nationalstrategies.standards.dcsf.gov.uk/node/47324 (accessed March 2010).

Goldin, G.A. (1998) Representational systems, learning and problem solving in mathematics, *Journal of Mathematical Behavior,* 17(2): 137–65.

Hiebert, J. and Carpenter, T.P. (1992) Learning and teaching with understanding, in D. A. Grouws (ed.) *Handbook of Research on Mathematics Teaching and Learning.* New York: Macmillan.

Hoyles, C. (1985) What is the point of group discussion in mathematics? *Educational Studies in Mathematics,* 16(2): 205–14.

Krauss, S., Brunner, M., Kunter, M. et al. (2008) Pedagogical content knowledge and content knowledge of secondary mathematics teachers, *Journal of Educational Psychology,* 100(3): 716–25.

Nuñes, T., Bryant, P. and Watson, A. (2009) *Key Understandings in Mathematics Learning.* London: The Nuffield Foundation.

Ofsted (Office for Standards in Education) (2008) *Mathematics: Understanding the Score.* London: Ofsted.

Piaget, J. (1968) *Six Psychological Studies.* London: University of London Press.

Shulman, L.S. (1986) Those who understand: knowledge growth in teaching, *Educational Researcher,* 15(2): 4–14.

Sierpinska, A. (1994) *Understanding in Mathematics.* London: Falmer Press.

Sowell, E.J. (1989) Effects of manipulative materials in mathematics education, *Journal for Research in Mathematics Education,* 20(5): 498–505.

White, R. and Gunstone, R. (1992) *Probing Understanding.* London: Falmer Press.

4 Thinking aloud means talking allowed: group work in the primary school mathematics classroom [1]

Frank Monaghan

Introduction

The 1980s saw a shift away from a view of mathematics as a teacher-directed activity where students were taught algorithmic routines that they then practised in splendid isolation towards a more collaborative, investigative, problem-solving approach. This change was reflected in, and disseminated further through, some key documents on the teaching of mathematics in schools such as the highly influential Cockcroft Report (*Mathematics Counts*) (DES 1982). These ideas have survived the various iterations of the national curriculum orders for mathematics, numeracy strategies and government reports such as the *Independent Review of Mathematics Teaching in Early Years Settings and Primary Schools* (the Williams Review) (DCSF 2008). In all these documents, the role of discussion in developing students' mathematical abilities is seen as central, as Cockroft (DES 1982: 72), for example, stated:

> By the term 'discussion' we mean more than the short questions and answers which arise during exposition by the teacher . . . The ability to 'say what you mean and mean what you say' should be one of the outcomes of good mathematics teaching. This ability develops as a result of opportunities to talk about mathematics, to explain and discuss results which have been obtained, and to test hypotheses . . . Pupils need the explicit help, which can only be given by extended discussion, to establish these relationships, even pupils whose mathematical attainment is high do not easily do this for themselves.

There are essentially two key aspects that have emerged from research into the explicit teaching of talk. The first is the potential benefits for individual learners of participating in effective group work, not only in terms of insights gained from the contributions of others but also through having an opportunity to externalize and make explicit their own thinking to their partners and to themselves. The second is the crucial role of teachers in enabling successful collaborative talk and using the insights gained from it in assessing their students' progress and planning for future learning. This chapter addresses both of these aspects through a description of an approach known as Thinking Together.

The Thinking Together approach

Thinking Together is a project that began in the mid-1990s at the Open University based on the work of Vygotsky (1986), who argued that children learn through their interactions with (more capable) peers and adults. He proposed that engagement in *intermental* activity (social interaction) fosters the development of *intramental* (individual) cognitive abilities. The research is thus founded on a sociocultural model of education, in which talking to learn is central. Its fundamental premise is that the ability to communicate effectively is a key skill that children need to develop in every aspect of their lives and one that lies at the heart of educational success. Central to the Thinking Together approach is the belief that talk for learning can and should be explicitly taught. A goal arising from this belief is to enable teachers and students to conceptualize talk as, in Neil Mercer's phrase, 'interthinking', which he defines as 'our use of language for thinking together, for collectively making sense of experience and solving problems' (Mercer 2000: 1).

The Thinking Together project has sought to investigate and apply these insights in classroom settings and has had a significant influence on educational policy and practice in the UK, having been incorporated into official guidance and training materials. The research and classroom experience of the Thinking Together team and the teachers involved in its various projects have shown that the key conditions for, and features of, effective talk are that:

- everyone is encouraged to contribute;
- everyone listens actively;
- ideas and opinions are treated with respect;
- information is shared;
- challenges are welcomed; reasons are required;
- contributions build on what has gone before;
- alternatives are discussed before decisions are taken;
- groups work towards agreement before an action is taken;
- it is possible for participants to change their mind;
- discussion is understood to be a way of learning.

Left to itself, classroom discussion rarely displays many of these positive features. Observation of children working in groups (but sadly not always *as* groups) has led to the characterization of three types of talk.

1 Disputational talk

Disputational talk is characterized by assertions, disagreement and short exchanges between participants in which there is little evidence of any explicit reasoning. Typical of this sort of talk will be the proliferation of utterances such as, 'That's wrong, it goes there, stupid', 'It's number 2, it's number 2', 'You're wrong, I'm right, end of story'.

2 Cumulative talk

Cumulative talk is characterized by self-repetition and elaboration leading to uncritical agreement, again with little evidence of shared meanings being created. Such talk is usually calm and unaggressive. It often arises when groups are organized on the basis of friendship. Typical utterances would be, 'Okay, well I suppose we might as well . . .' or 'That's fine, whatever, so long as you put in what I said as well . . .'.

3 Exploratory talk

As defined by Wegerif and Mercer (1997: 54), exploratory talk occurs when:

> Partners engage critically but constructively with each other's ideas. Statements and suggestions are offered for joint consideration. These may be challenged and counter-challenged, but challenges are justified and alternative hypotheses are offered. Compared with the other two types, in exploratory talk knowledge is made more publicly accountable and reasoning is more visible in the talk.

Typical utterances will be, 'What do you think?', 'Why do you think that?', 'I think x because . . .', 'Is there another way of looking at it?'

Exploratory talk is the most likely to display the features of effective talk described earlier. Students are, however, rarely explicitly taught how to engage in this kind of talk. A more typical pattern is one in which the teacher asks a question, a student responds and the teacher gives evaluative feedback. This form of 'triadic dialogue' (Sinclair and Coulthard 1975) is termed IRF (Initiation, Response, Feedback), and has been more informally described as 'guess what's in the teacher's head'; not necessarily the best strategy for developing reflective thought and practices!

In order to promote the development of exploratory talk, the Thinking

Together approach typically involves a series of lessons devised with teachers in order to provide a framework both for them and their students. Numerous studies (see Mercer and Littleton 2007) have repeatedly demonstrated that exploratory talk can be successfully developed in primary school children; that this training improves students' capacity to reason and solve problems both individually and in groups; and that this training also has positive impacts on knowledge and abilities in a range of curriculum areas.

The Thinking Together approach has been applied across the age range and in a number of curriculum areas, including mathematics. As Wegerif and Dawes (2004: 102) point out: 'Maths is not only a way of thinking inside an individual mind; it is also a kind of language. That is, maths can offer a form of social communication between people. To become fluent in that language, as with any language, children need guidance and opportunities to practise.' This principle guided the work of the project[2] described below whose aim was to develop an approach to enhance pupils' skills in talking and thinking in the mathematics classroom.

The study

The study was conducted in six primary school classes across four schools, two located in London and two in Milton Keynes. Two of the teachers in the Milton Keynes schools had previous experience of working on a Thinking Together project; the others were all new to the approach. The study involved the use of computer software programs produced by SMILE Mathematics[3] with which the teachers were not previously familiar. While integral to this particular study, the approach has been shown to be equally effective in non-ICT settings and would apply to other similarly constructed group-work situations, as will be evident from the transcripts of the teachers' and students' talk.

We held two training sessions for the teachers to introduce them to the software and the Thinking Together approach and then developed a series of lesson plans in collaboration with the teachers aimed at introducing their students to the approach and leading in to the mathematics lessons in which it would be applied. This consisted of three lessons of about 60 minutes duration, each including activities aimed at developing the skills needed to work and learn together effectively using ICT. It takes a high level of planning and commitment to ensure students work *as* groups and not just *in* groups.

Twelve lessons were video-recorded including a sequence of three lessons introducing the students to the approach as described below. We also recorded children working with various computer programs including the one focused on here called *3 in a Line*, which is a variant on the popular game Connect 4 involving the use of coordinates to identify where counters are to be placed on screen, a free version of which (but without the coordinates element) is available online at http://www.mathsisfun.com/games/connect4.html (accessed March 2010). Given the competing demands on classroom time, teachers needed some persuading to take time out of their Year 6 mathematics lessons in order to 'talk about talk'. The fact that they were willing to do so in the face of concern and pressure about preparations for the national tests spoke volumes about their commitment to the project.

Lesson one: talking about talk

The objective for this lesson, shared with the students, is to raise awareness of talk: 'We are learning to talk about talk.' In this lesson students discuss such questions as:

- Who thinks they are a talkative person?
- Who thinks they are a quiet person?
- Who do you like talking to? Why?
- When are you asked not to talk? Why?
- Why is it really helpful to be able to talk?
- What sort of things can we do by talking together?

The students work in groups of three, ideally not friendship based and preferably of mixed gender as this has been found to help avoid unhelpful stalemate or unconsidered consent. Each group is given a set of picture cards showing people engaged in various types of everyday talk activities. They discuss what sort of communication is taking place and try to describe the talk. They feed this back to the whole class. They then practise talking and listening to each other in pairs about a topic of their choice, and again feed back to the whole class. In groups, they discuss their understanding of a set of words related to talk such as, *decide, persuade, interrupt, discuss, listen, share, argue, reason,* and so on. The lesson ends with a plenary discussion on what makes a good talker and listener, and how these skills might be useful in class.

Lesson two: agreeing the ground rules for talk

The objective for this lesson is to establish a set of 'ground rules' for talk: 'We are learning to agree a set of ground rules for talking to each other.' The lesson begins with an introduction to the idea of 'ground rules' as basic rules everyone can agree to. There is a discussion of other kinds of rules, such as those used in a board game, and of what would happen if the rules were ignored or arbitrarily changed. At this point, the students consider what sort of rules might apply for talk in the classroom. They then work in groups of three and are given a set of cards with possible rules on them and have to decide whether they are good, bad or uncertain. They are asked to decide on the four they think are most important and then to devise a further two of their own. The outcomes are shared and they agree on a set of ground rules for their class.

Here, as an example, is a set of ground rules produced by a class in one of the previous studies:

Class 5D Rules for Talk

- Everyone should have a chance to talk;
- Everyone's ideas should be listened to;
- Each member of the group should be asked:
    - What do you think?
    - Why do you think that?
- Look at and listen to the person talking;
- After discussion, the group should agree on a group idea.

It is interesting to note how well these rules accord with the features of effective talk identified previously. The rules developed in each class in this study (and others) were all similar to this example.

Lesson three: practising the ground rules

The objectives for this lesson are to use the ground rules for talk on mathematical problems designed to address such problems as mentally adding or subtracting a pair of numbers; mentally adding several numbers; and solving mathematical problems or puzzles. The lesson begins with a whole-class session in which the children are asked to recall the ground rules for talk they have established. An emphasis is placed on applying the ground rules for talk in a mathematical context. The students are then introduced to (or revise) the concept of 'magic squares' – typically a 3 × 3 grid containing the digits 1–9 which students have to arrange in such a way that all rows, columns and diagonals have the same sum. We used a simple Word table to demonstrate this idea and the students then worked in groups of three on the task of completing the magic grid. The teacher's role was to monitor and intervene in their activity, always keeping the focus on using the ground rules for talk. The plenary required the students to report back on how they had solved the problems and how they had organized their group work. They were also asked to comment on how well they had used the ground rules.

Subsequent lessons followed a similar pattern, starting with a review of the ground rules; an introduction to the objectives (which always included a 'talk' objective) and the activities; group work around the computer; and a plenary to discuss the outcomes. In these lessons, students worked on programs chosen for their mathematical appropriacy and which were all strategy games that made reasoned discussion essential as they had to reach consensus before making a move.

Outcomes

Previous studies have established the benefits of the Thinking Together approach on a variety of measures (including the Raven's Progressive Matrices, a test of non-verbal reasoning, taken as pre- and post-tests) and on our own measures of change in language use by the children. In one study (Mercer et al. 1999) students were recorded doing one of the Raven's non-verbal tests prior to the Thinking Together lessons and again afterwards. Table 4.1 emerged, indicating significant changes in the use of key words associated with collaborative thinking.

These examples demonstrate how the children's use of key markers of exploratory talk increased significantly as a result of the intervention, for example, the fourfold rise in the logical connective 'because', indicating explicit reasoning, and the even more dramatic rise in the use of conditional verb forms, such as 'would' and 'could', that indicate hypothesis making.

In this project, however, we were more interested in examining the kinds of effective interactions and strategies that were developed by the teachers and students. To this end, we filmed 18 lessons, including initial sessions on developing the ground rules for talk and work on the mathematical activities. The analysis of the transcripts revealed some interesting insights into the role of the teacher in scaffolding effective collaborative talk; into how the students developed their own 'community of practice' (Lave and Wenger 1991); and into the students' conceptualizations of the computer as a partner in their activity. These insights are discussed below.

Table 4.1 Significant changes in the use of key words

Key word	Pre	Post
Because	25	100
Agree	7	87
I think	7	87
Would	1	15
Could	2	14

The role of the teacher

Teachers provide a key role in modelling appropriate language and behaviour to the students. In the following extract (which, incidentally, demonstrates the effective use of triadic discourse – not all IRF is bad!), the teacher both models and rehearses the sort of language and conduct that is expected:

Extract 1

1	Teacher	Anything else I might hear?
2	Students	I disagree because.
3	Teacher	'I disagree with you because,' good, well done. Esme?
4	Student 1	Have we got any more ideas to share?
5	Teacher	'Have we got any more ideas?' Maybe they're not the
6		only moves we can do. Maybe there are different ideas?
7	Student 2	Don't think in your head, think aloud.

The teacher here requires the students to make explicit the kind of language that will be needed and models its use herself by reflecting aloud on alternatives (lines 5–6), focusing on the need to explore and 'share' alternatives. Her own use of positive reinforcement to Esme (line 3) also serves as a model to the students of the social relations that she is seeking to encourage between the children.

Another crucial role for the teacher is that of monitor. Moving around the groups, the teacher is able to observe points at which an intervention would help, for example, to check the students' understanding and probe for shifts in thinking, as in this extract:

Extract 2

1	Teacher	Can I ask you a question? Did you place your counter in the middle?
2	J, T and C	Yes.
3	Teacher	Brian was the only one of you three who said you should . . .
4		Have you changed your idea about that?
5	J	Yes.
6	Teacher	Why?
7	J	Because then you can anywhere. You can go there,
8		there and there . . .
9	Teacher	What do you think Claire?
10	C	If you do it (4,4) you've got more chance. You can do it
11		anyway. You can block the computer too.

The teacher here is not only checking their mathematical strategies and ability to justify their reasoning, she is also making explicit the advantages of thinking together. By bringing her students to acknowledge that Brian had been right to pose an initially unpopular alternative, she creates space for the 'outsider' to be included and makes being able to change one's mind a sign of strength rather than weakness. Her question to Claire (line 9) also models the desirability of including all participants and allows Claire to externalize her understanding to the group.

In addition to this sort of direct intervention, teachers have also found other ways to support the Thinking Together approach by providing students with cue cards on Post-it notes so that they can refer to the ground rules during the lesson. This strategy has the positive effect of providing an aide-mémoire for students during the activity, which has also helped students with challenging behaviour by giving them a structure to work within as they develop a new 'self' as an effective member of the mathematics discourse community.

Exploratory talk in action

In the following exchange between two boys (one of whom, R, is learning English as an additional language), it is possible to see how a student is encouraged to shift position as a result of positive engagement with a fellow classmate.

Extract 3

1	A	So we move this one to here.
2	R	Yeah. Move that one to there.
3	A	Wait. Why do you think that?
4	R	Because the feeling's right. The computer hasn't gone
5		nowhere yet so we can move there and there. All you can do is
6		move them there and there so we might as well move that one.
7	A	So you're saying if we can move that one there we can move
8		that one as well.
9	R	No. I saying if we move that there and move that there, first
10		move that, then move this here.
11	A	But what if the computer moves that?
12	R	We've still got a chance. This one can move, that one can . . .
13	A	I agree now. I get what you're saying.

R shifts from a position where he initially appears to be relying solely on an unarticulated, instinctive response ('the feeling's right', line 4) to one where, in the face of A's positive engagement with, and persistent requests for, clarification of his strategy ('So you're saying . . .', line 7, 'But what if . . .', line 11), he is able to explain his reasoning and convince A to follow it. A's challenge in lines 9–10 as to the motivation behind the suggested move leads R to make his thinking visible to A and possibly also to himself. This then allows A to rehearse alternative scenarios (line 12) which R responds to (line 13), demonstrating that he has now thought through his move and its possible outcomes. Through dialogue he shifts from a casual 'might as well' approach to a clearly articulated strategy.

Shaping a reflective community of practice

A further important feature of the approach is the use of the plenary to consider explicitly what has taken place during the lesson and how it reflects the aims for the session. The plenary allows the teacher to foreground the talk objectives and to review how successfully they have featured in the day's work. The teacher is able to celebrate the good practice that has occurred; enable students to hear from their peers the sorts of behaviours that constitute the targeted discourse; and assess what more needs to be done. This is useful in shaping the community of practice in that it allows the students to come together and reflect jointly on what they have been doing and what they have learned from it, not just in terms of the mathematics but how the mathematics is explored through language and social behaviour. The following extract is taken from the end of a lesson. The teacher has gathered the students in a circle on the mat:

Extract 4

1	Teacher	Do you want to sit yourself down, A? S, we're just
2		waiting for you to come and join us on the carpet. Now I
3		had four secret spies amongst you . . . Can you explain to
4		people what you were doing this afternoon G?
5	G	We were going round visiting the people and seeing
6		what we heard.
7	Teacher	Right. So I had four people who were going round, and
8		they are going to help me judge whether or not we gave
9		good explanations because they have been gathering
10		evidence all through this afternoon's session. They have
11		been looking for all these phrases to see if we are using
12		them, and from the looks of their sheets I think I'm going
13		to have a really big smile on my face the same as
14		everybody else. Can you explain what you found out?
15		What sorts of things are we seeing . . . those people who
16		have been monitoring?
17	H	'That would be good because.'
18	Teacher	'That would be good because'. That's one we didn't
19		even come up with here, but which some people were
20		using really effectively to give reasons and back people

21		up. Thank you very much. A, what did you find out?
22		What was the most popular way of giving an explanation?
23	A	'Because'.
24	Teacher	Simply 'because'. Okay. How many times did you hear
25		that this afternoon?
26	A	Eight times.
27	Teacher	Eight different times in just the groups that you were
28		listening to.

The teacher here has apparently handed over a level of control to the students by having them monitor each other's performance and gather evidence of how it conforms to expectations of their role as collaborative thinkers and mathematicians. The message is that the language they use is an important constituent of this community of practice. The teacher locates this use of language not just in its function as a medium of thought, but also in its interpersonal functions in sustaining solidarity within the group, as seen in her evaluation of one of the phrases used by the children to 'give reasons and *back people up*' (lines 18–22, my emphasis). Her use of monitors to gather examples of exploratory talk (lines 7–16) might also serve to remind the children of the need to monitor their own use of such language.

Students were also involved in reviewing the use of the ground rules so that they become conscious and reflective about their own practices. In the following extract, taken from the very end of a lesson, the teacher has reviewed their mathematical strategies and the class have discussed what did and did not work. The teacher continues with a discussion of how effectively the students have used the ground rules:

Extract 5

T Let's finish off. Let's go back to our rules. We're looking to apply our ground rules for talk. I'm going to be very interested to look at [the] footage to see how well we've done there, but what's your assessment? Let's see the thumb vote. Compare it to this time last week when we tried somewhat unsuccessfully to apply those ground rules. Think of that last session. Think of how you interacted with your partners. Yes, [thumb up] I applied the rules as well. Okay [thumb horizontal], but definitely room for improvement. Let's have a thumb vote. Okay, [addressing one pair] you're not happy with the ground rules but your partner is. That's interesting. Maybe we need to clarify that. We've got a lot of thumbs up, the majority. Okay, thank you. I'd generally agree. I think we're getting better at the ground rules. There was a lot of conversation there, there were a lot of people listening to each other's ideas and also giving reasons for those ideas.

This sends out a very different and far more engaging message about how the teacher sees their students' role in becoming members of this particular community of practice than one finds in lines from the poet W.H. Auden: 'Minus times minus is plus, the reason for this we need not discuss'; or the Hungarian mathematician von Neumann's icy put-down of an inexperienced journalist: 'One does not understand mathematics, young man, one just gets used to it'. The students engaged in Thinking Together group work are expected to reflect not only on the day's performance but also to see it as part of a continuous process of conscious learning and adaptation. They learn that to get it they need to discuss it.

Implications for teaching and learning

The transcripts of the students' and teachers' talk provide evidence to support our belief that the explicit teaching, agreement and practice of ground rules for talk will lead to effective group work in the primary mathematics classroom. The extracts have provided evidence about the contribution that the Thinking Together approach can make to students' abilities to articulate their mathematical thinking to make it visible to both their partners and themselves. It has also shown how, through the explicit teaching and agreement of 'ground rules' for talk, teachers can provide a solid basis for effective group work and support the development of reflective practice in their students. While the linguistic development of students learning English as an additional language was not a focus of this research, some evidence has emerged from the data that this approach may also have advantages for them by exposing them to models of collaborative talk and thinking in a socially supportive and linguistically scaffolded context.

These findings also tally well with the principles of other approaches and initiatives such as assessment for learning (see Hodgen and Askew, Chapter 10) and guided group work, the latter promoted in the Williams Review (DCSF 2008: 67) which states:

> Guided group work in mathematics, where teachers work with smaller groups of children within the class, offers an organisational approach where attention can be given to particular children who may require additional support or challenge to ensure they continue to progress in learning. Working with a group can provide assessment information that is more difficult to capture in the whole class context; it provides an opportunity to discuss the mathematics in more detail with individuals in the group. The focused attention given to a group helps to inform future planning and teaching. It also gives children who are not active contributors to the whole class the

opportunity to participate more directly, share their ideas and extend their learning within a small group of peers.

Given all the above we can be confident of concluding with the following observation from Wegerif and Dawes (2004: 102):

> Children working in groups can offer one another chances to explore their conceptions, to employ their new vocabulary, and an audience for explanation, planning, suggestion and decision-making. In this way children learn to speak the language of maths. Challenges and explanations in groups, guided by teachers, can lead children to learn more expert ways of talking.

Notes

1   This chapter grew out of research into group work in mathematics with Year 5 and Year 6 primary school students (9- to 10-year-olds). It draws on and describes the Thinking Together approach to teaching children how to engage in effective collaborative talk and thinking as developed by Neil Mercer, Karen Littleton, Lynn Dawes, Claire Sams and Rupert Wegerif (Mercer and Littleton 2007; Wegerif and Dawes 2004) together with many teachers and their students. I would like to take this opportunity to express my indebtedness and thanks to them all.
2   For a full description of the project including sample lessons and DVD footage visit http://smile.open.ac.uk/project.htm (accessed March 2010).
3   SMILE Mathematics is no longer in operation but work is under way to provide freely downloadable digitized versions of the materials.

References

DCSF (Department for Children, Schools and Families) (2008) *Independent Review of Mathematics Teaching in Early Years Settings and Primary Schools* (Williams Review). Nottingham: DCSF. http://publications.teachernet.gov.uk/eOrderingDownload/Williams%20Mathematics.pdf (accessed March 2010).

DES (Department of Education and Science) (1982) *Mathematics Counts: Report of the Committee of Inquiry into the Teaching of Mathematics in Schools* (Cockcroft Report). London: HMSO. http://www.dg.dial.pipex.com/documents/docs1/cockcroft.shtml (accessed March 2010).

Lave, J. and Wenger, E. (1991) *Situated Learning: Legitimate Peripheral Participation.* Cambridge: Cambridge University Press.

Mercer, N. (2000) *Words and Minds: How We Use Language to Think Together*. London: Routledge.

Mercer, N. and Littleton, K.S. (2007) *Dialogue and the Development of Children's Thinking: A Sociocultural Approach*. Abingdon: Routledge.

Mercer, N., Wegerif, R. and Dawes, L. (1999) Children's talk and development of reasoning in the classroom, *British Educational Research Journal*, 25(1): 95–111.

Sinclair, J. and Coulthard, M. (1975) *Towards an Analysis of Discourse*. Oxford: Oxford University Press.

Vygotsky, L.S. (1986) *Thought and Language*. Cambridge, MA: MIT Press.

Wegerif, R. and Dawes, L. (2004) *Thinking and Learning with ICT: Raising Achievement in Primary Classrooms*. London: Routledge.

Wegerif, R. and Mercer, N. (1997) A dialogical framework for researching peer talk, in R. Wegerif and P. Scrimshaw (eds) *Computers and Talk in the Primary School*. Clevedon: Multilingual Matters.

5 Making connections: teachers and children using resources effectively

Kev Delaney

Introduction

Concrete objects such as counters, buttons and beads have been used for a great many years in the teaching and learning of early number (although fingers probably go back a lot further). We know that nineteenth-century educationalists like Tillich and Froebel advocated the use of practical apparatus for teaching elementary arithmetic, and that in the early twentieth century Montessori used practical apparatus such as bead bars, rods and counting frames in her 'alternative' schools. More recently, the Association for Teaching Aids in Mathematics (now the Association of Teachers of Mathematics) was formed in 1952, and, true to its name, set about arguing a strong case for the use of 'teaching aids' and structural apparatus in mathematics classrooms. Caleb Gattegno, the driving force behind the new association, was particularly enthusiastic about Georges Cuisenaire's coloured rods for the teaching of number.

During the 1950s and 1960s, educationalists were gradually becoming aware of the work of educational psychologists such as Piaget and Bruner. Piaget's work was interpreted as being about 'learning by doing', and Bruner's as being concerned with three distinct modes of representing the world: enactive (actions), iconic (pictures) and symbolic (words and numbers). These interpretations, along with the work of the Association for Teaching Aids in Mathematics, the myriad courses organized by the enthusiastic HMI, Edith Biggs, and the publication of the Plowden Report in 1967 (see Brown, Chapter 1) led to great emphasis being placed on the use of structural apparatus for the teaching of number work, to the extent that it would not have been surprising to find structural equipment such as Tillich blocks, Stern rods, Dienes multibase arithmetic blocks or Cuisenaire rods in a great many primary schools in the late 1960s.

The Cockcroft Report (*Mathematics Counts*) (DES 1982: 84) recommended the use of practical equipment throughout the whole of the primary school (and beyond), and was unequivocal in its view on the value of practical work: 'For most children practical work provides the most effective means by which understanding of mathematics can develop.' Askew and Wiliam (1995: 10), in a review of research findings, concluded that 'practical work can provide images that help pupils contextualise mathematical ideas'. The *National Numeracy Strategy Framework for Teaching Mathematics from Reception to Year 6* (DfEE 1999a: 29) includes number tracks, 'washing lines', number lines, number squares, digit cards, place value cards, addition and subtraction cards, sets of shapes, construction kits, base-ten apparatus and the spike abacus in a discussion of classroom resources. The resource focus of the *Independent Review of Mathematics Teaching in Early Years Settings and Primary Schools* (the Williams Review) (DCSF 2008) is mainly on multi-sensory equipment for under-attaining children involved in the Every Child Counts project (see Dunn, Matthews and Dowrick, Chapter 17). Interestingly, we appear to have come full circle, in that the Williams Review (DCSF 2008: 61) provides a glowing account of work in one particular school that uses Cuisenaire rods!

The brief historical overview outlined above would appear to suggest that there is a consensus (see also Ollerton, Chapter 6, and Beishuizen, Chapter 13) that apparatus of different kinds can enhance the teaching of mathematics. However, there are several writers who raise caveats, one of which is most interestingly expressed by Ball (1992: 17) who argues that 'Although kinaesthetic experience can enhance perception and thinking, understanding does not travel through the fingers and up the arm.' Elsewhere (Delaney 2001: 124), I comment that mathematics can only be *brought to* a resource by children and teachers interacting with it: ultimately it is the child who must own the awarenesses made possible in this way.

In Chapter 2, Askew describes the Effective Teachers of Numeracy project (see also Askew et al. 1997) whose aim was primarily to identify those factors that enable teachers to put effective teaching of numeracy into practice. What seemed to distinguish some of the effective teachers from others was what the project team described as a propensity to make connections, such as:

- connections between different aspects of mathematics, for example, addition and subtraction or fractions, decimals and percentages;
- connections between different representations of mathematics, moving between symbols, words, diagrams and objects (see Barmby, Harries and Higgins, Chapter 3);
- connections with children's methods – valuing these and being interested in children's thinking but also sharing their methods.

The researchers found that this connectionist theme was more important than either the teachers' style of organization for teaching mathematics or the level of mathematical qualification they achieved. The set of connections between

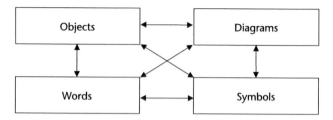

Figure 5.1 Making connections.

different representations of mathematics described above can be illustrated diagrammatically (Figure 5.1).

Is there a rationale for using resources within the Primary National Strategy?

Neither the *Primary Framework for Literacy and Mathematics* (DfES 2006) nor the mathematics pages of the National Strategies' website currently offer a clear rationale for the use of resources in primary mathematics, despite the fact that models, images and practical resources are recommended for various blocks of work in different years. However, it does seem reasonable to assume that current expectations about resources are substantially underpinned by various training materials produced by the original National Numeracy Strategy (NNS) in 1999.

As these are available in every school and have been extensively used for training purposes within schools and initial teacher education institutions, it is interesting to consider the way in which resources are used in the videotapes for Books 1 and 2 of the NNS professional development materials (DfEE 1999b), which were part of the first NNS training pack provided for primary schools. While there have been developments within primary mathematics since the introduction of the NNS, particularly with the advent of electronic resources, it seems reasonable to argue that these tapes still represent aspirations for the use of resources within the revised *Primary Framework for Literacy and Mathematics* (DfES 2006).

There are a number of problems surrounding the viewing of films of teachers in action, particularly when they are clips of edited films of mathematics lessons. We need to be cautious about how we interpret these sequences, given the reduced relationship they have to 'reality'. The purpose of these clips was to illustrate aspects of the NNS's approach to teaching and learning, and so it makes sense to question the relationship that they might have to the teachers' 'natural teaching style'. Because they are just 'snapshots' it is also all too easy to speculate as to what might have happened before or after the actions that we see in the videos. It is easy to be seduced into feeling that we are actually 'there' in some sense or other. However, because the video clips are still widely available, this makes them a useful focus for discussing the possible use of resources.

In one extract (Video clip 4, tape 1) Roger uses a counting stick (this is a wooden stick about 1 metre long, usually marked into ten sections) to help a Year 4 class with learning the multiples of 7. Roger is keen that his pupils come to perceive relationships between the various multiples of 7 and connect this with work previously done on doubling and halving. By inviting children to add on 7, he establishes that the first and second divisions on the stick are 7 and 14. He then affixes appropriate labels using Blu-Tack (Figure 5.2).

Figure 5.2   Multiples of 7 on a counting stick.

Next, he asks what number they think will appear at the end of the stick, relating this to the children's previous knowledge of multiples of 10. Based on the responses of the children Roger affixes the number 70 at the end, and then moves to the middle of the stick, establishing it as a half of 70 and also as a useful reference point that will enable them to calculate further multiples. To emphasize this he leaves his thumb on the mid-point. He then starts to draw attention to doubling relationships, first finding 4×7 from 2×7 and then 8×7 from 4×7. By now 7, 14, 28, 35, 56 and 70 have been labelled, and Roger continues to label the rest by adding or subtracting 7s. He then removes half of the labels and children recite the 7 times table forwards and backwards.

It is useful to consider how Roger has used this resource and what other approaches he might have taken. The first thing that is clear is that he is using the counting stick for demonstration purposes. He also leaves us in no doubt that it is *his* agenda that is being followed ('I'm going to teach you to . . .'). He believes that certain multiples of 7, in relation to the stick, are important, and he is 'coaching' the children to operate with his awareness of this and of doubling and halving relationships in order to arrive at the whole set of multiples to 10. He does *not* ask the children to offer their own views on arriving at particular multiples.

There is no doubt that Roger is a thoughtful and skilful teacher who has clearly considered relationships between different multiples, and has transmitted his awareness of these relationships in a highly focused manner. However, it is not possible to ascertain, except in a very limited way, the extent to which this has connected with the children. In the main, his approach seems to be determined by the structure of the daily mathematics lesson (the section we see appears to be of a mental/oral starter) with its emphasis on direct teaching. On the little evidence that we have, we cannot describe Roger as a connectionist teacher since he does not attempt to make connections with the children's methods. We cannot, of course, say anything about Roger's normal approach to teaching, but it *is* interesting to ask whether there are other approaches that he might have used with this particular resource. First, however, it is worth considering different approaches to the use of resources in general.

Two different views of resources

I believe that we first need to make a distinction between the use of a resource to *demonstrate* to a class and the use of a resource for children to *engage* with (Delaney 2001). The first approach emphasizes the resource as an aid or support for *teaching*, whereas the latter puts more emphasis on the resource as a support for *learning*, although clearly one cannot really make such a sharp distinction. Of course, both emphases are laudable and entirely justifiable – but they are different in the purpose they attribute to the resource, and therefore have different implications in terms of the actions and thoughts of the teacher and the learner.

Resources for demonstration purposes

The National Numeracy Strategy's professional development resources pack (DfEE 1999b: 20), suggests that resources can be used in what the document describes as 'Effective teaching' – which is seen to involve:

> *Directing* – explaining what has to be done and when;
> *Demonstrating and modelling* – showing children how to do something or providing an image to help them understand something;
> *Instructing* – running through a procedure or process to be followed;
> *Explaining and illustrating* – providing reasons and giving examples;
> *Evaluating children's responses* – giving them feedback and dealing with misconceptions and errors.

These are 'traditional skills' to which all teachers would wish to aspire. However, there is an assumption in the list that the teacher has appropriate insights into the nature of some mathematical idea or procedure which they will pass on to pupils. In this idealized picture, the pupil is initiated into these insights by the demonstration of ideas or processes by means of appropriate resources. Explanations and illustrative examples are provided by the teacher and the child's responses are measured against a range of correct responses that the teacher has in mind. If this were the only diet offered to the children it would be viewed as a purely transmissive mode of teaching mathematics, with all the limitations that this implies.

Provided they are balanced with other modes of teaching that involve pupils more actively, the categories listed above seem entirely appropriate. It is perfectly reasonable for a teacher who understands the mathematics that they are teaching to offer their view of how things could be fitted together (as Roger does, for example, in the video clip already discussed). Such demonstrations are worth having for those children who are able to make sense of the connections that teachers draw to their attention by their choice and use of resources and language. Of course, each child still has to reconstruct the mathematics in their own mind, despite the teacher's intention of 'pre-digesting' the mathematics being presented. For those children who are not able to make these connections so easily, opportunities to *engage* with the resource individually will give them space for making connections in a different way; 'quicker' children are also likely to benefit from this opportunity.

Resources for 'engagement' purposes

There is nothing more frustrating than being obliged to watch someone else manipulate a resource when you really want to explore it in your own way. It is probably the case that the least productive method of engaging in your own meaningful way with a resource is in the context of a fast-paced, direct teaching session, where someone else has the resource and your attention is constantly being called to *their* concerns. Even in the context of a whole-class lesson, slowing the pace and *asking questions* that invite children to *notice* and *describe* are more likely to engage children in using the resource to make meaning for themselves.

Ultimately we all have to make individual sense of whatever mathematics we learn. Those teachers who have observed children working in groups will have noticed how children often engage with the group for a while then withdraw to consider the matters under discussion in order to make sense of them individually, before finally re-engaging with the group.

A list was provided above that considered the ways that resources might be used with an emphasis on *demonstrating*. A complementary list, focusing on children *engaging* with resources, might look like this:

> *Playing around with and getting a sense of* – how does this resource help me visualize this calculation, these patterns, this relationship . . .?
> *Noticing and describing* – patterns, structures, similarities, differences . . .
> *Discussing and showing* – this is how I do it/see it. How do you do it/see it? Is there some way that we could make sense of this together?

Articulating – putting different kinds of relationships into words.

Asking questions – of yourself and others and trying to find answers to these questions. How does this work? Why does it work? Does it always work? Are there other ways of doing this?

Testing out – conjectures, hypotheses, approaches and ideas – both your own and those of others.

Convincing – yourself, and others, about these conjectures, hypotheses, approaches and ideas.

Practising and consolidating – can I do further examples with increasing understanding, confidence and fluency? Can I repeatedly carry out this procedure reliably?

Developing new situations and contexts – what would happen if . . .? Are there any other situations similar to this?

This list feels very different. The *demonstrating* list involves someone else presenting you with their view of the world, whereas with the *engaging* list there is a feeling of personal involvement in making decisions and choices. Highly focused engaging with resources is probably best done individually and in a situation where time is available. But part of the organizing skill of a teacher is to arrange situations in such a way that, when you go into that individual space, ideas have already been seeded and your reflections are as productive as they could be.

When you are unable to grasp, for example, the fact that any two numbers added together give the same result independently of the order in which they are added – what we call the 'commutative property' of addition – it may be no use to contemplate this on your own without some supporting structure. A particularly useful structure for this situation might involve an initial demonstration, using Multilink blocks or Cuisenaire rods, that, for example, 3 + 5 and 5 + 3 have the same sum. This could be followed by an invitation to investigate whether this is true for any other pairs of small numbers. Working with a partner as part of this invitation to produce such pairs of numbers is very likely to generate productive discussion.

If the participants encounter a problem, then a well-timed intervention by the teacher might well produce a different focus. An apposite question could lead to a more constructive discussion between members of the group. However, throughout all these events the final 'making sense' belongs to the individuals who must withdraw, for however short a time, into a more private space to persuade themselves that the newly acquired awarenesses are correct and in some way fit with their previous knowledge. Resources play a crucial role in this process, as does the teacher. However, if intervention is limited to yet another demonstration rather than fostering the possibilities in the second list, then a crucial opportunity is lost.

If Roger had at some stage decided to involve the children in finding a useful method to arrive at multiples of 7, he could have done this within his own agenda, for example, he might have asked them:

- If you know that 2 sevens are 14, how could you work out 4 sevens . . . and 8 sevens?
- Do you remember the work we did on doubling – can anyone see how we could use that idea to work out some of the missing multiples?

Or in a more open way:

- How could I work out 6 sevens (for example) from what we already know?
- How else could we find 6 sevens?

The children could have used a paper image of the counting stick and worked in pairs to decide on different ways of finding multiples. The children (and Roger) might have learned something from sharing in these ways.

The training videos include a strong emphasis on demonstrating or modelling mathematics and on explaining and illustrating a piece of mathematics (DfEE 1999b: 20), and Roger is operating effectively within the spirit of that principle by using a resource to *demonstrate*. However, it would be interesting to know whether he also uses resources to *engage* the children in making meaning for themselves by acting as facilitator. Of course, we cannot know the answer having watched just a few minutes of video film.

A more flexible use of resources

In another clip (Video 2, clip 1c) Mary works with a Year 1 class using a range of resources in order to show different aspects of place value. Her aim is to show how number names give us information that we can use to write the numbers. In order to achieve this aim she makes use of the Gattegno grid (see Figure 5.3) to encourage children to say two- and three-digit numbers using the grid.

The next step is to emphasize the difference between saying and writing numbers. For this step she uses place value cards (sometimes called Gattegno cards) (Figure 5.4) to show children how we 'squeeze numbers together' when we write them.

1	2	3	4	5	6	7	8	9
10	20	30	40	50	60	70	80	90
100	200	300	400	500	600	700	800	900

Figure 5.3 A Gattegno grid.

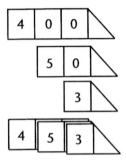

Figure 5.4   Place value cards illustrating 'squeezing together'.

Later in the lesson, she uses the computer program *Developing Number* (ATM 1999) to show the links between the two pieces of apparatus that she has used thus far. *Developing Number* is an animated combination of both the Gattegno grid and place value cards, and demonstrates how to combine, for example, 400 and 50 and 3 to make 453. In order to ensure that the children have the opportunity of also seeing numbers as quantities, Mary uses the plenary session to involve the children in using bundles of straws in hundreds, tens and ones in order to move away from the essentially abstract images of the place value cards and Gattegno grid. A discussion of the difference between the *quantity value* and the *column value* aspects of place value can be found in Thompson (2003).

Towards the end of the lesson, she also asks the children to visualize what numbers are formed as she says 'eight hundred and eighty-eight'. She is trying to help them internalize the useful mental images that the resources have hopefully made available. Some children draw what they have visualized, and it becomes clear that the resources that Mary has offered have indeed been a rich source of images for internalizing. It is also interesting to consider in this lesson how many connections have been made in terms of Figure 5.1.

Mary's teaching session successfully involves the children and engages their ideas, although the context is probably more limiting than finding multiples of 7. The lesson certainly involves direct teaching in a whole-class format for the purpose of establishing familiarity with the apparatus to be used and with specific ideas of place value. However, children are also given some space in pairs to choose numbers on an adapted Gattegno grid for their partner to make with the place value cards. This enables them to make their own connections in a less public way. A great deal of discussion is apparent in the film, although unfortunately none of it is audible.

The impression is very much that we are watching a connectionist teacher at work, especially given Mary's invitation for children to have their own images in the plenary section of the lesson, although we can always ask questions about alternative uses and timings of the resources she chooses. Once again, analysis of this clip is perhaps most usefully seen not as an end in itself but as a means of throwing light on important issues about the appropriateness of resources; ways of combining their use; and the order of use for particular purposes.

Towards a rationale for resources

It is interesting to compare the approach to resources exemplified in these videos with curriculum development work in other European countries. Rousham (2003) has compared the development of the use of the empty number line in England and the Netherlands, and it is revealing to compare the approach to the use of resources in Germany and England. Wittman (1995) was in a position to adopt a much more sensible timescale in developing a rationale for the use of resources in the Dortmund-based Mathe 2000 project. Working within the principle of what, in this country, we might translate as 'guided active discovery', Wittman lays down the following set of criteria for the selection of teaching aids:

- The visual aids offered within a given school year should be compatible and small enough in number for pupils to deal with them thoroughly in the time available.
- Each and every aid should incorporate the basic ideas of the topic under consideration, and should be exploited intensively over a long period of time in order that the structure it offers can be assimilated.
- Teaching aids need to be structured as clearly as possible and be easy to handle.
- Wherever possible, teaching aids should be available as a large model for class demonstration and as small models for individual pupil use, with dialogue concerning different examples using these two versions encouraged.
- Every pupil should have their own individual set of resources (the suggestion is made that this is generally only possible where the resource is made of paper).

What is different about the Dortmund approach is that time has been made available to think through important issues about the fine detail of their approach to numeracy, and in particular to the provision of teaching and learning resources within the project. The Mathe 2000 project began in 1987, and even at that stage, it was based upon substantial earlier research by key members of the development team. A similar situation obtained in the Netherlands with the development of the Wiskobas and Realistic Mathematics

Education (RME) projects of the 1970s. Interestingly, the approach to learning resources in both these projects – with their focus on a limited number of well-researched resources – conflicts with the English approach that is clearly spelled out in the *Independent Review of Mathematics Teaching in Early Years Settings and Primary Schools* (the Williams Review) (DCSF 2008: 54): 'Local authorities and schools found it useful to be provided with suggested resources and noted that it was helpful to include a *wide range of types of resource* [my italics] so that children can work with those that appeal to them. These should include resources for kinaesthetic activities.'

Implications for teaching and learning

It is the complementary nature of the demonstration and interaction approaches set out above which, in my view, offers the most powerful way forward in optimizing the use of resources. There has always been a tendency to emphasize demonstration. The heavy endorsement of this direct approach since the introduction of the NNS and the Primary National Strategy (PNS) has tended to turn parts of mathematics lessons into 'performance art', and this emphasis on exposition has been to the detriment of children 'playing with' underlying concepts in appropriately supported ways to further their understanding in a more embedded way. Some teachers work hard to hone their demonstrations, and this affords clear benefits for their classes. However, this essentially 'one way traffic' limits the possibilities afforded by more explicitly involving the children in their own learning (and potentially that of their peers) by facilitating their engagement with resources as well. This is clearly recognized by the Office for Standards in Education (Ofsted), who observed the negative effect of interactive whiteboards in reducing the use of practical resources. They further noted that 'Teachers generally under-used practical resources . . . to develop pupils' understanding of mathematical ideas and help them to make connections between different topics' (Ofsted 2008: 28).

The important focus of good (mathematics) teaching is to keep the interaction between teacher and learners high. A resource which facilitates demonstration *and* interaction mediates discussion in powerful ways. It offers the possibility for teachers to support their talk with appropriate actions and, in turn, to watch and listen to pupils interacting with the same resource, revealing their inherent understanding of important concepts as well as any potential misconceptions. It is the individual and changing nature of this interchange that keeps a teacher fresh and the potential for learning high. If one has the view of a teacher as essentially a researcher, then, within this approach, teachers are constantly assessing understanding and supporting a more grounded development of mathematical concepts.

References

Askew, M. and Wiliam, D. (1995) *Recent Research in Mathematics Education 5–16.* London: HMSO.

Askew, M., Brown, M., Rhodes, V., Wiliam, D. and Johnson, D. (1997) *Effective Teachers of Numeracy: Report of a Study Carried Out for the Teacher Training Agency.* London: King's College, University of London.

ATM (Association of Teachers of Mathematics) (1999) *Developing Number* (software). Derby: ATM.

Ball, D.L. (1992) Magical hopes: manipulatives and the reform of mathematics education, *American Educator,* 16(2): 14–18, 46–7.

Delaney, K. (2001) Teaching mathematics resourcefully, in P. Gates (ed.) *Issues in Mathematics Teaching.* London: Routledge Falmer.

DCSF (Department for Children, Schools and Families) (2008) *Independent Review of Mathematics Teaching in Early Years Settings and Primary Schools* (Williams Review). Nottingham: DCSF. http://publications.teachernet.gov.uk/ eOrderingDownload/Williams Mathematics.pdf (accessed March 2010).

DES (Department of Education and Science) (1982) *Mathematics Counts: Report of the Committee of Inquiry into the Teaching of Mathematics in Schools* (Cockcroft Report). London: HMSO. http://www.dg.dial.pipex.com/documents/docs1/ cockcroft.shtml (accessed March 2010).

DfEE (Department for Education and Employment) (1999a) *The National Numeracy Strategy Framework for Teaching Mathematics from Reception to Year 6.* London: DfEE.

DfEE (Department for Education and Employment) (1999b) *Guide for Your Professional Development: Book 2 – Effective Teaching and the Approach to Calculation.* London: DfEE.

DfES (Department for Education and Skills) (2006) *Primary Framework for Literacy and Mathematics.* Norwich: DfES.

Ofsted (Office for Standards in Education) (2008) *Mathematics: Understanding the Score.* London: Ofsted. http://www.ofsted.gov.uk/Ofsted-home/Publications- and-research/Browse-all-by/Documents-by-type/Thematic-reports/ Mathematics-understanding-the-score (accessed March 2010).

Rousham, L. (2003) The empty number line: a model in search of a learning trajectory? in I. Thompson (ed.) *Enhancing Primary Mathematics Teaching.* Maidenhead: Open University Press.

Thompson, I. (2003) Place value: the English disease? in I. Thompson (ed.) *Enhancing Primary Mathematics Teaching.* Maidenhead: Open University Press.

Wittman, E. (ed.) (1995) *Mit Kindern Rechnen.* Frankfurt-am-Main: Der Grundschul- verband e.V.

6 Using problem-solving approaches to learn mathematics

Mike Ollerton

Introduction

Problem-solving or more open-type tasks enable children to find different approaches and different solutions to puzzles and problems. When children have opportunities to discuss ideas and share methods, to offer alternative explanations, by working together, this provides a different, richer experience of learning mathematics than working individually through an exercise from a textbook or worksheet (see Monaghan, Chapter 4). The *Independent Review of the Primary Curriculum: Final Report* (the Rose Review) (DCSF 2009: 68) places: 'a greater emphasis . . . on developing mathematical understanding through more practical, problem-solving activities'. This chapter, therefore, is about the value of using problem solving as the vehicle to support children's learning of mathematics.

Problem solving is something people 'do' at all ages and in all walks of life, socially, academically, in employment and in retirement. Problems are of all shapes and sizes, ranging from doing a jigsaw, a crossword, a sudoku or a kakuro, to reading a map, organizing rotas in the workplace or building a carbon-neutral house. The innate need to solve problems is the fundamental basis for the existence and the construction of mathematics. We invented numbers so we could count and measure; we created and defined properties and names of shapes so we could construct and communicate our understanding of the world. In brief, mathematics has been constructed through the ages in order to solve problems.

In this chapter I link the teaching and learning of mathematics through problem-solving approaches and the broader qualities which I believe are desirable for children to develop to support their learning. I consider how, through problem solving, we can simultaneously help children make sense of mathematics and develop these qualities. I argue that by using problem-solving approaches we can challenge some of the prescribed orthodoxies, such as teaching in 'three-part lessons' and the flawed notion of differentiation occurring at three different levels in classrooms. Using problem-solving approaches teachers can embrace issues of differentiation by outcome and simultaneously enable the practice and consolidation of key numerical concepts. I offer examples of problems to demonstrate how these learning qualities and issues can be worked on. Finally, I consider the issues of problem solving and 'real-life' mathematical contexts.

Learning mathematics through problem solving

I draw upon the concept of multiplication in order to illustrate how mathematics can be learnt using a problem-solving approach and how an important shift can take place away from the kind of situations where only one 'right' answer is possible. For example, asking: 'What is six times four?' is a closed question for which there is only one answer. Those children who can speedily provide the answer of 24 may inevitably be seen as the 'successful' ones. However, speed of calculation can mask deeper understanding. If we pose a problem such as 'Tell me some ways of multiplying numbers together so the answer is 24', this question has a range of answers, one of which might be $1 \times 2 \times 3 \times 4$, at which point a teacher might take this as a learning opportunity to explain that such a calculation can be written in a mathematical shorthand as 4! (factorial four).

A starting point for such a question might be to give pairs of children 24 square pieces of card (such as those produced by the Association of Teachers of Mathematics, atm.org.uk) and ask them to make different rectangles using all 24 pieces. Clearly there are just four solutions (24×1, 12×2, 8×3 and 6×4) unless, of course, we count the reverses which would clearly be an important consideration if these pairs of values were to be plotted as coordinate points on a graph, thus enabling learners to see what a picture of the function $x \times y = 24$ looks like.

If this task were to be extended to making 'L' shapes, the resulting diagrams could be translated into mathematical sentences such as $ab + cd$. For example, the mathematical sentence for the diagram in Figure 6.1 is $5 \times 2 + 7 \times 2$ and some children may be ready to write this as $(5 + 7) \times 2$.

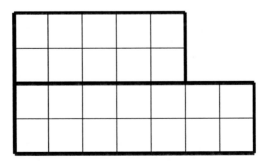

Figure 6.1   Diagram illustrating $5 \times 2 + 7 \times 2$.

Of course a different dissection could produce the sentence $5 \times 4 + 2 \times 2$ as illustrated in Figure 6.2.

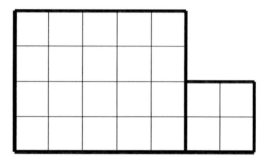

Figure 6.2 Diagram illustrating $5 \times 4 + 2 \times 2$.

Such a situation could be reversed and this would create other challenges. For example, if the sentence is $3 \times 4 + 2 \times 6$, what could the picture look like? How many different 'L' shaped diagrams are there for $3 \times 4 + 2 \times 6$?

A development task could be to provide children with 24 linking cubes and ask them to make all the different solid boxes. Using this equipment the third dimension comes into play; again it is important that the solids made are described in terms of multiplication. The solutions are: 24 by 1 by 1, 12 by 2 by 1, 8 by 3 by 1, 6 by 4 by 1, 6 by 2 by 2 and 4 by 3 by 2.

Asking children to explain why they think they have found all the solutions might also be pursued, and this could develop into a proof by exhaustion based upon the divisors of 24. A further development could be to consider the different surface areas of these cuboids and for children to produce calculations pertaining to them. As an example the surface area of the 6 by 4 by 1 cuboid (see Figure 6.3) could be written as $6 \times 4 + 6 \times 1 + 4 \times 1 + 6 \times 4 + 6 \times 1 + 4 \times 1$, or as $(6 \times 4 + 6 \times 1 + 4 \times 1) \times 2$

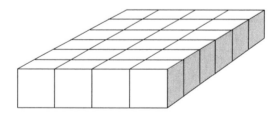

Figure 6.3 A cuboid 6 by 4 by 1.

This type of work enables children to actively engage with pictorial representations of the concept of multiplication (see Barmby, Harries and

Higgins, Chapter 3). The sense-making process is essential for learners to see how abstract concepts can be accessed through concrete manipulatives (see Delaney, Chapter 5). Furthermore, because a range of answers is possible, all children will have opportunities to achieve some degree of success. Success, in turn, breeds confidence and confidence underpins competence.

Learning qualities and problem solving

When I read a school's mission statement I always feel curious about how words in the statement are translated into actions in classrooms. What is it teachers do to support learners to 'live-out' the intentions behind a mission statement? How do teachers' daily interactions with learners, the types of lessons they plan and the tasks children subsequently carry out, fulfil the words in a mission statement? I have another question about what any school's aims are and this is, what learning qualities does a school want its children to develop? You may wish to construct your own list before reading on.

My list would contain the following qualities:

- resilience;
- perseverance;
- being able to cope with 'stuckness' and ambiguity;
- independence;
- sharing with and supporting others.

In my experience teachers are keen to celebrate learners' success; this might involve drawing attention to particular achievements or positive behaviours that individuals exhibit. Recently, I was working with a Year 2 class using an activity about number bonds to ten based upon playing cards. I gave the children, working in threes, 18 playing cards. The cards were two of the four suits with the 10, J, Q and K removed, leaving the cards from 1 to 9. Cards were placed face down and the children took turns to turn over two cards. If these cards totalled ten, then the child kept them as a pair; thus the children were practising number bonds to ten.

I noticed one child had not been able to collect any pairs of cards. I also noticed she was not daunted; indeed she seemed keen to play another game in the hope she might gain at least one pair of cards that totalled 10. When we gathered around at the end of the lesson I chose to bring this event and the qualities I felt the child exhibited to the attention of the rest of the class; I wanted to show that this seeming 'failure' had in fact been a great success in terms of the desirable personal quality of perseverance the child had shown.

Of course the game itself could hardly be described as a problem-solving activity, apart from trying to memorize where certain cards were when a pair did not total 10 and therefore had to be turned face down again. However, by asking the children to work out how many pairs there would be altogether that total 10, and following this up with a question about what all the numbered cards add up to in a complete pack of cards was a planned development and one which the class teacher planned to follow up in the next lesson. A further development would have been to turn over three cards and see whether any two of these cards totalled 10; this would potentially involve the children in carrying out three addition calculations at each turn.

Mathematical qualities and problem solving

Alongside the development of these qualities I also want children to develop ways of thinking mathematically. These include:

- gathering and ordering information;
- analysing information by searching for patterns and seeking connections;
- making conjectures;
- offering generalities.

Mathematics, as mentioned above, is intrinsically a problem-solving discipline: it has been constructed in order to make sense of the social, physical and economic world. Teaching and learning mathematics through the central medium of problem solving is, therefore, symbiotic. Consequently, mathematical thinking skills can only be developed when children are provided with problems to solve; the skills cannot be developed as disembodied entities. A typical problem-solving task which I call 'Exploring addition' is based on adding together two two-digit numbers and is described in Figure 6.4. The task provides children with opportunities to engage with each of the mathematical thinking skills listed above.

As learners are working on this problem, perhaps in pairs or in a group of three, I can circulate among them and, depending upon how any pair or group is 'getting on' with the task, I can ask a series of questions such as:

How many different totals have you found?
Do you think you have found all the different possible totals?
How can you be sure you have found them all?
What are your minimum and maximum totals?

Questions such as these are intended to focus learners' attention on what

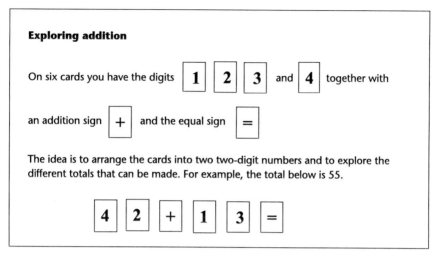

Figure 6.4 Exploring addition.

they are doing; to cause them to analyse the information they have gathered; and ultimately to try to construct a proof. Of course, different pairs/groups of learners will take different amounts of time to work on such questions; with this in mind I need to use the knowledge I construct about the members of a class. This is dependent upon the 'signs' I see and hear, the observations I make and the discussions I have with learners.

Through such interactions I can determine the nature of the questions I might ask and further problems I might pose. For example I might be delighted if some children begin to demonstrate a confidence in adding two two-digit numbers together while I may expect others to construct a robust proof that they have indeed found all possible solutions. This is, obviously, an aspect of the teacher responding to differentiated learning outcomes.

Development tasks could be:

- Arrange your totals in order from smallest to largest and calculate the difference between successive pairs.
- Choose four other consecutive digits and see what kind of answers you find.
- How do these answers compare to the answers for the digits 1, 2, 3 and 4?
- Suppose you started with the digits 3, 4, 6 and 7.
- What will the minimum and maximum totals be now?
- What happens to the differences between successive answers?
- Suppose you had the 'values' a, b, c and d, where $a < b < c < d$.
- How would you arrange these to minimize and maximize totals?

This final question is clearly one for the most confident mathematicians and would challenge many KS3 or KS4 students. Indeed, I have seen adults write a generalization such as: $da + cb$ instead, of course, as $10d + a + 10c + b$ or in a slightly more elegant form: $10 (d + c) + a + b$.

The balance between teaching and learning mathematics

When mathematics is learnt through problem solving, the focus is on children's activity, their explorations and their explanations. This contrasts with children trying to follow a teacher's predetermined pathway. Problem solving in classrooms shifts energy from teacher as 'deliverer', using mainly didactic approaches, to teacher who lights the blue touchpaper and retires a strategic distance – which is probably a convoluted way of describing a 'facilitator'! The teacher can still see and hear the action and can, therefore, intervene when they deem it appropriate. Working on shifting the energy in classrooms, therefore, from the authority of the teacher to responsibilities of the learners involves the teacher working strategically to create space for children to develop qualities of resilience, perseverance, and so on. This approach mirrors Gattegno's 'subordination of teaching to learning' (1971: ii): 'A radical transformation occurs in the classroom when one knows how to subordinate teaching to learning. It enables us to expect very unusual results from students – for instance that all students will perform very well, very early on . . .'

The important issue here is the act of 'doing' by contrast to something that is 'done to' individuals. The parallels with teaching and learning are that teaching is something teachers do and learning is what learners do; the teacher clearly cannot do the learning for the learners. When problem solving is used as a teaching strategy it is the learners who must solve the problems; the teacher cannot do this for them. Using a problem-solving pedagogy, therefore, requires the teacher to use less didactic methods and employ a greater range of facilitative approaches. As such, teaching must, in some ways, be subordinated to learning. Broadly speaking, the role of the mathematics teacher is to help learners develop skills inherent within problem solving: organizing, analysing and generalizing. As Mason et al. (2005: 297) argue: 'a lesson without the opportunity for learners to express a generality is not in fact a mathematics lesson'.

It is this emphasis on generality that needs to be encouraged in mathematics classrooms from the earliest age. A simple example would be to ask learners what they think it means to add two numbers together. Asking such a question is likely to require learners to do fewer 'sums' and instead spend time thinking about what it means 'to add'. If, in response to such a question, the learner draws a picture or reaches for some linking cubes in order to demonstrate the act of 'putting togetherness' or 'totalling up', then generality is taking place.

Building on this, the learner needs to be encouraged to describe situations, contexts or suggest models where concepts appear. If a learner has secure knowledge of the process behind a concept then, in theory, they should be able to apply this process to any situation involving addition. The same is true whether the concept is multiplication, Pythagoras' theorem, trigonometry, logarithms or calculus. No matter how complex a concept is, the issue is about the learner being able to explain concepts as well as carry out calculations connected to a concept. The big challenge is whether learners recognize when it is appropriate to 'use and apply' their knowledge when solving a problem.

Teacher autonomy and professional decision making

A further important issue concerns teacher autonomy and the type of minute-by-minute decisions they make in the 'busyness' of classrooms. Problem-solving approaches do not fit into prescribed three-part lessons or into the ubiquitous notion of planning for three different 'ability' levels within any class. When children embark upon a problem they do not all achieve similar depths of understanding; neither do they progress at a specific rate or at three different rates. Understanding occurs on as many different time continua as there are children in a class. Of course, when working in pairs or small groups children can support one another. However, to construe a notion that at some point in a lesson it is time to stop everyone in order to hold a plenary is counterproductive to learning per se across a class. Problem-solving approaches work hand-in-hand with differentiated outcomes and these, as argued, occur at different speeds and to different depths of understanding. Trying to match any problem with three different levels of ability within a class is nonsensical; what we need is a range of starting points that every child can access together with a sequence of developmental tasks and questions that cater for different speeds and depths of cognition. Two tasks to illustrate these issues are shown in Figures 6.5, 6.6, 6.7 and 6.8. The first is about sequences and the second is about place value.

Sequences task

This task (Figure 6.5) is based on creating sequences of numbers and asking children to analyse the outcomes. They can be given the option of building the sequences using linking cubes.

Sequence A generates numbers one more than multiples of two. Sequence B produces multiples of four. Sequences C and D both generate square numbers from 4 onwards, using different methods. Sequence E generates multiples of three from 6 onwards. We can obviously make up many more

For each of the following sequences:
Continue the pattern;
Write down what you notice about each set of answers;
Try to explain the pattern you notice.

Sequence A
1 + 2 =
2 + 3 =
3 + 4 =

Sequence B
1 + 3 =
3 + 5 =
5 + 7 =

Sequence C
1 + 3 =
1 + 3 + 5 =
1 + 3 + 5 + 7 =

Sequence D
1 + 2 + 1 =
1 + 2 + 3 + 2 + 1 =
1 + 2 + 3 + 4 + 3 + 2 + 1 =

Sequence E
1 + 2 + 3 =
2 + 3 + 4 =
3 + 4 + 5 =

Figure 6.5 A 'sequences' task.

such addition-type patterns, though it would be of greater value for children to create their own. Indeed, the idea of children creating sequences feeds perfectly into the notion of differentiation by outcome. As a teacher I can have a minimum expectation that everyone will work through the examples I offer, whereas some may develop their own and others might consider sequences involving multiplication as well as addition.

Here the strategy of offering learners concrete manipulatives, such as linking cubes, provides an important opportunity for learners to physically see a structure. This, in turn, serves to enhance numerical patterns so created. The issue is about shifting from the concrete to the abstract – something so central to children making sense of concepts.

Place value task

This task requires children to be given an enlarged version of the grid in Figure 6.6, perhaps copied onto card, or even laminated. The problem can be used with various grids according to the complexity of the work a teacher may wish to offer children. The idea is to give pairs of pupils a copy of one of the three grids (Figures 6.6, 6.7 and 6.8). Ask them to place cards with the numbers 2 and 5 somewhere on the grid and carry out an addition calculation.

Again, the value of children being able to physically shift numbers around on a grid cannot be overstated. Holding, placing and moving actual numbers around is a very different kind of activity from just writing numbers down; this is about offering children a first-hand engagement with numbers, making decisions about where to place the numbers and thinking about creating a systematic order. The initial challenge is to find how many different answers can be made. This task will create opportunities to discuss which zeros are unnecessary or redundant – an important aspect of place value, particularly when working with decimal values.

The first two grids produce sets of answers that contain exactly the same digits, but those gained from the HTU grid are ten times larger than the corresponding set of answers achieved using the TU•t grid.

For each grid pupils can order their answers from smallest to largest and analyse the differences between adjacent pairs of values. Development tasks can easily be created by using two digits which when added 'bridge a

100	10	1
Hundreds	Tens	Ones
H	T	U
0	0	0
0	0	0

(+ shown to the left of the fifth row)

Figure 6.6   The HTU grid.

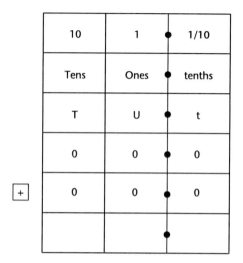

10	1	•	1/10
Tens	Ones	•	tenths
T	U	•	t
0	0	•	0
0	0	•	0
		•	

Figure 6.7 The TU•t grid.

10	1	•	1/10	1/100
Tens	Ones	•	tenths	hundredths
T	U	•	t	h
0	0	•	0	0
0	0	•	0	0
		•		

Figure 6.8 The TU•th grid.

10'; by placing three digits on a grid; or by using a grid with more columns (see Figure 6.8).

Asking pupils to try to explain how they know whether they have found all the possible answers is aimed at causing them to think of working systematically and to become more adept at explaining their reasoning.

Problem solving and 'real-life' contexts

So far, all the problems I have offered have arisen from 'pure' mathematical contexts, about exploring mathematics in a similar way to how we might tackle puzzles or play games. Of course, children also need to engage with 'applied' or real-life problems where they can use their knowledge to work on problems which could be described as cross-curricular contexts. However, the phrase 'real-life' trips easily off the tongue yet is shark infested in its manifestations. This is because teachers' 'adult' contexts are rarely those which children might be concerned with (VAT, shopping, paying the plumber, average fuel consumption of a car, and so on) or, indeed, even interested in. The Rose Review (DCSF 2009: 75) argues that: 'Children use and apply mathematics confidently and competently in their learning and in everyday contexts. They recognise where mathematics can be used to solve problems and are able to interpret a wide range of mathematical data.' With this in mind it is important to create problem-solving situations which children can actively engage in, such as:

- measuring their height changes month by month during the course of a school year;
- making maps of their immediate environs;
- creating scale drawings of themselves;
- calculating how far from the school they live;
- drawing diagrams showing what they do and how long these activities take over the course of a day or a week;
- carrying out experiments and recording data.

Discussing with children the kind of real-life tasks they are interested in finding out about is another useful starting point. For example, we may find some children are keen to engage in environmental issues such as working out how much it costs to transport them to and from school. Some children might want to find out about the environmental cost of litter; indeed, asking them to work out how the amount of litter in the school grounds could be 'measured' would be a significant challenge.

Conclusion

When problem solving is used as the fundamental approach in mathematics classrooms, many changes to, or developments of, practice are potentially achievable. These are about placing an emphasis upon the development of both wider learning qualities and mathematical thinking skills. Because problems will be solved at different rates and to different depths we can break away from some of the teaching approaches prescribed by national initiatives. This is because problem solving – just like life – rarely follows or adheres to neat sets of rules or narrow, imposed frameworks. As teachers we have to work things out for ourselves, and so do children when they are learning mathematics; this is the prime motivation for creative thinking to emerge. Problem-solving approaches offer children the 'buzz' of working things out for themselves, of making sense of situations and doing so at a pace and a depth appropriate to their capability. When accessible and interesting problems are used in classrooms, opportunities arise for children to participate in, and demonstrate, what they are capable of achieving.

References

DCSF (Department for Children, Schools and Families) (2009) *Independent Review of the Primary Curriculum: Final Report* (Rose Review). Nottingham: DCSF. http://publications.teachernet.gov.uk/eOrderingDownload/Primary_curriculum_Report.pdf (accessed March 2010).

Gattegno, C. (1971) *What We Owe Children: The Subordination of Teaching to Learning.* London: Routledge and Kegan Paul.

Mason, J., Graham, A. and Johnston-Wilder, S. (2005) *Developing Thinking in Algebra.* London: Paul Chapman Publishing.

7 The role of ICT

Richard English

Introduction

When published in June 2008, the recommendations of the *Independent Review of Mathematics Teaching in Early Years Settings and Primary Schools* – the Williams Review – (DCSF 2008) substantially exercised the minds of the government, local authorities, primary practitioners and those involved in initial teacher training. This should have come as no surprise since the review represented one of the most significant government reports into the teaching of mathematics in primary schools since the Cockcroft Report (*Mathematics Counts*) (DES 1982). The key issues highlighted included the provision of a mathematics specialist for every primary school; the need for greater emphasis on the use and application of mathematics; a renewed focus on oral and mental mathematics; and the promotion of high-quality discussion, particularly in the early years. Some of these would have been instantly recognizable to those familiar with the Cockcroft Report, and so one could have been forgiven for thinking that little progress had been made during the 26 years separating the two publications. The debate about 'progress' (or lack of it) will not be initiated here; instead, an interesting contrast between the two publications will be highlighted, that is, the almost total absence of any discussion by Williams about the role of Information and Communications Technology (ICT) in the teaching and learning of mathematics. Cockcroft, however, affords a whole chapter to this, as well as giving it frequent coverage elsewhere in the report.

One interpretation of Williams's lack of reference to ICT is that he was aware of the prominent position that it would be afforded in Jim Rose's subsequent *Independent Review of the Primary Curriculum* (DCSF 2009a), which recommended that ICT should be embedded throughout the primary curriculum and, along with literacy and numeracy, should form the core knowledge, skills and understanding for children. Another interpretation is that we had reached the stage where educators acknowledged ICT as being simply a resource to support teaching and learning. Perhaps we no longer felt the need to highlight

ICT's potential because practitioners were aware of this already and were exploiting it fully. Office for Standards in Education inspection evidence suggested otherwise. In its 2008 mathematics report it concluded that 'the potential of ICT to enhance the learning of mathematics is too rarely realised' (Ofsted 2008: 27). A later report by the DCSF concluded that 'A high proportion of ICT applications in mathematics centre around games, puzzles and revision/practice web-sites which often provide little more than the practice of basic skills' (DCSF 2009b: 25) and recommended that 'Pupils' experiences of ICT could be extended to support deeper and enhanced learning in mathematics' (DCSF 2009b: 27).

Survey evidence indicated that the availability of ICT resources in primary schools had continued to improve (Smith et al. 2008), but the reports from Ofsted and the DCSF cited above suggested that this improvement had not been matched in terms of effective utilization in the classroom. Nowhere is this more clearly evident than with the use of interactive whiteboards (IWBs). Smith et al. (2008) report that the average number of interactive whiteboards per primary school rose to 18 in 2008 compared with just eight in 2007, but in a review of the literature on the introduction of interactive whiteboards as a pedagogic tool, Higgins et al. (2005: 65) conclude that there is 'a clear preference for IWB use by both teachers and pupils', but 'it remains unclear, however, as to whether such enthusiasm is being translated into effective and purposeful practice'. This view is echoed by my own observations in primary schools where the interactive whiteboard is used as an effective presentation tool to convey large amounts of information in an attractive, engaging manner, but with little meaningful interaction between the teacher and the pupils or between the pupils themselves. When the expression 'interactive whiteboard' first entered our language the 'interaction' was referring to the ability to touch the whiteboard, to move things around and to generally make things happen, but the most important interaction is that between the teacher and the pupils. In the hands of an effective teacher an interactive whiteboard can significantly improve the quality of interaction in the classroom, but it cannot compensate for bad teaching.

The aim of this chapter is to explore some of the issues identified above by, first, providing a justification for using ICT to support teaching and learning, and, second, discussing the role of ICT in addressing some of the key priorities raised in the Williams Review.

Why use ICT?

If you want to argue the case for an ICT-rich primary curriculum then you need look no further than your own lifestyle, starting with what is in your jacket pocket or handbag. Many of us carry around a single, compact device that combines the capabilities of a mobile phone, a high-resolution digital video camera, a CD-quality music player, and a high-specification computer with email and Internet access. Looking beyond our pockets and handbags there is the wider high-technology world in which we live, for example, the wealth of electronic gadgetry that we have in our homes, as well as the technology we encounter when we go through the self-service supermarket checkout, fill the car with petrol, withdraw money from the bank, make a hotel or restaurant reservation online, borrow a book from the library, and so on.

Our working lives provide further evidence of the vital role of technology, with very few occupations not utilizing it in some form or another. We therefore owe it to pupils to prepare them to be citizens in a technology-rich world and this should start in the earliest stages of their schooling. Aubrey and Dahl (2008: 4) provide evidence to suggest this is already happening, when they state that 'most young children aged from birth to five years are growing up in media-rich digital environments in which they engage actively from a very early age'. So preparation for the realities of their future adult world should be sufficient justification for ensuring that all children see and experience the full potential offered by ICT, not just in mathematics but in all areas of the curriculum.

The availability of ICT in primary schools allows purely mechanical tasks to be carried out very quickly and efficiently, thus freeing the user to concentrate on higher-level things such as analysis, interpretation, reasoning and problem solving. One example of this is pupils' use of data-handling software to sort, search and graph data that they have collected. The speed of a computer also allows real-life situations to be modelled effectively. For example, random numbers on a spreadsheet can be used to simulate the rolling of dice, hundreds or even thousands of times. If two dice are involved, then the spreadsheet can add the scores, produce a graph of the outcomes and calculate the average score, all in a matter of seconds. As well as being fast and powerful, computers can also store and retrieve huge quantities of information, both locally, for example, using hard disks, DVD-ROMs and memory sticks, and remotely via wireless networks, intranets and the Internet. Teachers, pupils and parents therefore have access to a wealth of resources that were simply not available a few years ago. Technology also allows the information to be presented more accurately and more attractively than by traditional means, thus engaging the target audience. Why rely on a hand-drawn pie chart on the board when you can produce a far superior visual aid with a computer? Technology is also inclusive in that the information can be presented in a variety of ways according to the size of the audience and the particular needs of individuals. One can also combine various media such as text, graphics, sounds, animations and video in an interactive way, to capture the interest of the user and motivate them to want to learn.

It is not possible within the constraints of this chapter to conduct a discussion of the many theories about learning that have been put forward over the years, so instead one simple observation will be offered: children learn what they choose to learn. We cannot force pupils to learn and it is this optional feature of learning that requires us to inspire, to motivate, to encourage and to make them want to learn. ICT can play a key part in achieving this. Many teachers will have anecdotal evidence of how children are motivated by ICT, but there is a growing body of research literature to support these beliefs. This evidence suggests that ICT can have a positive impact on pupils' levels of concentration, self-confidence, self-esteem, independence and behaviour. This applies to all pupils, but there are particular benefits for those who are reluctant learners or have special educational needs. One reason for this is that the ICT-based approach requires pupils to employ different sorts of skills from those needed when using traditional tools such as pens, pencils, rulers, pro-tractors, graph paper, and so on. These pupils adapt to the ICT-based approach more readily than the traditional approach and so have an opportunity to savour some much needed success, thus raising their self-esteem. Similarly, ICT also provides access to the curriculum for those with a special educational need of a physical nature, for example, those with poor motor-control who find it difficult to produce legible work by hand, or those with a visual impairment.

ICT can also benefit pupils with special educational needs in other ways, particularly when they are using computer-based learning materials. First, such materials often break down the skills and content being taught into small, achievable steps, thus allowing the learner to demonstrate measurable progress and enjoy the praise that results from it. Second, there are advantages in terms of the learning taking place 'in private', particularly at a time when whole-class teaching approaches continue to be encouraged. The child can work at their own pace without fear of appearing slow or holding back the rest of the class. If a mistake is made then the child does not have to worry about looking foolish in front of everyone else and they can simply have another go, usually after being given additional hints or clues by the computer. The com-puter is no substitute for good quality interaction with an effective teacher but the instant, impartial feedback it offers is something that the teacher is not always able to provide.

When engaging in computer-based activities, pupils are also more likely to experiment and take risks, which is precisely what we want them to do, particularly when carrying out investigative, open-ended, problem-solving activities which encourage the pupils to make decisions, predictions and gen-eralizations, and to employ skills such as trial and improvement, estimation and reasoning. A spreadsheet can be used by the pupils or the teacher to model particular mathematical situations, for example, how the volume of a box changes as its dimensions are altered, or how a bank deposit appreciates in value over time depending on the interest rate. ICT also enables pupils to get to grips with tricky mathematical concepts quickly, for example, the use of a programmable floor robot makes the concept of angle as an amount of turning accessible to young children. Another example, involving older children, is the use of data-logging equipment which opens up complex scientific and mathematical concepts such as the warming and cooling of liquids and the graphical representation of these changes over a period of time.

To summarize, ICT enables teachers to access or create stimulating resources; to distribute or display them attractively to individuals, groups and whole classes of pupils; to capture the interest of their pupils and motivate them; to address the issue of inclusion by providing all pupils with access to the curriculum; to share resources with colleagues; and to carry out the many administrative demands more effectively and efficiently. Essentially, there are many things that are done better with ICT than without it although, as we will see in the next part of this chapter, ICT does not always provide the best solution.

ICT and the Williams Review priorities

Of the key issues highlighted by the Williams Review, three will now be examined more closely in terms of the role that ICT can play: the need for greater emphasis on the use and application of mathematics; a renewed focus on oral and mental mathematics; and the promotion of high-quality discussion, particularly in the early years.

The use and application of mathematics

The lack of opportunities for pupils to genuinely use and apply mathematics continues to be an issue in primary schools, as noted by Ofsted in its 2008 report into the teaching of mathematics, stating that 'the majority of pupils had too few opportunities to use and apply mathematics' (Ofsted 2008: 6) and that as a consequence of this 'achievement and standards in "using and applying mathematics" remain lower than in other areas of mathematics' (Ofsted 2008: 35). Since the advent of the National Numeracy Strategy in 1999 there have been improvements in pupils' abilities to carry out the mechanical processes of mathematics, for example, those relating to mental and written calculation, but the majority of teachers still do not acknowledge that the whole point of learning mathematics is so that we can use and apply it (see Ollerton, Chapter 6). This problem is compounded by national testing structures which 'do not require pupils to use and apply mathematics in substantial tasks' (Ofsted 2008: 35), which in turn limits tasks that pupils typically engage in to no more than tackling 'word problems'.

Using and applying mathematics encompasses far more than the ability to identify the operation hidden within a word problem. It includes the ability to represent and communicate mathematical ideas effectively; to solve problems through careful planning and enquiry; and to employ logical thinking, reasoning and deduction skills. The consequence of not providing pupils with opportunities to develop these skills is identified by the Williams Review (DCSF 2008: 62) which states that: 'if children's interests are not kindled through using and applying mathematics in interesting and engaging ways, and through learning across the full mathematics curriculum, they are unlikely to develop good attitudes to the subject'.

Improving both the quality and frequency of pupils' engagement in the use and application of mathematics is clearly a challenge for schools, but it becomes an even bigger challenge when ICT is included in the discussion, given that most examples of pupils' ICT use are restricted to 'closed' drill and practice type activities which could not be further removed from the notion of using and applying mathematics. Meeting this challenge will depend on teachers' subject and pedagogical knowledge and thus the availability of high-quality initial and in-service training, all of which are beyond the scope of this chapter. However, by way of illustration, a few examples of how ICT can be used to promote the use and application of mathematics are described briefly here.

Examples of how a spreadsheet can be used as a modelling tool have been mentioned already in this chapter. In addition to those examples, a spreadsheet can also be used to investigate the ratio between consecutive terms in adding sequences such as the Fibonacci sequence, or to investigate the sums of sequences created by repeated halving (that is, $\frac{1}{2}$, $\frac{1}{4}$, $\frac{1}{8}$ ...) or repeated division by three (that is, $\frac{1}{3}$, $\frac{1}{9}$, $\frac{1}{27}$ ...).

The ICT-based data-handling encountered by pupils is often restricted to the mechanical tasks of sorting, searching and graphing data. Instead of these closed tasks, why not offer more open alternatives? For example, if pupils have access to a data file containing their personal information (height, weight, arm span, shoe size, date of birth, gender, and so on) they could investigate whether there is any evidence to suggest that boys are taller and heavier than girls, or whether the older pupils have bigger arm spans and bigger feet than the younger ones.

A data file providing nutritional information for different types of food could be used to investigate which types of food are good for us, or the relationship between calorific value and the amount of fat foods contain. Climate data for weather stations around the world (average temperature, average rainfall, altitude, latitude, and so on) could be used as a starting point for an investigation into relationships between latitude and temperature or altitude and rainfall. The key feature of all these examples is that pupils have to make decisions about the way they are going to tackle the problem; they need to employ a wide range of mathematical and ICT-related skills; and in terms of curriculum coverage the focus is not exclusively on mathematics.

The National Strategies website offers teachers a range of interactive teaching programs (ITPs) which are ideally suited for use with an interactive whiteboard, although equally they can be used by pupils sitting at computers. They tend to be used by teachers for demonstration purposes with the whole class, but there is a huge potential for more creative open-ended activities, such as:

- the ITP 'Area', which could be used to investigate the relationship between the area and perimeter of different shapes, or the number of different rectangles of a given area that can be made;
- the ITP 'Fixing Points', which pupils could use to investigate how many squares of different sizes can be created on a 6 by 6 arrangement of pins and also find ways of working out the area of each one (the sides do not have to be vertical and horizontal!);
- the ITP 'Number Grids', which is typically used by teachers to demonstrate the visual patterns when the multiples of 2, 3, 4, and so on are shaded on a hundred square. A far more productive task would be to ask pupils to investigate the patterns produced when the width of the grid is altered for a given multiple, leading to the pupils making valuable predictions and general statements.

Most of the examples provided above could be carried out by pupils manually using pens, pencils, rulers, squared or spotty paper and an electronic calculator, that is, entirely without ICT. However, for the reasons outlined earlier in this chapter, ICT offers a range of benefits which ultimately enhance the learning experience for pupils.

A renewed focus on oral and mental mathematics

This is one of the key recommendations identified in the Williams Review, although one could be forgiven for initially questioning the reason why (see Thompson, Chapter 12). With the oral–mental starter being a resident feature of the daily mathematics lesson since the inception of the National Numeracy Strategy in 1999, surely pupils' oral and mental skills have improved. Well, yes they have, but a closer examination of the situation reveals that progress has stalled to some extent and so there is still room for much improvement.

Two government publications (DfES 2007a; DCSF 2007) identify recurring issues in relation to oral and mental mathematics: mental methods seemed to lose importance once formal written methods were introduced; pupils tended to use a limited range of traditional algorithms in preference to mental approaches in the belief that they were better; and pupils often lacked confidence with regard to mental methods and so were reluctant to use them. These findings are mirrored by those of Ofsted which noted a 'reliance on formal written methods and a reluctance to use informal or mental strategies which are sometimes more efficient' (Ofsted 2008: 21).

To remedy this situation:

- pupils must be provided with a wider repertoire of approaches to calculation, with a continued emphasis on mental methods throughout Key Stage 2;
- teachers must encourage pupils to explain, compare and contrast methods, perhaps sometimes using a pupil's inefficient method as a stimulus to discuss better alternatives;
- time for discussion should be planned for and implemented through paired, small-group and whole-class activities;
- discussion should be encouraged through the use of open rather than closed questions that require only brief responses (see Ollerton, Chapter 6), and accompanied by sufficient thinking time for pupils to formulate their responses;
- correct mathematical vocabulary should be modelled and reinforced by the teacher and pupils should be encouraged to use this in their discussions and explanations;
- there needs to be a move away from the belief that the desired outcome at the end of every mathematics lesson is an exercise book full of correct answers.

Interestingly, ICT has contributed to the issues described above rather than provided a possible solution. The widespread availability of interactive whiteboards, combined with the preponderance of drill and practice type resources, has resulted in the oral–mental starter often being reduced to no more than a quick-fire question and answer session based around closed tasks that provide little or no opportunity for discussion. The same resources are also used by pupils themselves at other times during the lesson, but again the activities are not structured by the teacher in a way that promotes discussion. In the hands of a skilful teacher these sorts of resources can be used with the whole class to encourage reflection, discussion and the development of reasoning skills, and likewise a carefully planned computer-based activity for a pair of pupils can do the same, but this tends not to be the default position.

A skilful teacher will also acknowledge that oral and mental work in mathematics do not only take place in the oral–mental starter and do not only involve mental calculations. Pupils should be encouraged to reflect, explain, discuss, question and reason throughout the lesson, in whole-class situations, in pairs or in small groups, and in contexts covering the complete mathematics curriculum as well as other subjects, but this does not necessarily require the use of ICT. For example, when exploring aspects of place value the teacher can use large place value cards for modelling, questioning and discussion purposes as a low-technology alternative to the National Strategies ITP 'Place Value'. A counting stick, with number cards stuck to it provides an effective visual aid when considering mathematical concepts based around a number line (see Delaney, Chapter 5). Interactive whiteboard tools can be used to produce attractive number lines, but the counting stick allows the teacher to move around the classroom, targeting particular individuals or groups, and providing a focal point for the pupils' attention.

When considering the properties of two- and particularly three-dimensional shapes there is no substitute for being able to hold and examine real models, no matter how attractively they can be presented and animated on an interactive whiteboard. The key point to be drawn from these examples is that the teacher must make an informed professional decision as to whether the ICT approach is the most appropriate one, but the overriding consideration should always be fitness for purpose and the resulting quality of the pupils' learning experience.

Promoting high-quality discussion

This has already featured in the preceding section but will be continued here with specific reference to the early years since this was afforded particular attention in the Williams Review. Within its early years chapter the review recommends that 'Early years settings should ensure that sufficient time is given to mathematical discussion' (DCSF 2008: 36) because high-quality mathematical learning is supported by 'opportunities for open-ended discussions of solutions, exploration of reasoning and mathematical logic' (DCSF 2008: 37). The review also identifies the key role of staff, stating that as part of effective mathematical pedagogy 'practitioners' use of mathematical language in open-ended discussions is essential' (DCSF 2008: 34).

The Early Years Foundation Stage (EYFS) curriculum has a strong emphasis on communication, language and literacy; indeed it is identified as one of the six areas of learning and development. Mathematics in this phase appears as 'Problem Solving, Reasoning and Numeracy' (PSRN) and there is a section for ICT within the 'Knowledge and Understanding of the World' area of learning and development. The challenge for early years practitioners is in bringing these three areas together so that high-quality discussion can be developed in mathematics, possibly through the utilization of ICT.

A study by Aubrey and Dahl revealed that those working in the EYFS are 'generally positive about the role of electronic media and ICT' (2008: 4) but goes on to say that those interviewed during the study tended to associate the use of ICT with the development of children's language and literacy skills rather than mathematics. In defence of those working in the early years, the content and structure of the EYFS guidance documents do not help to alleviate this problem. The 14-page PSRN section of the *Practice Guidance for the*

Early Years Foundation Stage (DfES 2007b) makes no reference at all to the use of technology. This omission is mirrored in the two-page ICT section within 'Knowledge and Understanding of the World', which similarly makes no reference to mathematics. The ICT section does refer to the role of talk, but this is restricted to encouraging teachers and children to talk about the ICT apparatus, rather than the effective use of ICT to promote high-quality discussion. The PSRN section is also extremely limited in terms of promoting high-quality talk/discussion, with most of the examples provided being of a closed nature, focusing on the learning of mathematical vocabulary.

If we want early years practitioners to use high-quality discussion in mathematics, possibly supported by the effective use of ICT, then much needs to be done in terms of providing clearer guidance that highlights the interrelated nature of language and mathematical development, otherwise the two will continue to be viewed separately. Meeting this challenge will be dependent upon establishing practitioners with high levels of subject and pedagogical knowledge.

The importance of high-quality discussion is identified by Williams (DCSF 2008: 65) when he states that it 'develops children's logic, reasoning and deduction skills, and underpins all mathematical learning activity' and research suggests that this is possible to develop this with young children. For example, Mercer and Sams (2006) have shown that children can be inducted into a collaborative style of reasoning in mathematics, and Monaghan (2006: 15), working in the same Thinking Together project, showed the extent to which primary children, who had benefited from explicit instruction in how to talk in a group, proceeded to work together playing a game against a computer, and managed to 'articulate their mathematical thinking and make it visible to both their partners and themselves' (see Monaghan, Chapter 4).

Conclusion

The first part of this chapter put forward the case for utilizing ICT in mathematics teaching and learning and concluded that many things are done better with ICT than without it. The second part has considered three of the key issues identified in the Williams Review and discussed the role that ICT can play in addressing them. Here, the case for fully embracing ICT is not so strong and there are some cautionary words. This is partly because the issues themselves are not fundamentally related to ICT and this is possibly the reason why the Williams Review makes no direct reference to the role of ICT in the teaching and learning of mathematics. Instead, the issues discussed present more immediate challenges that can be tackled initially without the need to consider the ICT dimension. That is not to say that ICT has no role to play, but for many teachers the development of their subject and pedagogical knowledge in relation to ICT as well as mathematics may present too big a challenge in the short term. A longer-term view is therefore needed in which the role of the teacher or early years practitioner is seen as crucial in improving the quality of teaching and learning. However, to achieve this, current levels of mathematics subject and pedagogical knowledge among the workforce at all levels will have to be improved.

References

Aubrey, C. and Dahl, S. (2008) *A Review of the Evidence on the Use of ICT in the Early Years Foundation Stage.* Coventry: Becta.

DCSF (Department for Children, Schools and Families) (2007) *Getting There – Able Pupils Who Lose Momentum in English and Mathematics in Key Stage 2.* Nottingham: DCSF.

DCSF (Department for Children, Schools and Families) (2008) *Independent Review of Mathematics Teaching in Early Years Settings and Primary Schools* (Williams Review). Nottingham: DCSF. http://publications.teachernet.gov.uk/eOrderingDownload/Williams%20Mathematics.pdf (accessed March 2010).

DCSF (Department for Children, Schools and Families) (2009a) *Independent Review of the Primary Curriculum: Final Report* (Rose Review). Nottingham: DCSF. http://publications.teachernet.gov.uk/eOrderingDownload/Primary_curriculum_Report.pdf (accessed March 2010).

DCSF (Department for Children, Schools and Families) (2009b) *Beyond Engagement: The Use of ICT to Enhance and Transform Learning at Key Stage 2 in Literacy, Mathematics and Science.* Nottingham: DCSF.

DES (Department of Education and Science) (1982) *Mathematics Counts: Report of the Committee of Inquiry into the Teaching of Mathematics in Schools* (Cockcroft Report). London: HMSO. http://www.dg.dial.pipex.com/documents/docs1/cockcroft.shtml (accessed March 2010).

DfES (Department for Education and Skills) (2007a) *Keeping Up – Pupils Who Fall Behind in Key Stage 2.* Nottingham: DfES.

DfES (Department for Education and Skills) (2007b) *Practice Guidance for the Early Years Foundation Stage.* Nottingham: DfES.

Higgins, S., Falzon, C., Hall, I., et al. (2005) *Embedding ICT in the Literacy and Numeracy Strategies.* Newcastle: University of Newcastle upon Tyne.

Mercer, N. and Sams, C. (2006) Teaching children how to use language to solve maths problems, *Language and Education*, 20(6): 507–28.

Monaghan, F. (2006) Thinking aloud together, *Mathematics Teaching*, 198: 12–15.

Ofsted (Office for Standards in Education) (2008) *Mathematics: Understanding the Score.* London: Ofsted.

Smith, P., Rudd, P. and Coghlan, M. (2008) *Harnessing Technology: Schools Survey 2008.* Coventry: Becta.

8 Shaking the foundations: does the Early Years Foundation Stage provide a secure basis for early mathematics?

Sue Gifford

What are the issues for the Early Years Foundation Stage?

There are vast differences in children's pre-school mathematics learning. Lewis, aged 2, when asked to count backwards, recited 'one two three four five six seven eight nine ten' while walking backwards! Although he cannot actually count backwards, he is well set to do so by the time he goes to school and he is beginning to say 'three!' when he sees three things. However, many 4-year-olds struggle to recite numbers forwards to 10 (Threlfall 2008). Pre-school children can vary enormously in their experiences of numbers and they all need a lot of practice to use counting confidently and with understanding. According to Aubrey (2008), research shows that those who start behind in Key Stage 1 get further behind. She argues that differences between children's early experiences are exacerbated by formal education and in reception 'the whole-class teaching contexts . . . are precisely those that research has shown accentuate initial variations in mathematical attainment rather than decrease them'.

In England, official recommendations for whole-class teaching for 5-year-olds may have overlooked the fragility of some children's mathematics and exposed them to failure. Rather than creating secure foundations for mathematics, this may build anxiety and negative attitudes: as Dowker (2009: 6) argues, 'when children fail at certain tasks, they may come to perceive themselves as "no good" at mathematics'. Children in other countries who start formal schooling later than in the UK subsequently do better in mathematics. However, this does not mean they receive no mathematical education, just that they may do so at home or pre-school in informal contexts.

The implications are that pre-school settings need to provide experiences for the mathematically disadvantaged, and that teachers in Reception and Key

Stage 1 need to cater for children sensitively as individuals, so no child is left behind. They need to be able to assess early mathematical understanding so they can plan for and monitor individual learning. Research also shows that early number learning is a complex process, requiring the synthesizing of many skills and concepts, which are challenging in terms of verbal and spatial memory, coordination and reasoning (Gifford 2005). Children with difficulties or delays in any of these areas are going to take longer to master these skills. Young children need both frequency of experiences and time in order to gradually develop understanding of counting, number relationships and symbols.

Young children who have mastered the skills of counting still may not be able to use counting to solve problems: for instance, when comparing two lots of sweets, a young child may be able to count both groups but not be able to say whether five is larger than four. It seems that children need some time to make connections between the results of counting and number size: they do not necessarily realize that numbers are ordered so each is worth one more than the previous number (Gifford 2008).

Without awareness of the complexities of early number understanding, it is easy to assume that children who can count and recognize numerals are ready to move on to addition and subtraction. In this way mathematics teaching and learning are built on shaky foundations, and children are unlikely to feel confident in later learning and may well go backwards, as Aubrey found. Therefore early years educators need to be knowledgeable about children's developing mathematical understanding, as advocated in the *Independent Review of Mathematics Teaching in Early Years Settings and Primary Schools* (the Williams Review) (DCSF 2008a).

With regard to whole-class teaching, currently, there is hope that UK official guidance is changing. There is increasing emphasis on personalized learning and formative assessment (see Hodgen and Askew, Chapter 10), which should empower teachers to monitor children's learning according to *their* needs, rather than those of tests and targets. There have also been expert recommendations to continue the informal approach of the Early Years Foundation Stage (EYFS) into Year 1 and even to defer the start of formal schooling, according to *Children, their World, their Education: Final Report and Recommendations of the Cambridge Primary Review* (Alexander 2009). With the demise of the Primary National Strategy and its directives about whole-class numeracy lessons, there may be much more freedom for teachers to decide how to teach. The issue then becomes whether the EYFS provides guidance on what to teach as well as how.

The Early Years Foundation Stage

Since 2008, educators in England are in the rare position of having a mathematics curriculum for children from birth to 5 in the Early Years Foundation Stage. Some may have wondered why singing number rhymes to the unborn has been ignored! While a statutory curriculum for children so young is in danger of threatening childhood freedoms, it nevertheless provides an entitlement for all children to learn mathematics. It should also empower educators to preserve children's freedoms by indicating what is not appropriate for young children. For too long, some parents lovingly and successfully taught their children to count and understand numbers at home, while some pre-school educators hesitated to teach disadvantaged children mathematics for fear of over-pressurizing them.

The EYFS sets out principles for early years education which could go some way to prevent inappropriate mathematics teaching. Its four themes – *a unique child, positive relationships, enabling environments, learning and development* – are linked to principles which emphasize emotional well-being, individualized provision, partnership with parents and respect for home cultures. There are pedagogic 'commitments' of *play and exploration, active learning, creativity* and *critical thinking*, which are very relevant to mathematics. Mathematics is one of six areas of learning in the EYFS and is (curiously) entitled 'Problem solving, Reasoning and Numeracy'. While we might welcome the emphasis on problem solving and reasoning (and wonder why spatial mathematics is ignored) the titles allocated to the other curriculum areas unfortunately signal that 'communication' and 'creativity' are separate from mathematics.

Within the mathematical area of learning, there are three strands: *Numbers as labels and for counting, Calculating* and *Shape, space and measures*. In the *Practice Guidance for the Early Years Foundation Stage* (DfES 2007: 64–74), there are lists of key competences for each of these, named 'development matters', grouped for overlapping age ranges, such as 30–50 months and 40–60+ months, culminating in the Early Learning Goals, which are the focus of assessment at the end of the Reception year (see Table 8.1). These key aspects of development are arranged on a grid alongside 'look listen and note', 'effective practice' and 'planning and resourcing'. At first glance it seems that key competences are ordered down the left-hand side in developmental progression, matched with examples of assessment pointers, provision and adult role. While this would be useful, there is no alignment of the 'development matters' points with the relevant points in the other columns, so that examples are not provided for each of the competences.

In Table 8.1, it would be useful to suggest contexts where children might represent numbers in their own way, as in scoring games and making labels.

At 40–60+ months, estimating, counting objects, the numerosity of zero

Table 8.1 An example of a page from the *Practice Guidance for the Early Years Foundation Stage*

	Development matters	Look, listen and note	Effective practice	Planning and resourcing
40–60+	– Begin to represent numbers using fingers, marks on paper, or pictures – select a numeral to represent 1–5, then 1–9 objects – recognize numerals 1–9	Children's methods of counting out up to six objects from a larger group, for example, when children do a jigsaw together and share out the pieces, counting to check everyone has the same number	Ensure that children are involved in making displays, for example, making their own pictograms of lunch choices. Develop this as a 3D representation using bricks and discuss the most popular choices	Create opportunities for children to experiment with a number of objects, the written numeral and the written number. Develop this through matching activities with a range of numbers, numerals and a selection of objects

and rote counting are mentioned without exemplifying either the mathematics or the pedagogy. This does not help in explaining ambiguous phrases like *Using ordinal numbers in different contexts*, which practitioners might think includes using vocabulary like 'third', which is not to be expected at this age (see Gifford 2005).

The key competences are also not helpfully organized. *Numbers as labels and for counting* lists several aspects of early number, including counting, estimating, 'ordinal numbers' and numeral recognition, some with several competences. These are all mixed up together and with no discernible progression. While it is true that children learn all these aspects in parallel and not in the same order, it would be more helpful to have a clear structure which helps educators identify the progressive knowledge, skills and understanding involved in counting. For instance, *Count out up to six objects from a larger group* precedes *count actions or objects which cannot be moved* and the Early Learning Goal *count reliably up to ten everyday objects*. However, counting out from a larger group is more demanding, because it requires understanding that the 'stopping number' gives the number of the set, whereas counting actions and objects requires only skills.

Confusingly, the 'Look, listen and note' example offered (see Table 8.1) involves counting several groups formed by sharing, then comparing them, which is a more challenging counting problem, involving several sets but no counting out from a larger group. A more useful framework for counting would emphasize progression in understanding, for example:

- know some number names;
- say numbers in order;
- coordinate saying one number for each object (including actions or sounds);
- keep track of which ones have been counted (fixed and irregular arrays);
- count out a number from a larger group;
- use counting to solve problems.

The last two demonstrate understanding of the cardinal principle – that the last number of the count gives the number in the group. Examples of problem-solving purposes would also help practitioners plan, for example:

- to get the right number of things (setting up an activity, in a game);
- to compare two groups;
- to check that shares are fair;
- to check if any are missing.

Problem solving is one of the early learning goals, and is important for fostering understanding and positive dispositions, but according to Williams (DCSF 2008a) it needs developing in pre-school settings.

The list relating to numerals also seems in reverse order:

- begin to represent numbers using fingers, marks on paper, or pictures;
- select a numeral to represent 1–5, then 1–9 objects;
- recognize numerals 1–9;
- know that numbers identify how many objects in a set.

Inviting children to represent in their own way is a useful assessment of understanding, involving problem solving, communication and metacognition, and so would be better emphasized as a higher-level activity. The example given in Table 8.1 includes *the written numeral and the written number*, which confuses understanding the meaning of numerals with reading number words. However, the Early Learning Goal 'recognize numerals' does not require children to understand the meaning or cardinal value of numerals. It would be helpful if there were some meaningful examples, like using numbers on labelled containers to check contents when tidying up; using numeral dice to play collecting games; or buying priced goods with penny or pound coins.

Calculating has more appropriate Early Learning Goals: these include comparing numbers and finding 'one more or one less than' numbers to ten. Research has shown that understanding the relative size of numbers is a key predictor of later success or difficulties (Locuniak and Jordan 2008). However, understanding the 'one more than' relationship between consecutive numbers requires children to integrate understanding of both the cardinal value of numbers and counting, and is a later development. 'One more than-ness' is such a basic feature of the number system that it may be overlooked, with provision moving from number friezes of randomly arranged ducks and frogs to abstract number lines, without helping children explore how numbers grow by ones. This involves the important idea that each counting number includes the previous number and one more. Trundley (2008:19) refers to this as the 'successor function' and describes 3-year-old Alice, when told there are four toilets in the changing room, looking at one toilet door and asking 'where are the other three?' Alice can also mentally partition numbers: this implies understanding part–whole relationships and seeing numbers as made up of other numbers.

Another listed competence for calculation is being able to 'select two groups of objects to make a given total of objects'. This requires a knowledge of number bonds which seems a more appropriate expectation for Year 1. However, the ability to visualize numbers as wholes made up of parts is important to develop, especially since a reliance on counting in ones characterizes the calculation strategies of older children with number difficulties. Young children can readily recognize small numbers of objects without counting, that is, they can *subitize*. Through playing dice games or finger rhymes, they come to see six as made up of three and three or five and one. Locuniak and Jordan (2008) found that knowing number combinations at 6 years is a good predictor of later arithmetical achievement: subitizing seems a painless way of learning these, building on children's intuitive skills.

It also seems that dot patterns are effective with children who find learning number facts difficult. The *Practice Guidance for the Early Years Foundation Stage* (DfES 2007) does recommend using fingers to help children understand that five and five make ten and using egg boxes to show three and three make six (although it is not clear what activity children would actually *do*). There could be more encouragement for subitizing, for instance, in dice and domino games and making arrangements for a number in different ways with shells or matchsticks.

Recommendations for recording calculations include encouragement of children's own recording but also demonstrating recording calculations, 'using standard notation where appropriate'. Aubrey's (2008) finding that children who start formal schooling later are mathematically more successful suggests that the ability to write equations at an early age is not important. Furthermore, there is little evidence that such young children can do so with understanding. However, Worthington and Carruthers (2006) have shown the importance of children recording in their own way both as a means for children to develop their own understanding and for teachers to understand children's thinking, especially after the age of 5, alongside the introduction of standard notation. The danger here is that written 'sums' are seen as appropriate, whereas evidence indicates the contrary. Unfortunately, they are also seen as evidence of high achievement in the *Early Years Foundation Stage Profile Handbook*.

With *Shape, space and measures*, there is also a mixture of aspects including data handling, although this is not mentioned in the strand title. Williams notes the Early Learning Goals' focus on language with little mention of exploring capacity or time. There is an emphasis on sorting and vocabulary, which can result in children merely 'barking at shapes'. Young children can intuitively discover relationships between shapes by investigating how shapes fit together, combine to make other shapes, contain shapes within them and can be dissected. Children will readily create three-dimensional (3D) shapes using linking shapes such as Clixi, discovering properties of nets. If educators were more aware of these mathematical relationships they would be better able to evaluate and provide for children's exploratory shape play: they are not guided in this by the *Early Years Foundation Stage Profile Handbook* (DCSF 2008b).

This EYFS profile, which is used to gather assessments of children by the end of the Reception year, has nine *scale points* for each of the three strands. These are based on the Early Learning Goals, which comprise the middle four points on each scale, with points 1–3 for children who have not reached these. So for instance where point 6 is *count reliably ten objects*, point 2 is *count three objects reliably* and point 3 is *count five objects*. The eighth point in each strand is *Using developing mathematical ideas and methods to solve practical problems*. The ninth point on each scale, for example, *the child recognizes, counts, orders, writes and uses numbers up to 20* is for high-achieving children, at a level above the Early Learning Goals.

The *Early Years Foundation Stage Profile Handbook* (DCSF 2008b) provides a range of examples which emphasize the need for understanding, by, for instance, including *counting out from a larger group* as evidence for *count reliably*. However, the points at the 'top' of the scales encourage practitioners to emphasize writing and recording, for instance, in writing numbers to 20, or the example of a child setting out 'addition sums'. This gives unfortunate messages as to what mathematical achievement looks like in the early years, suggesting that young children need to produce written mathematics in order to be recognized as high achievers. With shape, space and measures, the scale points focus almost exclusively on language, whereas investigative play could have received more emphasis, especially for higher achievers. However, the examples include a wide range of contexts, as it is recommended that assessment takes place mainly in child-initiated activities.

Conclusion

The current EYFS has much to recommend it in principle. In practice, it is muddled, and fails to give clear messages about key content and what the principles look like in practice. As argued elsewhere (Gifford 2008), the examples in the *Practice Guidance for the Early Years Foundation Stage* (DfES 2007) are rather pedestrian and do little to foster commitment to exploration, creativity or critical thinking. The *Early Years Foundation Stage Profile Handbook* (DCSF 2008b) provides better exemplification, including useful videos, and the emphasis on child-initiated activity should deter inappropriate whole-class teaching. However, the scale points narrow the focus, and with shape, space and measures there is a missed opportunity to identify mathematical relationships in exploratory and creative play. The *Practice Guidance* is also muddling, with no clear progression or exemplification which will help educators look for significant learning and plan accordingly. This does not support an approach which might reduce the differences in expertise between children from an early age.

There could also be more guidance on appropriate assessment such as puppets making errors to correct and explain; watching children play games in pairs; inviting children's own recording; and ideas for problem solving. It would be more helpful to assess understanding of a few key mathematical ideas, such as cardinality and relative number size, through exploratory activities and problem solving. This assessment then needs to be carefully built on in Key Stage 1, so that children develop confident understanding and are not rushed into abstract manipulation of numbers too soon.

This is what the *Numbers and Patterns* materials (DCSF 2009), produced by the National Strategies, aim to do: they bridge the EYFS and the Framework for Year 1, by identifying key aspects of number from both. The materials include a new structure of key competences listed in six developmental phases, roughly corresponding to the EYFS age phases, with phase 6 listing objectives from Year 1. There are two new strands, *Number words and numerals* and *Counting sets*, which seem based on ordinal and cardinal number, and include calculation in the latter. Progression through the phases is helpfully identified for groups of skills and related to *Potential difficulties* and *Learning and teaching approaches*. There are also useful suggestions for developing areas of play provision and *Adult-led activities*, which include playful and outdoor activities, like squirting water bottles and finding a number of things hidden in the sand. The key messages for the adults' role emphasize modelling, the use of language and the importance of repetition, and allowing time for learning. Unfortunately, despite mention of subitizing and estimation, there is more emphasis on skills of rote counting, numeral recognition and sequencing than on understanding number meanings and relative values and supporting problem solving. Despite the title, there is very little advice on developing awareness of pattern or on exploration and investigation. It is also unfortunate that practitioners are to be given yet another structure to grapple with, in addition to two existing ones. It remains to be seen whether this will make transition easier.

It would also be helpful in the EYFS if the commitments to *play and exploration, active learning, creativity and critical thinking*, were more rigorously adhered to in the mathematical examples. Young children's mathematical potential should not be underestimated; babies are hard-wired to spot patterns and to investigate shape and space, and young children are usually keen to learn to count and get excited by large numbers. The pedagogy of play is important for investigative work and for developing positive attitudes in mathematics; playing with numbers and shapes is one description of what mathematicians do. In the Foundation Stage and later key stages there could be clearer encouragement for:

- role play with adult modelling, for example, shops, garden centres and cafés;
- playing with measuring equipment and structured apparatus;
- games in pairs;
- physical skills and games outdoors to develop and score;
- pattern spotting and creating;
- children's own recording;
- construction and pattern making with shapes.

More generally, there is a need for more open-ended, exploratory and extended activities (see Ollerton, Chapter 6), which may be adult initiated and child developed, and unobtrusively structured. If they are based on observation and assessment, they can be challenging and aspirational. These are more likely to maintain positive attitudes to learning and self-esteem. This is what mathematics should be about: independent enquiry, risk taking, and prioritizing positive identities as successful learners. If these aspects were emphasized more, then the somewhat shaky mathematical foundations of the EYFS would build more secure mathematical futures for all children.

References

Alexander, R. (ed.) (2009) *Children, their World, their Education: Final Report and Recommendations of the Cambridge Primary Review*. Cambridge: University of Cambridge.

Aubrey, C. (2008) Still not getting it right from the start? in I. Thompson (ed.) *Teaching and Learning Early Number*, 2nd edn. Maidenhead: Open University Press.

DCSF (Department for Children, Schools and Families) (2008a) *Independent Review of Mathematics Teaching in Early Years Settings and Primary Schools* (Williams Review). Nottingham: DCSF. http://publications.teachernet.gov.uk/eOrderingDownload/Williams%20Mathematics.pdf (accessed March 2010).

DCSF (Department for Children, Schools and Families) (2008b) *Early Years Foundation Stage Profile Handbook*. http://nationalstrategies.standards.dcsf.gov.uk/node/113520?uc=force_uj (accessed March 2010).

DCSF (Department for Children, Schools and Families) (2009) *Numbers and Patterns: Laying Foundations in Mathematic*. Nottingham: DCSF.

DfES (Department for Education and Skills) (2007) *Practice Guidance for the Early Years Foundation Stage*. Nottingham: DfES. http://nationalstrategies.standards. dcsf.gov.uk/node/84490?uc=force_uj (accessed March 2010).

Dowker, A. (2009) *What Works for Children with Mathematics Difficulties? The Effectiveness of Intervention Schemes*. London: Department for Children, Schools and Families. http://nationalstrategies.standards.dcsf.gov.uk/node/174504 (accessed March 2010).

Gifford, S. (2005) *Teaching Mathematics 3–5: Developing Learning in the Foundation Stage*. Maidenhead: Open University Press.

Gifford, S. (2008) 'How do you teach nursery children mathematics?' In search of a mathematics pedagogy for the early years, in I. Thompson (ed.) *Teaching and Learning Early Number*, 2nd edn. Maidenhead: Open University Press.

Locuniak, M.N. and Jordan, N.C. (2008) Using kindergarten number sense to predict calculation fluency in second grade, *Journal of Learning Disabilities*, 41(5): 451–9.

Threlfall, J. (2008) Development in oral counting, enumeration and counting for cardinality, in I. Thompson (ed.) *Teaching and Learning Early Number*, 2nd edn. Maidenhead: Open University Press.

Trundley, R. (2008) The value of two, *Mathematics Teaching*, 211: 17–21.

Worthington, M. and Carruthers, E. (2006) *Children's Mathematics: Making Marks, Making Meaning*, 2nd edn. London: Paul Chapman Publishing.

9 Home–school knowledge exchange

Jan Winter

Introduction

Olivia loves Beanie Babies. She has well over a hundred and they are carefully organized and displayed in her bedroom. She has a file of information about them – prices, particular characteristics, those she wants to buy, the rare ones she is looking out for and how much they might cost her. Her mum works in a day centre for people with learning disabilities and each week Olivia counts the takings from the coffee bar and sorts it ready to be banked.

Nadia has learned, from her Bengali family, a way of counting up to 30 on her hands, using finger joints rather than just whole fingers. She also uses a similar method in which each finger represents four, so that she can count to 40. She doesn't use these methods in school though, just at home.

The teachers of these two girls, who are both in Year 4, don't know much about these parts of their lives. Both Olivia and Nadia are good at mathematics and actively use it in their lives out of school, supported by their families and their very different social backgrounds. These two stories illustrate what we all, of course, know: that learning is not just something that happens in school and that children manage to integrate what they learn in school with what may be quite different kinds of learning taking place outside school. This chapter is about how teachers can make connections with this wider learning going on in children's lives, so that their learning can be more effective. There has been research showing the 'disconnection' between school learning and out-of-school use of mathematics in real-life situations (Carraher et al. 1985).

In a research project at the University of Bristol, we worked with four schools, two in Bristol and two in Cardiff, to develop ways of sharing knowledge between homes and schools. In the mathematics strand of the project (which also looked at literacy in Key Stage 1 and transfer to secondary school) we worked with one class in each school, going through from Year 4 to Year 5 over two years. A seconded teacher-researcher worked with the class teachers to develop and implement ways of sharing knowledge. We also followed some of the children, who we called 'target children', such as Olivia and Nadia, and talked to their families to understand better how they learned and used mathematics out of school, so that the activities we developed would meet their needs.

Life for families is often busy and complex – so contact between schools and home is not straightforward. Parents' contact with their children's teachers reduces as children go through primary school. The familiar picture of parents in classes supporting reading and other activities in Key Stage 1 is far less common in Key Stage 2. Some families we worked with had significant barriers to their involvement in their children's learning – perhaps through work commitments or through language issues. What is also true, but sometimes not recognized, is that children's out-of-school learning is rich and varied whatever the context. We gained a different perspective on children's learning through the wide variety of their family backgrounds. We drew on ideas of 'funds of knowledge' (Moll et al. 1992) which emphasized the diversity and abundance of the contributions to learning from family contexts rather than taking a perhaps more typical view of a deficit model of families in less advantaged economic circumstances.

The rest of this chapter will look at the mathematics we found being done out of school and then consider in more detail some of the issues we found talking to parents – what did they want to know more about and what difficulties were there in doing this? Then we offer examples of some of the activities we developed and how schools and families used them. Finally, implications for how this might work more widely are discussed.

Mathematics at home

In this section we look at what mathematics we found being done out of school. We collected this information in various ways – through interviews with parents and with children and through videos which our target children made with cameras we provided for them to take home. We categorized the mathematics we saw into three main groups: *play and games*, *authentic household activities* and *school-like mathematics*.

Play and games

Perhaps this is the most obvious way in which we would expect mathematics to be used by children outside school. Many games have strong mathematical elements, as do sport and other play activities. We saw examples of children playing card games, board games, strategy games, activities involving spatial skills and scoring, as well as games they invented themselves.

A boy showed us a photograph of himself playing Scrabble, a game which is not necessarily considered mathematical, and wrote about how he was trying to make a high score using triple letter scores and other features of the board. Monopoly was another game recognized by some of our target children as mathematical with the use of money being an obvious link for many. The more strategic aspects of the game may not have been so quickly identified as using mathematical skills. Carrom is a South Asian game with some similarities to pool. It involves 'potting' pieces which are pushed across a board and one of our target children showed us, on video, a game between him and his brother, clearly recognizing the spatial skills involved.

In Ryan's video, he and his friends played a game they had invented themselves, 'Kerbs'. In their quiet street, they took turns in throwing a ball at the opposite kerb. The aim was to hit the kerb, scoring 20 points. A near miss gave the player a second attempt, from the middle of the road, from where a hit was worth 10 points. The group were well-practised at playing this and very competitive. Interestingly, later in the project Ryan told us they no longer played – they had moved on to other activities. Children's worlds are fast-evolving places.

We have already heard about Olivia's use of mathematics in recording her Beanie Baby collection. She took this very seriously and was methodical and accurate in the details she kept. Indeed, this recording itself seemed to be an activity she enjoyed:

> I write down their names and I just have, well, in my room it's kind of shelves but it has boxes and stuff and they're in there. So I just name the boxes, box 1, box 2, box 3 and there's 18 boxes and stuff, and I just say like one, two, three, four, five, six in a box and then just add them up all together and keep a total and just cross out the old total and put in the new total when I get a new one and stuff.

Another target pupil, Chloe, played at being an estate agent, collecting information about houses and then matching them to what 'pretend' people want to buy:

> I'll go on like the laptop and I'll look and see what one's the best quality and they have to choose and something like that. Then I write it all down, like where they're moving and how much they really want to spend, and then how much it costs, and then they have to write me a cheque out, and then I'll pretend to fax the cheques off, and then I'll do other stuff . . .

Authentic household activities

Here we saw lots of activities related to money – an area in which parents clearly want their children to become confident. Children were given gradually increasing responsibility for money in various ways – relating to managing their pocket money and taking part in household spending.

Nadia would often accompany her mother on shopping trips, as her mother's English was relatively modest. Nadia would check prices and ensure they received the correct change. Her father would also use Nadia's pocket money to give her the opportunity to practise her skills: 'She needs a pound every week. We give her one pound every Monday, so sometime, I give her 20p, 22p, 29p and so "what's left over?", so we say "it's 60p left" and she says "no dad, it's 70p". So she knows how much is left, so we can't cheat her!'

Ryan would be given money for his trips to the local swimming pool and his mother told us how he knew how much he would need, although Ryan was not necessarily aware that he was using mathematics: 'He knows how much I'm giving him, because if he goes to the baths, he needs £1 to get in, 50 pence for the locker and then £1 for sweets (laughs) although he gets his 50 pence back, so he knows he needs £2.50. So he's counted there. And he doesnae know he's doing it obviously like.'

Other household activities involved, for example, programming the DVD recorder – with inevitable examples of children being more competent than their parents in doing this! Bryn said he was the only one in his family who understood how to manage Sky Box Office and explained all the mathematical skills this involved – both using money and time calculations. In another video we were shown how Ellie calculated the amount of cat food she needed to leave for a neighbour to feed her cat while the family were on holiday. This involved weighing the cat, which was not very cooperative, so Ellie held the cat in her arms and then subtracted her own weight from their combined weight. The amount of food needed was then calculated, with an unfortunate final error in units meaning that Ellie announced her cat would need 700 kilograms of food for the fortnight they were away! We also saw videos of children cooking with their families and working out the distance they would travel to a holiday destination and how long the journey would take.

Although some of these situations were set up for the videos, they were all a real part of the families' lives and the outcomes mattered. Children were using the mathematics they had learned in real ways to contribute to the running of the household. A side effect of collecting some of this data was that some parents told us they were made more aware of the mathematics that both they and their children did as part of their everyday lives.

School-like mathematics

The final category that we identified was that of children doing 'school mathematics' at home. Other researchers working in this area have distinguished between the *site* of an activity (school or home) and the *domain* (also school or home). They would therefore call this 'school–domain mathematics on the home site' (Street et al. 2005). A common example of this, of course, is children doing homework that is sent home by their school – a possible source of conflict. Ryan has written, in a vertical 'sum', 43 – 15 = 32.

> Mother: I don't think that's right, that one there *(points to the subtraction sum)*. You can't take five from . . .
>
> Ryan: You have to take three away from five . . . four, three, two . . . You don't get it, do you?
>
> Mother: If I was doing a take-away sum, . . .
>
> Ryan: *(getting cross)* It's the way I do it, we do it a different way.
>
> Mother: *(tries to explain how she would do it)* To be able to take five away from three, you have to put one unit off the four, and put it on the three, do you not?
>
> Ryan: No.
>
> Mother: You have to.
>
> Ryan: *(in a plaintive voice)* You don't, not at my school you don't.

Parents are very aware that school methods have changed (we'll hear more about this later) and they may not be very confident in their own mathematical skills. Sometimes other family members provide support: Olivia would call her grandparents who lived nearby; Nadia would ask her elder sister; and Saqib would sometimes ask an aunt for help.

At the end of the project, Chloe described how she had been set the task of learning her times tables at the end of Year 5:

> 'Cos in Year 6 now, we have to learn . . . this summer holidays, we had to learn our times tables like our name. Like if we say 'what's your name?' and we say 'Chloe' really quick, we have to learn the times tables like that. So if we say '7 × 9?' we have to go whatever the answer is really quickly . . . I just need to learn my 6s and my 9s . . . no, my 8s. That's all now, 'cos they're the hardest. I can't remember . . . I can't remember the pattern in them. So tonight I'll probably go up to my bedroom . . . I'll have a bath, I'll go up to my bedroom and then I'll probably just sit at my desk and just do it until I know them.

We also saw parents who set school-type problems for their children. In Nadia's video she worked through a sheet of problems set for her by her elder sister and Olivia described car journeys with her mother where Olivia would do mental calculations set for her. Some families used commercially available workbooks of examples or mathematics software packages for extra practice.

So, we saw a wide range of uses of mathematics in children's lives. Part of the aim of the project was to find ways of sharing these with children's teachers. We also wanted to find out what parents' concerns and priorities were, although traditionally the flow of information from school to home has been the dominant direction. It still may not be that the information going home about their children's mathematics learning was really what parents wanted. The next section will look at what emerged from our discussions with parents.

Parents' memories of mathematics at school

Everyone went to school. So most parents feel they know quite a lot about how schools work. Some did not go to school in this country, so are not confident about how different it may be here. Some have bad memories of school and do not really want to be reminded of these. And most are aware of how teaching methods have changed in recent years, especially in primary mathematics, where the National Numeracy Strategy has had a big impact. Here are comments about what three parents remember:

> He's brought some maths home before and I'm no too bad at maths, but some . . . I don't know if it's just the way they pronounce some things and he's explaining it to me and I just hav'nae a clue and I just can't help him.
>
> (Ryan's mother)

> Oh, it was horrific, it was horrible . . . we used to have chalk thrown at us and things for getting it wrong and be humiliated in the classroom by being asked to stand up and say your times table, and if you got it wrong repeating it until you said it, time and time again.
>
> (Olivia's mother)

> The simple questions I understand because it's adding, subtracting, multiplication, but when it's a question written in English, I don't understand. I've studied maths up to 6 or 7 class, junior/infants, isn't it? But after that I didn't go to school but I was taught how to do basic maths.
>
> (Saqib's mother)

So in our project, we tried to find out about how some parents felt about their children's mathematics learning and what information they felt would help them contribute more effectively to it. The combination of parents' ideas and our discussions with teachers led to the development of a range of activities, over the two years of the project. These were different in each school, with some overlaps as teachers heard about what was working well in other schools. The next section describes some of these activities and their outcomes.

Activities taking knowledge from school to home

As we mentioned before, this is the traditional route of information – school reports tell parents and carers about children's progress, and at parents' meetings it is usually the teacher who is providing information to parents, rather than the reverse. So this was where we started, building on strategies teachers already used and developing them to try to meet the needs parents had identified.

Classroom visits

In one school, sessions were set up for parents to be taught calculation methods in the same way that children were being taught. This helped parents understand their children's experience of learning this topic. These sessions were targeted towards the parents of children who were finding this difficult – the parents valued something specifically aimed at meeting their children's needs, rather than a general approach aimed at all. Where a small group of parents is singled out, care must be taken that the selection criteria are not presented in such a way that the children or the parents might be stigmatized by inclusion in the group. One parent's response was:

> They had an afternoon where some of the mums went in and they actually taught us for an hour how they teach children, and it helped so much. We got all these sheets and we came home and once I had it in my head – this is how she's got to do it. I mean the answer came out the same whether I did it my way or her way but it was nice to know how they're being taught, how they break it all down. And she really did . . . even her teacher said they noticed such a huge difference, once I knew what she was doing and was able to give her more help . . . it was just breaking it all down and showing you how to do it.

Linked to this, we also worked with parents who spoke English as an additional language. We visited some parents at home with an interpreter which proved to be a very successful way of 'breaking the ice' in involving mothers who had been wary of contact with schools. This led to sessions in school where mothers came in and worked with their own children in making mathematical games that were then taken home to play. There is more detail about this, and all the other activities, in the project book (Winter et al. 2009). The Ethnic Minority Achievement Service (EMAS) teacher observed: '(At first) they met up in the yard beforehand and they came in en masse, now they come in on their own, and . . . walk upstairs and they're not bothered if they're by themselves.'

The children enjoyed having their mothers in the classroom and their behaviour and standard of work improved when parents were present. This applied to all the children whether their parents were able to attend or not. The EMAS teacher said that the whole experience had been a 'real eye-opener' for her: 'Well it's been absolutely wonderful to have the parents coming in and working with the children, and you can't believe how pleased and proud the children are. They still . . . I mean they still get really thrilled when their mums come through the door . . .'

Videos of teaching

Of course, it is not convenient for all parents to come into school – work and care commitments can be difficult to manage. We decided to make some videos which parents could see, to illustrate classroom strategies. Commercially produced videos were available, so, following the success of the videos children had made of their home mathematics, we decided to make videos in which the children would demonstrate the ways they learned mathematics at school.

This idea was very popular: the children thoroughly enjoyed 'being teacher' and parents enjoyed watching children take this responsibility. We made some videos in children's home languages with Pakistani or Bangladeshi heritage children working together. One child used the opportunity to give his teacher some advice: 'I tried to make it as fun as possible when I could, just to make him (the teacher) see I made the people I was teaching laugh, and I thought that would show him that they enjoy it much more when they're allowed to laugh and have a little joke but do work as well.'

A parent told us:

> One time she had the chance to be a teacher on her own, so she had to think properly what to explain to the rest of the kids. She said she did find it difficult 'cos the way the teacher says it is really easy but when it comes to the children's turn she found it quite difficult but she did get the hang of it . . . I did enjoy it 'cos it was like a whole new different thing they were doing, and it gave more chance for the children to speak out or have their own self confidence in front of the video.

Home–school files

A final example in this category is the home–school file. Each child had an A5 ring-binder with their own photograph on the front. Teachers sent home a variety of materials in the file – for example, weekly sheets describing the mathematics being covered, what activities were being used in school and suggestions for activities to do at home. This regular direct focus on what mathematics was being done at school was valued by families and teachers, although it was demanding to produce the sheets regularly. An example of one of the weekly sheets can be found in Figure 9.1.

Comments could be made by parents on the activities they did at home, and children enjoyed bringing these to show their teachers. One activity suggested measuring the dimensions of the family car and then suggesting dimensions for a garage. One parent, a builder, commented in the file: 'Without any help from me Jay has designed almost exactly a standard single garage. Well done. Dad.'

Activities taking knowledge from home to school

This section offers three examples of sharing knowledge predominantly in the opposite direction – from home to school.

Photographs of everyday mathematics

One successful activity involved giving children disposable cameras to take photographs of mathematical activities at home. Children were given a camera at the start of the summer holiday and asked to record any mathematical activities they engaged in over the summer. They also had a diary in which to record brief details in case they forgot by the time the picture was developed! When the cameras were returned the photographs were developed and then children were able to choose which ones they wanted to share. This element of privacy was important in creating trust in the process. In one school the photographs were used to make a class album and in another, a large wall display.

The range of mathematical ideas was very wide. For example:

- a photograph of bus timetables and description of the time calculations Olivia and her mother made about the journey;
- a photograph of a child's grandparents, another of a picture of their wedding day and a calculation of how long they had been married;
- a photograph of a pair of trainers and a calculation of how much had to be saved to buy them;
- a photograph, mentioned earlier, of playing Scrabble and the scoring system.

As digital cameras have become more cheaply available, this activity might now be easier for schools. Parents, and even some children, may have cameras on their mobile phones, thus removing the need to provide them.

Sometimes, different members of the family got involved. Ryan's mother took several of the photographs while Ryan did the mathematics:

School   **Class**

Topic: Percentages   **Date**

Key Words: fraction, percentage, per cent, tenths, hundredths, halves, quarters (century cent centimetre)

Objectives:

To understand that a percentage is a fraction of one hundred, e.g. 35% is 35/100. Per cent means 'out of a hundred'.

To remember simple fractions as percentages, e.g. ½=50% ¼=25%, ¾=75%.

To know that finding 50% of an amount is the same as finding ½ of it.

To know that finding out 10% or 1/10 of an amount makes it easier to find 20%, 30%, 40% etc.

Class Activities:

- Using a hundred square to demonstrate that a percentage is a hundredth e.g. 46% = 46/100.
- Shading in fractions and percentages of squares and comparing them to show that ¼ = 25% etc.
- Calculating 50% of an amount by halving it e.g. 50% of £60 is £30.
- Calculating 20% and 30% of an amount by first working out 10% or a 1/10 by dividing it by 10, and then multiplying by 2 or 3 to find 20% and 30% e.g. 20% of £60 (10% is 6 because 60 ÷ 10 = 6, 6 x 2 = 12) is £12.

Home Activities:

Percentages are displayed all around us when we go shopping or look at advertisements of sales. Being able to calculate how much an amount is reduced by when there is 25% off, is a real life skill.

To help your child calculate the percentage of a number remind them per cent means 'out of a hundred' and that 1% is 1/100, and 10% is 10/100 or 1/10. Let them practise calculating percentage increases and reductions of goods in a catalogue or advertised in the paper e.g. 10% off all prices means a game costing £30 now costs £30 − £3 = £27, whilst a 20% increase in price would be £30 + £6 = £36.

Parent / Teacher Comments:

(This space is for both parents and teachers to comment on the topic or the activities related to them. Please feel free to ask any questions or make any comments.)

Figure 9.1   Weekly sheet sent home.

Ryan: Remember that day we had to . . . if you do any sort of maths . . . like if I give the woman a tenner and then what change I'd get back, we had to (take a photo of it) with the camera . . .

Mother: Oh yeah, you were actually doing maths . . . if you were going to an ice-cream van or something . . .

Saqib's teacher said:

> When they brought the photographs in, I think they were quite a big . . . they were a big thing for me because they showed . . . gave me an insight into their homes and actually made me think of . . . um . . . yes, you know when you have a maths lesson in class, say of weighing scales, whatever, and you talk about maths at home and children tend to sort of – 'oh miss' – they sit there and you're thinking, you know, you're trying to draw it out of them and then you have these pictures where they are actually using maths at home, and you can see it.

Using games

We have already seen that this is a well recognized use of mathematics in the home. So it was a natural focus for activities which would bring that home experience into school.

We have mentioned earlier the activity in which parents came into school to work with their children on making games that they then took home to play. In Nadia's class children designed games that they then made. This was a further development of the mathematical challenge – designing a set of rules which makes a game that is fun and 'works' is no easy task!

We also provided games for children to take home and then report on in their home–school file. In some schools children brought in games from home to play – this let them be 'the expert' in their game and provided breadth of activities in which teachers could encourage the development of collaboration and group work. In one school an after-school mathematics club was set up, focusing on fun activities. Games were widely used in this context.

Creating and using mathematics trails

A range of activities using mathematics trails was used in project schools. In one a trail around the school and grounds was developed that parents were invited in to follow with their children. In another, a 'family maths trail' was developed, using children's ideas. For example, they suggested including questions about family members: their ages, heights, and so on. Children customized these to include specific questions about their own areas and families and then carried them out at home. When they brought the completed trails back to school they were keen to share information that they had gathered. Saqib's teacher noted that children who rarely participated fully in mathematics lessons were fully engaged in the activity, actively seeking help from others when necessary rather than passively letting other children take the initiative.

One of the mothers who came in to take part enjoyed the occasion and showed some ingenuity in her approach to solving the problems:

> I felt it was great . . . but there was one where there was a line . . . people were making the assumption about how many centimetres and I said 'I don't think they are', and I lay down . . . fortunately it was a dry day, because I know I'm more or less roughly five foot, and I said 'Look, actually on my passport I think I'm 1.5 metres' . . . I think they had to do something like find where two metres was . . . and I said that's not right because I'm one and a half metres, and I was really enjoying it.

Conclusion

This project tried to bring together children's two worlds – home and school. It recognized that learning takes place in both and that learning can be enriched by better connections. The activities we developed with the schools were based on what parents and teachers wanted – but of course the main agents in making them work were the children themselves. A note of caution: it is important to remember that children may not want these two worlds to come too close together. Remember Nadia, who did not want to use her 'finger counting' method in school. Children may need to be different people in these two worlds and this must be respected. How often do teachers hear 'She's not like that at home!' in discussions at parents' meetings? So there is a balance to be struck here between sharing knowledge and letting children develop their own identities as they move between these parts of their lives.

Some of the activities were quite time-consuming to develop, so it is also important to focus on what needs are for individual schools and classrooms. We hope that the insights we gained through our close collaboration with families and children can help others to make these decisions and enrich learning in their classrooms through better understanding of the contexts within which children's learning is taking place.

Acknowledgements

This chapter draws on the work of the Home School Knowledge Exchange (HSKE) Project, which was funded by the Economic and Social Research Council (reference number L139 25 1078) as part of the Teaching and Learning

Research Programme (TLRP). We are very grateful to the children, parents and teachers who participated in the project and to the LAs of Cardiff and Bristol for their support. The HSKE project team consisted of: Martin Hughes (project director), Andrew Pollard (who is also director of TLRP), Jane Andrews, Anthony Feiler, Pamela Greenhough, David Johnson, Elizabeth McNess, Marilyn Osborn, Mary Scanlan, Leida Salway, Vicki Stinchcombe, Jan Winter and Wan Ching Yee.

References

Carraher, T.N., Carraher, D.W. and Schliemann, A.D. (1985) Mathematics in the streets and in schools, *British Journal of Developmental Psychology*, 3: 21–9.

Moll, L., Amanti, C., Neff, D. and Gonzalez, N. (1992) Funds of knowledge for teaching: using a qualitative approach to connect homes and classrooms, *Theory into Practice*, 31(2): 132–41.

Street, B.V., Baker, D.A. and Tomlin, A. (2005) *Navigating Numeracies: Home/School Numeracy Practices*. London: Kluwer.

Winter, J., Andrews, J., Greenhough, P., Hughes, M., Salway, L. and Yee, W.C. (2009) *Improving Primary Mathematics: Linking Home and School*. London: Routledge.

SECTION 3
Assessment issues

Until the mid-1990s assessment was either 'summative' or 'formative'. Summative assessment is carried out periodically, at the end of a unit of work, a term, a year or – particularly with reference to the English education system – at the end of a key stage. Results of this type of assessment are reported in terms of marks, grades or levels to a range of different audiences. Formative assessment, on the other hand, takes place in the classroom at all times, and is concerned with the generation of information that can be used as feedback to influence the nature of the teaching and learning activities taking place. The key message is that formative assessment is concerned with using the information gathered to improve learning in the classroom. Alternative descriptors for these two aspects of assessment are 'assessment *of* learning' (summative) and 'assessment *for* learning' (formative).

The original material produced by the National Numeracy Strategy (NNS) in 1999 advises teachers to think of assessment as being at three connected levels: short, medium and long term. Within the list of purposes ascribed to short-term assessment, teachers are told to check whether their children have any misunderstandings that 'need to be put right'. In Chapter 11, Julie Ryan and Julian Williams offer a different perspective on 'errors and misconceptions', suggesting how they can be used to develop classroom discussion. They argue that an understanding of children's (developmental) errors and misconceptions may provide teachers with insight into their current mathematical thinking and inform teachers' decisions about the starting points for productive 'next steps' in teaching and learning. The authors report on the results of their own research involving the large-scale testing of children in England from 4 to 15 years and small-scale research of discussions with children. They present a classification of errors that may exemplify cognitive development and, finally, point to a dialogic pedagogy that supports children in reorganizing their mathematical thinking.

The original NNS material discussed above identifies medium-term assessment as being concerned with reviewing and recording the progress that children are making over time in relation to key objectives. Long-term assessment is concerned with assessing children's work against the key objectives for the year and, at the end of a key stage, against national standards. Given this focus on the achievement of key objectives, it is clear that the major emphasis of the material is on the summative rather than the formative aspect of assessment.

In Chapter 10, Jeremy Hodgen and Mike Askew trace the shift in focus in England from summative to formative assessment (or what is now called 'Assessment for Learning' (AfL)). They argue that summative assessment is concerned with what children already know, whereas AfL focuses on what they need to do to learn more, and is much more interested in what they can achieve with the help of others. They give practical suggestions on issues such as the generation of higher-level questions, the optimization of 'wait-time' and the development of focused listening skills. They also discuss the different types of mathematical problem that can help generate discussion, which in turn can enable teachers to give constructive feedback to individual children.

10 Assessment for learning: what is all the fuss about?

Jeremy Hodgen and Mike Askew

Introduction: assessing progress or assessing learning?

One of us (Mike) remembers coming to the end of a project that had been developing case studies of pupils. At the end of several visits to a class to observe some of the children working on mathematics and to gather data on their understandings, the teacher commented on how much she had learned about the children during his visits. No particular skill or 'trick' had been employed during the visits: all Mike had done was sit with the children as they were working and say 'tell me what you are doing'. Eavesdropping on these conversations was how the teacher had learnt about the pupils. But she could have sat and had similar conversations herself. Why did it take someone else in the room to allow these conversations to happen?

One possible reason is that as a researcher Mike had the luxury of not being responsible for the overall management and control of the class. He could spend a few minutes with individual children and listen to them without needing to keep an ear open for what was going on elsewhere in the room. But this was a well-behaved and calm class: the teacher could have spent a few minutes with individuals.

Another possible reason is that the researcher had no vested interest in how successful the pupils were at completing the tasks. From the researcher's point of view a pupil misinterpreting a task provided valuable evidence into the child's thinking. From the teacher's point of view the same misinterpretation might be seen to be getting in the way of learning. So, rather than letting the child pursue their line of reasoning and seeing where that led (and often it leads to the child realizing something is amiss), the 'teacherly' thing to do is to help the child get 'back on track'. The researcher is curious about the child's thinking, the teacher has responsibility for the child's progress. These two perspectives are not irreconcilable. Good formative assessment requires teachers to be curious about children's thinking. So the question is: how can teachers be encouraged to adopt a more researcher-like attitude in their interactions with children?

Assessing pupils' progress

In England, Assessing Pupils' Progress (APP) is being officially promoted as the principal approach to teacher assessment that all schools should adapt. As the guidance to schools highlights: APP 'is not a "bolt-on" to existing arrangements. APP is all you need' (DCSF 2009: 2).

At first glance the APP initiative would seem to be a move in the direction of teachers becoming researchers into children's thinking. It is presented as a 'basic' and 'straightforward' three-step approach:

> Step one: Consider evidence
> Step two: Review the evidence
> Step three: Make a judgement

> (DCSF 2009: 3)

We will not go into all of the details of these steps here; the documents containing details are easily located on the Internet. We do think, however, that that final step – make a judgement – is one to consider in a little more detail.

At the end of the APP the objective is to decide which 'Level' (according to National Curriculum Statements of Attainment) a child has reached and whether or not their position in this level is 'high', 'secure' or 'low'. In case there is any doubt about this being the ultimate goal of the assessment, the Chief Advisor on School Standards in her Foreword to *Getting to Grips with Assessing Pupils' Progress* (DCSF 2009: 1) points out: 'The bottom line is that when you make a judgement, you use national criteria, and keep a note of the judgements made over time so that you can see how pupils progress.'

So the purpose of the assessment is clearly about judging, and judging, we suggest, entails a different mindset from being curious. In making such judgements, pupil progress is seen to be developing along predetermined lines (or up pre-positioned ladders as high, secure or low implies). But we know that development in learning is not that straightforward: learning does not always mean moving forward or up. Sometimes learning involves 'unlearning' something you previously held true. Another difficulty with such 'tracks' or 'ladders' metaphors of learning is the 'one route fits all' implication – there is only one route of progression, and that is as set out in official documents. But learners don't fit such models.

Anna Sfard (2008), in arguing for thinking being a form of communication, talks about the process of reification and alienation. A pupil's particular actions on a particular day become reified into general objects. For example, the observation that 'Mike answered 20 two-digit subtraction calculations' becomes reified into 'Mike understands two-digit subtractions'. The process of alienation, according to Sfard, makes a step one further away, and 'Mike understands two-digit subtractions' becomes a 'judgement' contributing to 'Mike is a secure level 3'.

At the end of these processes of reification and alienation what is the teacher left with that might inform teaching and learning? 'Mike is a secure level 3' is, on its own, of limited use-value. Such statements have 'exchange' value: the teacher can 'exchange' the records of her assessments for recognition of her children's 'progress', thus she has played her part in ensuring that 'every school has in place structured and systematic assessment systems for making regular, useful, manageable and accurate assessments of pupils, and for tracking their progress' (DCSF 2009: 4). In fact, APP is far less useful, manageable and accurate than the guidance suggests.

For assessment to have use-value the information needs to have value for the teacher and for the learner. Being told that you are a secure level 3 doesn't provide any useful information that can be acted upon. (Mike is reminded of getting the results of a cholesterol-level test that simply told him his score was 4.3. There was no scale provided and nothing to indicate whether this was good or bad.)

Deep down we suspect that most teachers intuitively know that the result of this process does not result in anything of 'use-value'. And so we turn our attention to formative assessment, which evidence shows does have use value.

What is formative assessment?

The interest in formative assessment, in the UK at least, originates in a substantial review of its effectiveness that was later summarized in a pamphlet by Black and Wiliam (1998). In this, they define formative assessment as assessment with the main aim of promoting learning. They distinguish formative from summative assessment. Summative assessment focuses on what children already know, whereas formative focuses on what they need to do to learn more. Formative assessment is much more interested in what children can achieve with the help of others. Vygotsky called this the *zone of proximal development* and argued that this is key to understanding learning.

Black and Wiliam describe the broad characteristics of formative assessment as including the use of rich and challenging tasks, a high quality of classroom discourse and questioning, feedback and the use of self and peer assessment. In particular, they argue that 'the quality of the interaction [between child and teacher] . . . is at the heart of pedagogy' (1998: 16). Teachers in primary classrooms do already spend a great deal of time interacting with children. They ask questions, listen to children's responses and give feedback. Often the majority of a teacher's time is spent on these sorts of activities. So what could teachers do differently? The research evidence suggests that what distinguishes more-effective from less-effective interventions are the kinds of questions asked, the ways in which these questions are asked and how the teacher responds.

Putting it into practice: questioning and talk

Asking better questions

Much classroom discourse consists of what Bloom (1956) terms low-level questions for which the teacher knows the answer (for example, asking children to recall facts and procedures: what is 8 times 6?). Generally, increasing the proportion of higher-level questions is associated with increases in children's understanding (Burton et al. 1986). Higher-order questions require children to think (for example, 'How would you work out 8 times 6 if you didn't know it?'). Such questioning is often focused less on what children already know (although this may be important) and more on what they need to do in order to learn more. But the situation is not straightforward. Whether a question is actually challenging depends on what the children already know. So, a high-level question for one class may be a low-level question for another. To come up with 'good' questions a teacher needs to know the children. But higher level questions are also 'harder'. Children need to think and thinking takes time.

Giving children time to think

One strategy for higher-order questions is to increase the wait time (the time between a teacher asking a question and taking an answer). The wait time is typically less than 1 second in most primary mathematics classrooms. For higher-order questions, increasing wait time to around 3 seconds can have very dramatic effects on the involvement of children in classroom discussion (Rowe 1974) – more children say things, and the things that they do say are longer and more revealing.

But, while wait time is very powerful, increased wait time is not an effective strategy for lower-order more straightforward questions (for example, recall of number facts). Somewhat paradoxically, increasing wait time to more than about 5 seconds can actually decrease the quality of classroom talk (Tobin 1986). In fact, if children cannot respond within 3 seconds, this may indicate that they need time to talk or work on the problem in pairs or small groups.

Listening to children

Listening to children is perhaps the most valuable source of assessment information. Typically, however, many teachers listen to children in a way that Davis (1997: 357) calls 'evaluative'. They ask a question, then listen for the correct answer. When children give partially correct answers, they say things like, 'Almost' or 'Nearly'. This encourages children to believe that the teacher is more interested in the correct answer, rather than finding out what they think and understand. A more useful approach is to listen *interpretively*, listening to children in order to work out why they respond in the ways they do.

Teachers are likely to find out far more about what the children can do by intervening less in order to observe them collaborate on a task. For example, in the APP Mathematics Standards file, the exemplification of standards includes a video of a teacher working with Babigail on ordering numbers on a washing line.[1] The clip begins as follows:

Teacher: Where are you going to put that one?
Babigail: Here.
Teacher: Put it there then. What number have you got, what number is that one?
Babigail: Twelve.
Teacher: No, this one sweetheart, what's that one?
Babigail: Five.
Teacher: Five, good girl, pop it there then.
Teacher: What have we got here then? Can you count them?
Babigail: One, two, three, four.
Teacher: What's the matter?
Babigail: Four.
Teacher: Is that number four? Where's number four then? Do you want to put that one in?
Teacher: Babigail, can you count them along for me? Starting at number one.
Babigail: One, two, three, four, five, six, seven, eight, nine, ten.

Although there are two other children present, this excerpt is typical of the assessment, which consists of the teacher asking questions with short, generally closed responses from Babigail. While the teacher does learn a great deal about what Babigail can and cannot do individually, she finds out much less about what the child can do with help and, thus, what she, as a teacher, could do to help Babigail do more.

Intervening less and observing more gives children more space to construct mathematics. Often, this will mean that children make mistakes, which allows the child or one of her collaborators to correct or comment on the error. This in turn tells you more about what children know rather than simply what they can do. Children then realize the teacher is actually interested in what they say and are thus encouraged to say more. When teachers spend less time talking, children's contributions tend to get longer. As a result, children have more opportunities to listen to and compare their own ideas to those of others. Where children are actively involved in discussion, not only do they learn more, but their general ability actually increases (Mercer et al. 2004).

Listening more also gives the teacher more time to think about the interventions she does make. In Babigail's video, for example, the teacher suggests that the child uses the strategy of reciting the numbers from one to help her order the numbers. Giving herself more time might help to generate alternative questions (for example, what is one more than four?), or to modify the activity (for example, put these numbers in order: 9, 5, 6, 2) or to ask the children to set themselves ordering challenges.

Responding to children

Providing feedback

Talking is central to teaching mathematics formatively. But talking is not in itself enough. Talking allows children to express what they know. But they then need feedback on what to do next. Providing feedback in mathematics can be tricky. Part of the power of mathematics is that ideas can be expressed very concisely. Yet, this strength can make mathematics difficult to teach and learn. Through exploring and 'unpacking' mathematics, children can begin to see for themselves what they know and how well they know it. By listening to and interacting with pupils, a teacher can provide feedback that suggests ways in which pupils can improve their learning.

Talk also provides opportunities for children to give each other feedback. This peer feedback is often even more useful to children simply because it is framed in ways that are 'closer' to their own thinking (see Monaghan, Chapter 4). Listening to children talk among themselves is invaluable for us as teachers as it provides us with richer information about children's understandings and more time to think about how we will intervene.

If we want to find out what children understand in mathematics rather than just what they can recite, then we need to challenge children with activities that encourage them to think and talk about their ideas. This may involve presenting children with the unexpected: an 'obvious' answer that is in some way inadequate, a problem that does not have just one correct answer or a teacher defending the 'wrong' answer. Sometimes a good problem is one in which, paradoxically, a pupil who knows more is more likely to get it 'wrong' and in doing so reveals to themselves or the teacher something about the way in which they understand the mathematics in question. But working formatively is about finding out how to help children learn, not simply about finding out what they can do currently. Hence, these activities also provide opportunities for feedback on what to do next.

Pose problems where the correct answer is not obvious

Much of school mathematics consists of exercises in which answers are either right or wrong. Posing problems in which there may be more than one answer encourages pupils to defend their ideas. The ensuing discussion can provide an opportunity for pupils to examine their ideas and how well they know them. In the following activity children are presented with four items and asked which is the odd one out (Figure 10.1).

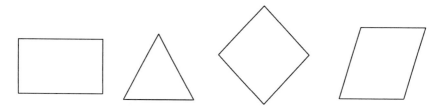

Figure 10.1   Find the odd one out.

Most will immediately choose the triangle, because it is the only shape with three sides. That is one possible reason for it being the odd one out. How many different reasons can the children come up with?

> Its angles add up to 180 degrees (the others all add up to 360).
> It has three lines of symmetry.
> It has the smallest area.
> It has the smallest perimeter.
> It has three angles.
> All its angles are acute.
> Six will fit together to make a hexagon.

But the triangle is not the only possible odd one out – what reasons can the children find for each of the other shapes? And what about these numbers:[2]

> 15   25   10   23

The next steps in learning are often indicated in the children's answers – either a child's own responses or those of others. The teacher has a crucial role to play in finding ways to make these next steps explicit. Doing so may involve questions which simply ask children to say more – and the strategy of silence is very powerful. Alternatively, it may involve asking pupils to think and, thus, extend their knowledge into new areas such as:

> Is the square the only shape with four lines of symmetry?
> How do we know 23 is prime?

The particularly important feature of this activity is that the challenges are directed at a wide range of ability and attainment levels providing an opportunity for pupils to learn from each other. This benefits all children – those who understand more get an opportunity to explain, while those who understand less can listen to and quiz these ideas. Asking pupils to generate different ways of solving a problem is one way of focusing their attention on the process of mathematics. The following activity asks pupils to find different ways of solving what is essentially a question about factors:

> Chocolates are packed in rectangular boxes and in a single layer. Design boxes that can hold 24 chocolates.

Through examining and comparing different techniques, the pupils can assess their own mathematical strengths. Knowing one solution can help pupils generate and understand another and this can enable them to understand the connections between different mathematical domains. Feedback might be in the form of a reflection on the activity:

> What are the advantages and disadvantages of the ways you looked for all the different solutions?
> What is similar . . . what is different about the ways of solving the problem?
> Did you find one method easier than another?

Encouraging pupils to unpack and share the ideas they consider easy and hard can provide pupils with some insight into strategies that they themselves find difficult. Problems with no solution can be equally productive. The following challenge has no solution:

> Create a quadrilateral with four equal sides and exactly one right angle.

Initially the children are likely to work by trial and improvement. The problem looks possible (and teachers do not pose impossible questions). As they begin to realize it is impossible they can be challenged to convince others.

Probing the children's knowledge might involve the teacher playing devil's advocate:

> I'm sure I've seen tiles like that. You mustn't have tried enough examples.

Used sensitively, giving children the opportunity to prove the teacher 'wrong' can be a powerful way of promoting independent learning. Alternatively, the teacher might ask a pupil to explain her thinking:

You say there's no solution. How do you know?

Feedback on ways of improving conceptual understanding might come in the form of teacher questions such as:

Can you show us what happens as you try to construct your quadrilateral?

Alternatively, feedback may come from the pupils themselves in listening to, adding to and improving the ideas of others.

Mistakes are often more informative for learning than 'correct' answers

Mistakes can often offer more opportunities both to assess how well a pupil grasps a mathematical concept and to offer feedback on how she could improve or adapt her ideas. Even successful pupils can have difficulties with what appear to be relatively simple ideas in new or less straightforward contexts. For example, faced with the question 'Jo got 15 spellings correct. Jo got three times more spellings correct than Sam. How many spellings did Sam get correct?', many children, even high achievers, give an incorrect answer of 45. Crucially here, the context is one that lulls the child into giving an incorrect response. The use of 'three times' leads the children to assume this is a multiplication problem. Asking a question (for example, what is confusing about that problem?) can focus children's attention on what they need to do to improve their understanding.

Often the context in which a problem is set can make it more or less straightforward. In their study of children's mathematics, Julie Ryan and Julian Williams (see Chapter 11) examined how 6-year-olds understood measurement using non-standard measures (see Figure 10.2). Ninety-one per cent of children correctly measured a toothbrush to be 7 paperclips when the paperclips were aligned with the ends of the toothbrush, but only 50 per cent correctly measured the comb to be 5 paperclips long when the ends were not aligned. Only 18 per cent could compare the length of the two correctly.

In primary mathematics, teachers often support children by giving more straightforward problems like the toothbrush problem. By posing the problem in less straightforward contexts like the subsequent examples, teachers can learn more about how well children understand mathematics and help them understand it better. Activities that focus on identifying and correcting common errors can be helpful in both the assessment and the feedback stages

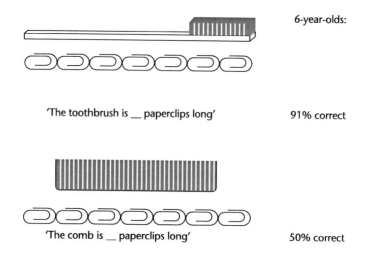

'The toothbrush is __ paperclips long'   91% correct

'The comb is __ paperclips long'   50% correct

'The toothbrush is __ paperclips longer than the comb'

18% correct

Figure 10.2 6-year-olds' understandings of measurement (from Ryan and Williams 2007: 95).

of formative assessment. For example, in the multiplication in Figure 10.3, the 'whole number' and fractional parts of the number have been multiplied separately.

This faulty calculation could be presented among a set of similar calculations – some with errors, others not – and children asked to identify which are correct or incorrect. Asking pupils to find what has gone wrong in this algorithm can help some pupils to identify the mistakes they themselves make. More importantly, by focusing on the process of the multiplication calculation rather than its result, pupils can identify why such errors are made. This in turn can help pupils understand what they know well and what they

$$
\begin{array}{r}
9\ 2\ .\ 7 \\
\times\ 3 \\
\hline
2\ 7\ 6\ .\ 2\ 1 \\
\hline
\end{array}
$$

Figure 10.3   A faulty calculation for 92.7×3 (correct answer: 278.1).

know less well. Feedback could take the form of pupils providing advice to others on why such errors happen and how to avoid them.

Mistakes and errors are a necessary part of learning. Children's misconceptions and errors are invaluable for teaching and learning – provided the classroom is one in which these mistakes are valued (see Ryan and Williams, Chapter 11).

Looking for similarities and differences

Identifying similarities and differences can enable pupils to begin to understand for themselves the big ideas in mathematics. For example, to experienced mathematicians and mathematics teachers all subtraction problems are essentially (mathematically) similar. This structure is much less clear to pupils encountering them in school mathematics lessons: why should 'Mike has £7 and Jeremy has £9. How much more does Jeremy have?' be linked to 'Jeremy has £9 and gave £7 to Mike. How much does Jeremy have left?' One teacher, for example, gave children a set of 20 word equations, each written on a card. She asked pupils in pairs to sort the equations into groups of no more than five. In the discussion that followed, the teacher's questions included:

> What do you think is similar about those two questions What mathematical sentences could you write for each problem?
> You put those two problems in different groups. What do you think is different about the two equations?

Two crucial factors in this activity's strength were that the teacher had structured it so that different groups of pupils grouped the problems in different ways thus providing some mathematical disagreement, and each pair had considered *all* the problems thus enabling *all* pupils to engage in the discussion.

'Closed' questions can sometimes be valuable

Closed questions have come in for much criticism in mathematics education, but some closed questions can be very powerful. The teacher could ask the following question (using say mini-whiteboards to get a response from all the class):

> Are all squares rectangles?

If all children get the answer correct, the teacher can move on. If no one gets it correct, then the teacher might re-teach the definitions. But if part of the class get it right and part get it wrong, then the teacher can organize a discussion:

You thought the statement was true. Why?
You thought the statement was false. Why?

The use of provocative statements (such as, can a third be bigger than a half[3]) is particularly powerful in mathematics and often more powerful than a direct question. This can provide an opportunity for pupils to challenge the teacher and for pupils to debate a particularly difficult aspect of fractions.

Finally

Implementing formative assessment is far from easy, but the benefits are substantial. Many teachers have found collaborating with other teachers helpful in putting these ideas into practice. Collaboration might involve joint planning, team-teaching or observing each other's classes. Another powerful tool is the children themselves. Some teachers have found time to interview a small group of children. They have found listening to children talk and grapple with mathematics to be an immensely powerful way of understanding how children learn.

Further reading

The Black Box series of pamphlets contain useful information and advice on questioning both in general and specifically in relation to mathematics and primary teaching: *Inside the Black Box* (Black and Wiliam), *Working Inside the Black Box* (Black, Harrison, Lee, Marshall and Wiliam), *Mathematics Inside the Black Box* (Hodgen and Wiliam) and *Inside the Primary Black Box* (Harrison and Howard) are all available from nferNelson (http://www.gl-assessment.co.uk). There is a great deal of published research on the way children understand mathematics on which teachers can draw. See Cockburn and Littler (2008) and Ryan and Williams (2007) for some of the difficulties primary pupils encounter. A good source of problems for the type of activities that we describe is Carpenter et al. (1999).

Notes

1   APP mathematics standards file: Babigail (Year 1 below level 1). Available from http://nationalstrategies.standards.dcsf.gov.uk/ (accessed March 2010).
2   The odd one out could be any of the numbers: for example, 25 as the only square number, 23 as the only prime, 15 as the only multiple of 3, 10 as the smallest. Children will generate even more reasons.

3   ⅓ can sometimes be 'bigger' than ½: for example ⅓ of £6 is larger than ½ of £3.

References

Black, P.J. and Wiliam, D. (1998) *Inside the Black Box: Raising Standards through Classroom Assessment*. London: King's College London, School of Education.

Bloom, B.S. (1956) *Taxonomy of Educational Objectives*. New York: Longman.

Burton, J.K., Niles, J.A., Lalik, R.M. and Reed, W.M. (1986) Cognitive capacity engagement during and following interspersed mathemagenic questions, *Journal of Educational Psychology*, 78(2): 147–52.

Carpenter, T., Fennema, E., Franke, M.L., Levi, L. and Empson, S.B. (1999) *Children's Mathematics: Cognitively Guided Instruction*. London: Heinemann.

Cockburn, A. and Littler, G. (eds) (2008) *Mathematical Misconceptions: A Guide for Primary Teachers*. London: Sage.

Davis, B. (1997) Listening for differences: an evolving conception of mathematics teaching, *Journal for Research in Mathematics Education*, 28(3): 355–76.

DCSF (Department for Children, Schools and Families) (2009) *Getting to Grips with Assessing Pupils' Progress*. Nottingham: DCSF.

Mercer, N., Dawes, L., Wegerif, R. and Sams, C. (2004) Reasoning as a scientist: ways of helping children to use language to learn science, *British Educational Research Journal*, 30(3): 359–77.

Rowe, M.B. (1974) Wait time and rewards as instructional variables, their influence on language, logic and fate control, *Journal of Research in Science Teaching*, 11: 91–4.

Ryan, J. and Williams, J. (2007) *Children's Mathematics 4–15: Learning from Errors and Misconceptions*. Buckingham: Open University Press.

Sfard, A. (2008) *Thinking as Communicating: Human Development, the Growth of Discourses, and Mathematizing*. Cambridge: Cambridge University Press.

Tobin, K. (1986) Effects of teacher wait time on discourse characteristics in mathematics and language arts classes, *American Educational Research Journal*, 23(2): 191–200.

11 Children's mathematical understanding as a work in progress: learning from errors and misconceptions[1]

Julie Ryan and Julian Williams

Introduction

Underlying our chapter is a positive and respectful view of children as learners in classrooms. Knowing about their errors and misconceptions gives teachers an opportunity to consider how children's mathematical thinking may be developing – such knowledge provides us with the starting points for productive teaching. That is, learning often starts with mistakes and those mistakes may provide us with a window to look into and see the child's thinking. We believe that children construct their own understanding of mathematics and that they may need considerable time in classrooms to express (think, speak) and reorganize that understanding (see Barmby, Harries and Higgins, Chapter 3). In this view, a teacher can productively plan for mistakes, provide opportunities for the testing and articulation of ideas, and support learners' growing mathematical identity.

Classrooms can be places where children see themselves as mathematical beings rather than simply receivers of pre-digested knowledge. The most wonderful moments for us as teachers have been when a learner exclaims, 'Ah, I get it now!' and when they then go on to explain their mathematics with clarity and confidence. Before these moments of clarity, the learner has *necessarily* made false starts or faulty connections. We, as teachers, may simplistically term these 'mistakes' or 'errors', but there is thinking behind these errors and much for teachers to interpret and understand as we support the learner in making the next steps. Dialogues provoked by 'mistakes and misconceptions' involve mutual learning by the teacher as well as the learner.

Errors and misconceptions as starting points for learning

When we as teachers first recognize a child's 'mistake', we may be tempted in the highly paced classroom flow to simply label the response as incorrect and resort to a teaching strategy to 'fix it' *and quickly*. But there can be more thoughtful and engaging reactions: we could identify the response, for example, as partially correct, partially misconceived, stumbling or tentative. Such labels might suggest that a particular pedagogical view is at work here: that here is a teacher who is trying to *make sense of the response* in order to create a learning experience that works *with* the child's ideas and helps to build on them.

So you can see that our professional vocabulary may be useful because it can guide our teaching response to learning. We must use some vocabulary to communicate, and words take on all sorts of meanings of course, so we state here that in our use of the terms 'errors and misconceptions' we are promoting a positive view of errors and misconceptions as productive starting points for learning. The word 'error' describes an incorrect response that you hear or see, while the word 'misconception' describes incomplete conceptions, or partial reasoning, usually hidden behind the error, and which may 'explain' the error: this may not be immediately accessible to the teacher. Questions such as 'Why has the child made this response?' and 'What is their reason for it?' help us to consider the current understanding of the learner. We believe that when children are learning mathematics they are trying to make sense of difficult ideas. They are usually trying to enter a world of thinking that is often quite puzzling and alien to their everyday experience. We, as teachers, can support them as they express their own ideas, their own explanations and, importantly, their own identity as independent learners, if we have a teaching strategy that explicitly values errors and seeks articulation of (mis)conceptions. This approach is usually called diagnostic teaching, because it involves a process of 'diagnosis', that is, the revealing of the underlying causes or explanations for errors (in this view errors are only symptoms, and we do not just 'treat' symptoms).

Learners' responses are not usually thoughtless or random – we are all thinking beings trying to make sense of the world. But there are several forces at play when we respond erroneously and the public classroom itself introduces a special dynamic to learning. We may be panicked to respond when we are not ready or confident; we may have been distracted, troubled or be daydreaming; we may have misheard or misread; we may have made a slip; or we may have dismissed ourselves already with negative beliefs, thinking 'I'm one of those people who can't do maths'.

Teachers can be sensitive to all these possibilities, both social and cognitive. We remember one story where a child wrote that the mathematical drawings presented to her were 'angels'. The sensitive teacher thought the child had made a spelling mistake and *did* know that the drawings represented 'angles'. On checking with the child, however, she found that she actually thought the drawings were flying angels. So teachers' first thoughtful responses can be erroneous, partial and misconceived too! We can all jump to the wrong conclusions.

Perhaps the challenge of discovering what a child is really thinking is what makes our profession so special – it is ongoing 'detective' work. Investigation starts with building up your teacher knowledge base by reading, researching and developing on-the-job experience about children's likely responses. A useful plan is to anticipate children's responses to mathematical tasks; create opportunities for the children to articulate their reasoning; keep an open mind about their understanding; and be prepared to change your mind based on the evidence.

We are promoting a pedagogy where teachers anticipate and identify likely errors and work with them; lesson design where children have opportunities to consider their own conceptions and work towards strengthening, refining or reorganizing their understanding, themselves. We call this approach diagnostic teaching.

Naming errors and misconceptions

Research over many decades has identified and named many common errors that learners make as we/they build mathematical understanding. The error diagnosed as 'decimal point ignored' is one of the most well-known errors in the research literature (for example, APU 1982; Ryan and Williams 2007) but the error has not been 'eradicated' since it was identified and named so long ago. Why? We think it is still a common error because there is reasonable (but partial) thinking behind it, that explains and so 'causes' it. Children of all ages make this error. Consider the question: 'Is 0.15 greater than 0.2?' Many children think 'Yes'. This is a reasonable suggestion if your experience to date is that the number 15 is greater than the number 2 and you ignore the decimal point. Understanding the new 'decimal numbers' here requires recognition that 15 and 2 are not whole numbers of a common unit when placed after a decimal point – their units are different, namely 15 is a number of hundredths and 2 is a number of tenths, that is, their 'place value' has changed.

How will teachers find out what the children are thinking about this question? How can teachers support children in reasoning their way through here so that they can justify the surprising new fact that '0.15 is less than 0.2'? How can teachers find carefully crafted tasks that provide enough (but not too much) cognitive conflict (that is, discomfort that something is not reasonable or consistent) so that children establish correct reasoning for the new number domain? (see Ryan and Williams 2007 for more on peer group discussion [pp. 31–9] and task design [pp. 44–5]) (see also Monaghan, Chapter 4, for more on group discussion).

A less common error in ordering decimals, and more likely as children get older, is the error called 'longest is smallest'. The reasoning here is that the more decimal places you have, the smaller the place value of the decimal fraction. So with this reasoning, 0.625 would be regarded as smaller than 0.25 because 625 (with three digits) is longer than 25 (with two digits), that is, simply because 'thousandths' are smaller than 'hundredths'. Could there be other reasoning? The 'teacher-detective' may uncover alternative reasoning drawn from generalization for *unit* fractions where 'the bigger the fraction denominator the smaller the fraction' which is correct but not complete (for example, $\frac{1}{625}$ is smaller than $\frac{1}{25}$). But *decimal fraction* form is different and 0.625 is greater than 0.25. How could children explore the reasoning here? Is there other reasoning behind this response that might also be misconceived? What will persuade children to change their mind? How will they articulate this?

Notice that the two errors and misconceptions – decimal point ignored and longest is smallest – sometimes give the correct answer, but not *always*. The decimal point ignored strategy gives the correct answer for 0.25 < 0.42, but not the correct answer for 0.25 < 0.4 because the strategy gives the incorrect statement 0.25 > 0.4. The longest is smallest strategy gives the correct answer for 0.625 < 0.8 but not for 0.625 > 0.5 because this strategy gives the incorrect statement 0.625 < 0.5. A generalization should be treated first as a conjecture, asking 'Does this statement work *sometimes*, *always* or *never*?' Children are then engaged in exploration, discussion and reasoning. Some children hold multiple rules for comparing fractions and switch rules according to the context. This is not an unfruitful strategy if the restrictions for the rules are known (knowing that this rule works 'sometimes' but 'not always'), but it can create an overload on working memory and prevent connections being made between rules. As learners we are striving for efficiency, and a universal rule (that works 'always') gives us some power and satisfaction.

A well-known counting error for young children involves 'counting the numerals' or, on a number line, 'counting the tick marks rather than the jumps'. For example, children asked to 'take 3 away from 9' might answer 7 by counting down three numerals: '9, 8, 7', giving 9 – 3 = 7. If teachers notice that children's counting answers are mostly one out, they may find that children are using this strategy. Or if answers are sometimes out by one or two, teachers may find that the children have an error somewhere in their counting sequence (for example, 'nine, eight, six, seven').

Some children have a conception we have called a 'unit fraction prototype', meaning they expect fractions to be 'unit fractions', that is to have a unit (one) in the numerator. For example, if they are shown six apples and three of them are put on a plate, and then they are asked 'What fraction of the apples is on the plate?' they may select ⅓ as the relevant fraction. Or if they are asked to 'Shade one-third' of a circle that is divided into six equal sectors, they may then shade one sector only. These are not unreasonable (mis)conceptions – they are early steps on the way to full understanding of fraction symbols.

Anticipation of errors and misconceptions: how are children likely to respond?

The 'wisdom of practice' that teachers build on the job and over time may include a growing store of knowledge of the errors that children commonly make in different areas of the mathematics curriculum, like those above. Researchers have systematically gathered and verified many of these errors and have sometimes uncovered errors and misconceptions that were not widely known by practising teachers (for example, see Williams and Ryan 2000).

Thus researchers' knowledge can complement and add to the knowledge base of the busy teacher quite significantly. Knowing what to look for – anticipating responses – can focus the professional view of the teacher and support their lesson planning. Classrooms are busy places and our experience suggests that teachers may not recognize all the common errors or the significance of the misconceptions behind them without first reading about them, naming them and considering different teaching strategies to work with them.

Japanese teachers have used a 'lesson study' approach to their lesson planning and evaluation for decades and their methodology makes use of *anticipation* of known errors and misconceptions for productive classroom learning. The lesson study approach involves a small team of teachers working together to plan and research their lessons, continually analysing each other's lessons and refining their plans and, through this research cycle, building their knowledge base of children's responses and productive learning. This is a collaborative approach supporting ongoing professional development and has been particular to the Japanese teaching culture. However it was taken up enthusiastically in the USA and Australia in the 1990s and later in England.

Teachers in the USA have reported that their subject-matter knowledge has been strengthened through lesson study as they became aware of missing knowledge that was needed to inform their pedagogical practice.

> Lesson study alone does not ensure access to content knowledge. But teachers are likely to build their content knowledge as they study good lessons, anticipate student thinking, discuss student work with colleagues, and call on outside specialists. Lesson study can help

educators notice gaps in their own understanding and provide a meaningful, motivating context to remedy them.

(Lewis 2002: 31)

As you can see, anticipation of children's thinking is a key focus of lesson study. But how do teachers build knowledge that helps them anticipate?

The research work discussed in this chapter was drawn from large-scale testing of children in England from 4 years to 15 years of age across the mathematics curriculum, as well as from smaller-scale research investigating children's underlying reasoning, and from research in real classrooms where teachers developed children's discussion of their errors and misconceptions (see Ryan and Williams 2007). The book's appendix 1 describes all the test questions, what percentage of children answered correctly, the common errors and the percentages showing how frequent each error was, as well as the inferred misconceptions, for each age group (Ryan and Williams 2007: 174–221). Appendix 2 has six prompt sheets for classroom discussion (Ryan and Williams 2007: 222–7). We will discuss several examples here, mostly with regard to number, but there are many other interesting errors to explore across the mathematics curriculum in measurement, shape and space, handling data and algebra.

We note though that the particular nature of a task or a test question can restrict how a child responds: test questions or tasks are not neutral, and context in particular can be misleading (Cooper and Dunne 2000). But we think that a well-crafted question can help uncover unstable knowledge and provide a starting point for a child to sort out their thinking and form more robust understanding of mathematical ideas.

Identification: classifying errors and misconceptions

When we studied children's erroneous responses to test questions, we tried to classify different types of response in terms of the thinking that (perhaps) lay behind them. There were, naturally, careless slips of memory or attention; jumping to conclusions; only dealing with one of the two conditions or steps in a task; and there were some errors that we could not diagnose. Many of these may be due to the assessment conditions – lack of motivation or high test anxiety. But there were several categories which we thought were significant in terms of cognitive development: they suggested there were underlying (mis)conceptions or conceptual limitations behind the errors. We explained these types of errors as due to modelling, prototyping, overgeneralizing or process-object linking. We concluded 'that the latter four types of errors are the result of intelligent constructions that should be valued by learners and teachers alike' (Ryan and Williams 2007: 13).

Modelling

We use the word modelling to refer to the way mathematics is connected with a 'real' everyday world – the everyday world being then represented by the mathematics. 'One can say perhaps when a child has a "modelling error" that the child has their own "model" of the situation, in conflict with the "mathematical model" expected in the academic context of school' (Ryan and Williams 2007: 16).

The representations and contexts we use in classrooms to model the mathematics – such as fractions of cakes, number lines, hundred squares, the context of money for decimals – ideally bring meaning by providing connections with what is already known intuitively by the learner and the mathematics under consideration. But such representations have their limitations: one model or context will not represent all of the mathematics and the learner will need to experience several models and be able to move flexibly between them to successfully build the mathematics (see Delaney, Chapter 5, and Barmby, Harries and Higgins, Chapter 3).

Prototyping

We use the phrase 'prototype of a concept' to mean a culturally typical example of the concept. For example, we will perhaps all share an image of a 'triangle' as an equilateral triangle oriented on its 'base'; think of a hexagon as always regular; read scales as marked in units; make a half-turn for 'turn'; or think of fractions as unit fractions. As a consequence, an error may result, for example, in not recognizing some triangular shapes because they are in untypical orientations; or a scale may be incorrectly read '1, 2, 3, . . .' because the unitary prototype is intuitively so powerful for the child.

Prototyping is an intelligent – even essential – element of concept learning and draws on early first experiences of concepts. Questions that challenge prototyping include:

- What makes this or that a triangle (or a hexagon)?
- Where is the whole unit on this scale?
- How much should I turn?
- What do the numerators and denominators in a fraction represent?

From the prototype we refine and broaden our conceptual understanding.

Overgeneralizing

Overgeneralizing is also an intelligent response to earlier experience and is closely related to prototyping – it involves an active attempt to build on previous learning. One of the most common overgeneralizations is that 'multiplication makes bigger' or 'division makes smaller'. These statements were correct for previous classroom situations and experiences but outside the domain of whole numbers they are no longer always true.

Almost all the overgeneralizations we have found in our research sprang from generalizing rules that worked for the whole numbers into domains like fractions, decimals and negative numbers. Consider these paired statements: $4 \times 2 > 4$ but $4 \times \frac{1}{2} < 4$ (the effect of multiplication by a whole number or a fraction); $42 > 5$ but $0.42 < 0.5$ and $2 > 1$ but $-2 < -1$ (ordering numbers). Clearly, generalizations of rules for whole numbers do not always hold in the new number domains of fractions and negative numbers. Mathematics is largely about generalizing, so an important focus in classrooms is testing a generalization and drawing attention to the domain in which it 'works'. Again, this involves refinement and development of mathematical understanding, in which the formulation and testing of false conjectures is an essential element.

We also found quite sophisticated overgeneralizations for decimals. Some children (and trainee teachers) read a decimal number as a pair of whole numbers separated by a point. This leads to a 'separation strategy'. This strategy works well for additions like $2.4 + 5.1$ where you add the two numbers to the left of the decimal point and then the numbers to the right giving 7.5. However, it no longer works in the case $2.4 + 5.8 = 7.12$. Similarly, $2.3 + 1.47$ does not equal 3.50.

Another overgeneralization occurs with the overuse of the 'additive strategy' when a multiplicative strategy is required. For example, children using an additive strategy for completing a fraction question like '$3/12 = 6/?$', may write 15 as the missing denominator. They see that 3 has been added to the numerator ($3 + 3 = 6$) so they add 3 to the denominator ($12 + 3 = 15$) rather than multiply by 2 ($3 \times 2 = 6$, and $12 \times 2 = 24$) to establish equivalence. This strategy is very resistant to change and is found across many mathematical contexts up to the age of 16 years for many children.

A key question we suggest for challenging generalizations in classrooms is: 'When does a particular generalization *not* apply?' For example, when does multiplication *not* make numbers bigger? Such questions foreground attention to *over*generalization and thus foster metacognition.

Process-object linking

Concept formation often requires that processes be made into new mathematical objects. If we ask young children 'How many toys are here?' the question may signal a response of counting, for example '1, 2, 3, 4, 5, 6'. What *we* are interested in is the 6-ness of the set of toys, that is, the cardinality of the set. We are hoping the child will make the link between the counting from 1 to 6 and the cardinality of the set of toys (6) by realizing that the last number name spoken answers the question we posed. Thus there is a need for a link between the process of counting and its object, the last number in the sequence (see Dunn, Matthews and Dowrick, Chapter 17).

Questions that teachers ask children may prompt process or object conceptions, and eventually require flexible switching between both conceptions. For example, in a sum such as $8 + 3 = ?$, the equal sign prompts the *process* of addition and the child perhaps says '8 plus 3 *makes* 11'. But a task like $8 + ? = 13$ requires a more sophisticated understanding of the equals sign and a conception of a number sentence recognizing there are relationships between the numbers. The processing or action needs to be 'extracted' from the number sentence object. Similarly, more difficult number sentences, like $9 + 3 = 6 + ?$, require a conception of equality that appreciates that the outcomes on both sides of the equals sign must be the same.

Here are three 10-year-old children discussing a number sentence task '? × 6 = 9 × 4' called 'missing numbers' in conversation with the teacher. They had earlier written their different answers to the task. Sonia had been correct and she moves flexibly between object and process in justifying her answer. Gareth had used a process conception and had answered '36', but with support from the teacher, and because he had listened to Sonia, he was moving towards an object conception of the number sentence. Robin has also reconsidered his earlier response and additionally shows mental flexibility with the arithmetic structure of multiplication facts.

Sonia:	I did 9 times 4 to get my answer of 36 and then saw there was 6 there so I thought to myself *what* times 6 equals 36 and then I thought of my 6 times table in my head and got 6.
Gareth:	Well, to be honest I didn't know 9 times 4 quickly, so I just changed it round and took 4 off 40, because 10 times 4 is 40, and it came out as 36. Then I thought 5 times 6 is 30 so I just added on a 6 to get 36.
Teacher:	So 36 is the answer to what?
Gareth:	9 times 4.
Teacher:	9 times 4, right.
Gareth:	And then I thought 36, and half of 10 times 6 is 30, so 5 times 6, then I added another 6. 6 times 6.
Teacher:	Robin, how did you do this one?
Robin:	I knew that 8 times 4 was 32. I added another 4 because it's the 4 times table. If you were changing it around as well, it would be the 9 times 4 – er, the 9 times table. 9 times 4 is 36. And then that would be *something* times 6 would be 36. And I 'looked' through my tables and then 6 times 6 equals 36.
Teacher:	So you've got a different way of getting that 36 from Gareth – he

>   went up to the 40 and you started at the 32, you said you knew
>   the 8 times 4 one. How did you know that one?
>
> Robin: Erm – just know it.

Process-object linking and understanding of mathematical structure is often a significant step. We think that if this step is not made confidently many children resort to formal manipulations or 'rules without reason'. The consequence may be withdrawal from mathematics that does not make sense to them and a loss of identity as a competent learner.

The patterns and structure of early arithmetic lay a strong foundation for algebra in the secondary school. For example, the counting numbers 1, 2, 3, 4 . . . go 'odd, even, odd, even . . .'. What can we say about the number after an odd number? Is it always the case? Are there images which can convince us that 'even + odd must be odd'? What about 'odd × odd'? Can such investigations of structure develop a 'feel' or confidence for number? For example, confidence in stating that 7 × 5 could not possibly be 32 because the answer should be an odd number, or being sure that the answer could not be 32 because multiples of 5 end in 0 or 5, or knowing that since 6 × 5 = 30 the answer should be 5 more. This is pre-algebraic number pattern awareness and everyday language is a powerful tool for describing it.

The four categories we have identified above have several features: they diagnose a learner's current understanding (tentative diagnosis); they demonstrate the learner's natural intelligent engagement with mathematical processes and concepts; and they signal a learning opportunity or potential for further development. Since the existing understanding is based on thoughtful construction and motivation, it is sensible to design teaching and learning opportunities that further engage children's reasoning. We will now discuss what we call a dialogic pedagogy.

Children reorganizing their thinking through argument-in-discussion

The test questions we used in our research were crafted as *diagnostic* questions, in the sense that they were written to uncover children's thinking in order to determine the next steps in their learning. We make a first guess (inference) about why a child responded in a particular way; but we then have an opportunity to check that inference by either *asking* the child to justify their response or, we think more productively, by setting up peer discussion and *listening* to children's reasoning. In such peer discussions children are asked to justify their response in order to persuade another child of their view or to consider changing their own mind. At the heart of our method is the child reorganizing or strengthening their understanding through *articulation* or through what we call argument-in-discussion. It is intended that persuasion through reasoning is required (Ryan and Williams 2007: 31–52).

Productive dialogue starts with a shared problem and different points of view – we call this a problematic. Our diagnostic questions can be a source of problematics if they provoke different responses from children. A discussion proceeds when all children have an opportunity to communicate, listen and consider different points of view. Children also need to have some criteria to decide what makes a good mathematical argument and some social rules to foster collaboration and respect. Finally, a reflection step should summarize or bring the discussion to some conclusion or temporary closure. We think it is useful to make these four steps explicit as the conventions for classroom discussion. Children of all ages are capable of reasoned discussion with appropriate support, but this does require teachers' attention (see Monaghan, Chapter 4).

Teachers we have worked with have organized groups for discussion in a range of different ways (see Ryan and Williams 2007: 45–7). One teacher set up peer discussion by forming groups of children who had given *different* answers to diagnostic test questions (that is, 'conflict groups'). She gave the children clear rules about social and mathematical interaction so that thinking and listening were maintained. Another teacher formed groups of children who had given the *same* response to the diagnostic questions. This gave the children an opportunity to articulate their positions first. She then regrouped the children into mixed-response 'conflict' groups so they could consider and argue with different views. Both teachers moved from small-group discussion to plenary whole-class discussion which reflected on the reasoning that helped children to change their minds (or not).

Summary

A dialogic pedagogy shifts attention from mathematical content to argumentation and consideration of changing one's mind. We do not say that this method should be used all the time or that it is the only way to address errors and misconceptions, but we suggest that there is much for teachers to learn from giving voice to children's errors and misconceptions and from providing more time for them to reason in order to establish secure understanding.

The teacher has a role to play in not just setting up classroom discussion but also has an active role in deciding what interventions and directions sustain discussion and move it forward: for example, what questions to ask and when to ask them; which models to suggest and at what particular stage; when to be silent; and when to reinforce. These are considerable professional decisions. A child's belief in their ability to reason mathematically will grow from thoughtfully designed opportunities provided in classrooms.

Note

1   This chapter introduces key ideas from chapters 2 and 3 of Ryan and Williams (2007), where they are developed in much greater detail and with full reference to the academic and research literatures on which they are based.

References

APU (Assessment of Performance Unit) (1982) *A Review of Monitoring in Mathematics 1978–1982*. London: Department of Education and Science.

Cooper, B. and Dunne, M. (2000) *Assessing Children's Mathematical Knowledge: Social Class, Sex and Problem Solving*. Maidenhead: Open University Press.

Lewis, C.C. (2002) *Lesson Study: A Handbook of Teacher-led Instructional Change*. Philadelphia, PA: RBS Publications.

Ryan, J. and Williams, J. (2007) *Children's Mathematics 4–15: Learning from Errors and Misconceptions*. Maidenhead: Open University Press.

Williams, J. and Ryan, J. (2000) National testing and the improvement of classroom teaching: can they co-exist? *British Educational Research Journal*, 26(1): 49–73.

SECTION 4
Calculation issues

In an attempt to provide a broader definition of the word 'numeracy' than that found in some dictionaries in 1999 – definitions such as 'Numeracy is the ability to do arithmetic' – the National Numeracy Strategy (NNS) settled on the following definition of the word:

> Numeracy is a proficiency, which involves confidence and competence with numbers and measures. It requires an understanding of the number system, a repertoire of computational skills and an inclination and ability to solve number problems in a variety of contexts. Numeracy also demands practical understanding of the ways in which information is gathered by counting and measuring, and is presented in graphs, diagrams, charts and tables.

Despite this broader definition, the key focus of the framework and the major thrust of the NNS teacher training materials were on the teaching of calculation: albeit with an emphasis on mental methods and informal written procedures as well as the standard written algorithms for the basic operations. This section considers the teaching of mental and written calculation.

In Chapter 12 Ian Thompson provides a brief historical account of the development of the teaching of mental calculation in school. After considering the reasons given in the literature for the teaching of mental methods he explores the range of interpretations of the phrase 'mental arithmetic'. A synopsis of the research evidence concerning children's mental strategies for addition and subtraction with numbers to 20 is followed by a more detailed consideration of strategies for dealing with the same operations with two-digit numbers. A model of mental calculation is offered, and is used as a vehicle for making suggestions as to how teachers might develop their pupils' mental strategies.

In Chapter 13 Meindert Beishuizen begins with a brief history of the development of the 'empty number line' (ENL) in mathematics education in the Netherlands, and provides a rationale for its role in the development of children's mental calculation strategies. Meindert outlines the knowledge, skills and understanding that need to be developed by young children learning to use the empty number line, suggesting practical activities to help teachers develop these specific skills and concepts in their pupils. Examples are given of the work of Year 3 children involved in an experimental programme at Leiden University to illustrate the point that the empty number line is a great help in making pupils' solutions clearer for the teacher. Not only does the use of the ENL facilitate whole-class discussion but also the individual diagnosis of mis-understandings and errors.

In 2006, the Primary National Strategy produced guidance papers for different aspects of mathematics teaching: using and applying mathematics; the use of calculators in the teaching and learning of mathematics; day-to-day assessment; and calculation. In Chapters 14, 15 and 16 Ian Thompson guides us through the paper on calculation, scrutinizing and clarifying the detail of the recommended progression in addition and subtraction (Chapter 14), multiplication (Chapter 15) and division (Chapter 16). During this 'guided tour' through the guidance paper Ian raises many questions.

12 Getting your head around mental calculation

Ian Thompson

Introduction

By the end of the nineteenth century the psychological theory of mental discipline had substantially influenced the content, scope and sequence of the developing mathematics curriculum in the USA and to a lesser extent in Britain. Advocates of the movement considered mental arithmetic to be an integral part of mathematics teaching, seeing it as an important form of exercise to develop the faculties of the mind. In the 1920s there was a backlash against the movement and the concept of 'mental discipline' was rejected in favour of the more sophisticated theory of 'transfer'. This led to a decline in the teaching of mental arithmetic. In the 1940s, however, when the social usefulness of mathematics was beginning to be recognized, there was a revival in the emphasis given to teaching the topic in schools. Mental arithmetic came to have its own separate heading on school reports, and mathematics textbooks written in England as late as the 1960s had exercises which perpetuated the 'mental, mechanical, problems' structure of earlier books.

The so-called 'decline' of mental arithmetic since the 1950s is often blamed on a variety of 'progressive' innovations, such as the move in the 1970s to individualized learning which, it is claimed, reduced the opportunity for teachers to communicate with the class as a whole group. Some argued that the teaching of modern mathematics, with its broader syllabus and focus on structure and understanding, placed much less emphasis on arithmetic in general and instant recall in particular.

A section devoted to mental arithmetic in the Cockcroft Report (*Mathematics Counts*) (DES 1982: 75) asserted that the topic, which was once a regular part of the mathematics curriculum, had come to occupy a far less prominent position by the late 1970s. The report argued for the reinstatement of mental arithmetic in the curriculum, explaining that the committee 'believe(s) that the decline of mental and oral work within mathematics classrooms represents a failure to recognise the central place which working "done in the head" occupies throughout mathematics'.

With the arrival of the National Curriculum in the late 1980s mental arithmetic – in theory at least – was back on the agenda: the ability to add or subtract mentally any pair of two-digit numbers was fixed at Level 4 in the very first version of the National Curriculum (see Brown, Chapter 1). However, in practice, because of the subject knowledge demands of the curriculum, mental arithmetic did not receive the emphasis that it deserved. Interestingly, in 1988 Level 4 was deemed to be the standard appropriate for an 'average' 11-year-old pupil. Unfortunately, over the next 20 years this level came to be known as the 'expected standard', leading to the extraordinary situation of a government minister, Lord Andrew Adonis (Curtis 2008: 4), bemoaning the fact that in 2008 *only* 78 per cent of primary school children had achieved this standard, that is, this *average* standard.

England's poor performance on the number sections of international tests and surveys in the 1980s was a major contributing factor to the swing back to mental arithmetic in the 1990s. The Bierhoff Report, a publication from the right-wing National Institute of Economic and Social Research, was published in the mid-1990s (Bierhoff 1996). This was ostensibly a comparison of primary school textbooks in Britain, Germany and Switzerland, and it emphasized, among other things, the importance that European countries attached to mental calculation and to the addition and subtraction of two-digit numbers in particular.

In 1996 the National Numeracy Project was launched. The project's approach to the teaching of numeracy was originally based on three key principles (later to become four): mathematics lessons every day; direct teaching and interactive oral work with the whole class and with groups; and an emphasis on mental calculation. The arrival of the Numeracy Project and its development into the National Numeracy Strategy succeeded in making 'mental arithmetic' the most important mathematics item on many school agendas.

In 2006 the National Numeracy Strategy became the Primary National Strategy and produced a revised *Primary Framework for Literacy and Mathematics*. The general introduction to the mathematics section of this framework (DfES 2006: 67) refers the reader to 'a detailed paper on mental and written calculation' available in the electronic version. However, the word 'detailed' is somewhat misleading: 14 pages outline a very detailed progression for teaching written methods, whereas just over half a page is devoted to mental calculation! It is therefore not surprising that in *Mathematics: Understanding the Score* (Ofsted 2008: 21), Ofsted inspectors noted 'pupils' reliance on formal written methods and a reluctance to use informal or mental strategies which are sometimes more efficient'. Also, the final recommendation of the *Independent Review of Mathematics Teaching in Early Years Settings and Primary Schools* (the Williams Review) (DCSF 2008: 66) is, 'This review recommends a renewed focus by practitioners on oral and mental mathematics'.

Why teach mental arithmetic?

The literature on mental calculation suggests the following reasons for an emphasis on the teaching of the topic:

1   Most calculations in real life are done in the head rather than on paper.
2   Mental calculation promotes creative and independent thinking.
3   It contributes to the development of better problem-solving skills.
4   It develops sound number sense. Maclellan (2001: 148), summarizing a discussion of the importance of mental calculation states 'The argument so far is that mental calculation is important because it promotes number sense'. Below, I suggest that, however true this statement may be, the opposite definitely is true: children's knowledge of number properties such as commutativity, associativity, distributivity and what I call 'partitionability' (that is, the property that allows numbers to be partitioned) is essential for the development of flexible mental calculation strategies.
5   It is a basis for developing estimation skills. Reys (1984: 549) argues that many of the skills required for successful estimation are developed when children improve their mental calculation skills.
6   Mental work is important because there is a natural progression through informal written methods to standard methods. The revised *Primary Framework for Literacy and Mathematics* (DfES 2006: 67) argues that 'These (mental) methods become more efficient and succinct and lead to written methods that can be used more generally'. However, I have argued elsewhere that there is little or no natural progression from mental to written calculation methods (see Thompson, Chapters 14, 15 and 16).

The language of mental methods

During the late 1990s the media and government ministers talked in terms of 'mental arithmetic' because of its air of respectability and tradition. However, because this phrase conjured up negative emotions in many adults' minds, reminding them of stressful times when they were unable to recall a number bond or tables fact quickly enough to avoid the wrath of their mathematics teacher, it was decided that the National Numeracy Strategy

(NNS) would use a different, more positive-sounding phrase. Consequently, 'mental calculation', with its suggestion of calculating or working something out in your head, came to be seen as a more accurate description of 1990s mental arithmetic. Given that you cannot really calculate unless you have something to calculate with, the phrase 'mental calculation' was seen to encapsulate the two important aspects of mental work, namely, recall and strategic methods.

When we compare the language used in England with that used in the Netherlands we find that, because there is no word equivalent to 'mental' in Dutch, they use the phrases 'working in the head' and 'working with the head' to distinguish what they see as the two different aspects of mental calculation. The former covers knowing by heart, or being able to work out very quickly, specific number bonds or tables facts. The latter is concerned more with the use of some of these known facts to work out unknown facts such as the sums of pairs of two-digit numbers. In England we came to use the phrases 'knowing facts' and 'figuring out' to describe these two different aspects of mental calculation.

Both countries had come to a similar view on the importance of knowing some facts and using these to work out others, but what made it all the more interesting was that they had reached this consensus from opposite ends of the spectrum: England from the facts end, the Netherlands from the strategies end. In England, even in the 1990s, mental arithmetic was interpreted by many in a limited way as being solely concerned with the instant recall of number bonds and tables facts. In 1991 the year of the first Key Stage 1 National Curriculum tests (formerly SATs) teachers were told to 'assess each child's ability to add and subtract by using recall of number facts, not by counting or computation', an instruction which flew in the face of research conducted over the previous 20 years. It was only in the 1995 Dearing version of the National Curriculum that the concept of 'deriving facts' was formally acknowledged as being an important component of mental calculation. On the other hand, Beishuizen (1997) explains that 1980s books in the Netherlands 'emphasised very much a variety of models and mental strategies at the expense of daily practice in mental recall of number bonds'.

What does research tell us about mental strategies?

Research since the late 1970s has provided a substantial amount of information about the mental calculation strategies used by young children, particularly for the addition and subtraction of one- and two-digit numbers. A brief description of some of these findings follows.

Addition and subtraction with numbers to 20

Carpenter and Moser (1984) identified the following levels of addition strategies used by young children when solving simple word problems:

- *count all* – where a child solving a simple addition problem such as 2 + 3 first counts out two blocks followed by another three blocks, and then finds the total by counting the number of blocks altogether;
- *count on from the first number* – where a child, finding 2 + 3, begins the count by repeating the first number and then continues counting from that number. For example, a child might say: 'Two . . . three, four, five. There are five', keeping a tally of how many number names have been spoken;
- *count on from the larger number* – where a child proceeds as in the previous example, but begins the count from 'three', reasoning that starting from the larger number will mean that less counting is involved;
- *use known addition fact* – where children give immediate responses to those number bonds that they know by heart – usually the simpler number bonds such as the smaller doubles like 2 + 2 and 3 + 3;
- *use derived fact* – where children use a number bond that they know by heart to calculate one that they do not know. In the initial stages there is a tendency to use the doubles, so that 6 + 5 might be found by saying: 'Five and five is ten and one more makes eleven', or 'Six and six is twelve, but it's one less, so it must be eleven'.

Thompson (2008: 103–5) has described levels for subtraction, but the developmental sequence is less clearly defined. The subtraction 9 – 3 is used below to exemplify the strategies:

- *count out* – where the child counts out nine objects, removes three and counts the remainder, or raises nine fingers, lowers three, and counts those remaining;
- *count back from* – where the child says 'Nine' and then counts back three numbers from nine: 'Eight, seven, six . . . It's six';
- *count back to* – where the child says 'Nine' and then counts back to three, 'Eight, seven, six, five, four, three', keeping a tally (probably on her fingers) of how many number names have been said. This tally (six fingers) is the answer;
- *count up* – where the child says 'Three' and counts forward to nine, keeping a finger tally: 'Four, five, six, seven, eight, nine'. This tally (six fingers) is the answer. (My own research suggests that this is not

a 'natural' strategy for children in England because of subtraction normally being interpreted as 'take away');
- *use known subtraction fact and use derived fact* are as for addition.

Addition and subtraction with numbers from 20 to 100

There appear to be four main two-digit mental addition and subtraction strategies used by children. In England the most common addition strategy is the *split* method, so-called because the numbers to be added or subtracted are split into multiples of ten and ones. This strategy is sometimes called the *partitioning* method, and in the Netherlands is known as the 1010 (ten-ten) procedure (Figure 12.1).

Scott   27 + 28

Two 20s is 40 . . . seven and eight . . . if there's seven . . . take three off eight which would be 10 . . . and three took off eight would be five . . . so the answer would be 55

Figure 12.1   Scott uses the split method for two-digit addition.

Scott has split the 27 into 20 and 7; has split the 28 into 20 and 8; has added the two 20s together; has added the 7 and the 8 together by *bridging through ten*; and has added the two subtotals together (40 and 15) to get the correct answer 55. Less common among children in this country – although it is the preferred method taught to children in the Netherlands – is the *jump* method (see Beishuizen, Chapter 13). The strategy is given the name *jump* because it can be easily represented practically or mentally on a number line, where you start at one number and move closer to the answer by jumping along the line adding or subtracting conveniently sized chunks of the second number, as Chris does in Figure 12.2. Alternative descriptors for this strategy in the literature are *sequencing* or *cumulative* methods (N10 in the Netherlands).

Chris   54 – 27

27 . . . I took 20 away from 54 . . . to make 34 . . . and I took four from 34 which made 30 . . . and I took another three away to make 27

Figure 12.2   Chris uses the jump method for two-digit subtraction.

Chris has split the 27 into 20 and 7; has subtracted the 20 from 54 to get 34; has split the 7 into 4 and 3; has subtracted the 4 from 34 and the 3 from 30 to get the correct answer 27. Because of the apparent superiority of this method for subtractions of this type (the split method leads to a potential problem with 4 – 7) some mathematics educators recommend that the jump method should be taught in preference to the split method. However, some splitters get round the problem by using a combination of the two strategies known as the *split-jump* method, the *mixed* method or, in the Netherlands, the 10S method (Figure 12.3).

Mark 27 + 28

55. Because, you know, I did 20 and 20 is 40 . . . and 48 and another two from the seven is 50 . . . and I've got five left, so 55

Figure 12.3 Mark adds two numbers using the split-jump method.

In this case Mark has partitioned both numbers: 20 plus 7 and 20 plus 8; has added the two 20s; has added the 8 (the larger of the two units) to the 40; has bridged to ten and has then added the remaining 5. A fourth common strategy for dealing with 'near multiples of ten' is the *over-jump, compensation* or N10C method used by Nigel (Figure 12.4).

Nigel 19 + 8

27 . . . Twenty and eight would be 28 . . . and take away one gives you 27

Figure 12.4 Nigel adds two numbers using the over-jump method.

Nigel has treated 'adding 19' as 'adding 20 and then subtracting one' – a useful strategy for the addition and subtraction of 'near multiples of 10' – but again, not as common with English children as with those from the Netherlands.

This research evidence provides a useful knowledge base to inform teachers' practice. Awareness of these strategies will help them better understand children's explanations and provide appropriate support to develop, where appropriate, more efficient strategies.

A model of mental calculation

The model shown in Figure 12.5 comprises four components which, it is argued, together contribute towards the development of an individual's range of mental calculation strategies. These components are facts, skills, understandings and attitudes, and it is conjectured that those who are most successful in mental calculation are likely to possess all four of these attributes. Weaknesses in any one area are likely to have an adverse effect on the development of a wide range of efficient mental calculation strategies. However, research is needed to test this hypothesis.

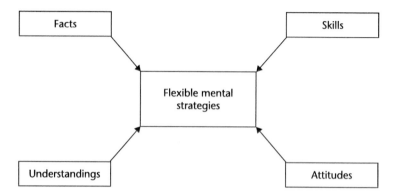

Figure 12.5 A model of mental calculation.

Facts

Included under this heading are: knowledge of specific number bonds, including doubles and complements in 10; awareness of addition and subtraction facts to 20; and knowledge of multiplication tables and division facts. It is sometimes difficult to tell which facts are known and which are calculated extremely quickly. For example, I think I know that 7 and 5 make 12, but I'm not too sure that I know what 17 − 9 is. I definitely *know* that 7 × 8 = 56, but I am sure that I do *not* know what 48 ÷ 6 is, as I have to use my multiplication tables to help me work it out.

Understandings

This heading refers to the many and varied properties of the number system that we might expect someone possessing good 'number sense' to be aware of – if not explicitly, then at least implicitly. These understandings range from those exhibited by very young children when they come to appreciate that they can count on from the larger of the numbers involved in an addition instead of counting on from the first number on each occasion, to those shown by Year 6 children when they realize that when you divide a number by a half it doubles in size.

Included under this heading are the properties of commutativity (3 × 4 = 4 × 3), associativity ((3 + 4) + 5 = 3 + (4 + 5)) and distributivity (3 × 24 = 3 × 20 + 3 × 4). Good mental calculators also need to understand the following:

- adding or subtracting zero has no effect (additive identity);
- multiplying or dividing by one makes no difference (multiplicative identity);

- subtractions can be solved by using a known addition fact (additive inverse);
- divisions can be solved by using a known multiplication fact (multiplicative inverse);
- adding together multiples of ten is similar to adding the corresponding single-digit numbers;
- because 3 + 6 makes 9 then 473 + 6 is 479;
- because 3 × 4 ends in a 2 then so does 13 × 14;
- a number ending in zero can be divided exactly by 10;
- to multiply by six you can multiply by three and then double;
- to divide by four you can halve and then halve again.

More sophisticated understandings would include the following:

- if you double one of the numbers in a multiplication and halve the other then the answer stays the same, so 3 × 18 is equivalent to 6 × 9;
- to multiply 23 by 9, you can multiply by 10 and then subtract 23;
- to multiply by 12 you can multiply by four and then by three, or by three and then double twice.

Skills

To be effective mental calculators children need to have acquired certain labour-saving skills or techniques, such as counting on as a development of counting all or subtracting ten from a number without counting back. To complete this section, the mental calculation skills used by Scott (Figure 12.6) and Chris (Figure 12.7) in their solution strategies discussed above will be analysed.

Scott   27 + 28

Two 20s is 40 . . . seven and eight . . . if there's seven . . . take three off eight which would be 10 . . . and three took off eight would be five . . . so the answer would be 55

Partition two-digit numbers	27 = 20 + 7
Add multiples of 10	20 + 20 = 40
Partition single-digit numbers	8 = 3 + 5
Know and use complements in 10	7 + 3 = 10
Add 10 to a number	10 + 5 = 15
Add multiple of 10 to a number	40 + 15 = 55

Figure 12.6   Skills used by Scott in calculating 27 + 28.

Chris 54 – 27

27 . . . I took 20 away from 54 . . . to make 34 . . . and I took four from 34 which made
30 . . . and I took another three away to make 27

Partition two-digit numbers	27 = 20 + 7
Subtract M10 from any two-digit number	54 – 20 = 34
Partition single-digit numbers	7 = 4 + 3
Bridge down through M10	34 – 4 = 30
Calculate/know complements in 30	30 – 3 = 27

Figure 12.7   Skills used by Chris in calculating 54 – 27.

Attitudes

An important, but neglected, ingredient in mental strategy use is confidence. Children can have all manner of facts and skills at their fingertips, but if they do not have the confidence to 'have a go' or take risks they are unlikely to use these facts and skills to generate an appropriate strategy. It is to be hoped that an emphasis on the teaching of mental calculation will effect a change in the attitude of children and adults towards mathematics. An ethos needs to be developed where people no longer have the attitude of 'I can't remember the method so I cannot solve the problem' – discussed in the Cockcroft Report (*Mathematics Counts*) (DES 1982) – but instead adopt the more positive attitude of 'I can't remember how my teacher did it, but if I . . .'.

Teaching mental calculation

In 1997, a School Curriculum and Assessment Authority discussion paper (SCAA 1997: 15) wondered whether 'strategies for mental calculation can actively be taught to pupils, or whether pupils develop them for themselves as a result of either maturation or experience'. The fact that most of the research reported in this chapter was carried out before the NNS was introduced suggests that some young children do develop them for themselves. Later in the same document we read that the development of mental calculation strategies 'should not be left to chance' (SCAA 1997: 29). In a similar vein, the *Primary Framework for Literacy and Mathematics* (DfES 2006: 68) states that 'It is crucial that mental methods of calculation are taught to children and not confined to starter activities in lessons'.

Less research has been done into the actual teaching of mental calculation than into the investigation of children's mental calculation strategies. Askew et al. (2001: 9) devised a successful intervention programme to improve the mental calculation strategies of a group of children operating at or below

Level 2 according to their SAT results. The intervention significantly improved the profile of techniques used by the pupils to arrive at correct solutions, and the researchers concluded that 'Through carefully targeted teaching, pupils who have not developed these strategies for themselves can indeed learn them'. Murphy (2004: 16) interviewed three young children after the direct instruction of a mental calculation strategy. She argued that 'mental strategies *can* [my italics] be introduced to children through whole class instruction but . . . their use of the strategies may be reliant on their personal knowledge'.

Ineson (2007) assessed the mental calculation abilities of a whole year group (n = 70) of Year 6 children in a north London primary school in 1999 (that is, pre-National Numeracy Strategy) and repeated the test in the same school in 2005 (n = 55). She found that 63 per cent of the second cohort correctly answered at least 15 of the 20 questions compared with 43 per cent of the first cohort – results that were significant at the 0.01 level. Using an equivalent written version of the same test the author found that on 16 of the questions a greater percentage of the 2005 cohort successfully used informal methods. These results – albeit for a relatively small opportunity sample – suggest that the teaching of mental calculation strategies can improve children's computational performance as well as their confidence to use informal rather than formal written methods.

Implications for teaching and learning

To summarize, it has been argued that a minimum requirement for children to be successful mental calculators is the development of the following:

- a secure knowledge of number facts;
- a good understanding of the number system – how it works, which operations are permissible and which are not – so that known number facts can be combined using appropriate operations to work out other facts;
- the ability to perform accurately the skills underpinned by these understandings;
- the confidence to use what they know in their own way to find solutions.

The teacher's job is to ensure that these aspects form an important part of their teaching. They need a good knowledge of the common mental strategies that children use so that they can understand their own children's methods; so that they can support them in refining these strategies; and so that they can help them develop more sophisticated methods if necessary. Teachers also need to hone their own teaching strategies for developing children's attitudes to calculation, particularly their pupils' confidence to use methods with which they feel happy. They need to create a suitable classroom ethos where children will be prepared to take risks. While working to develop efficient and effective strategies for mental calculation for all children, teachers need to ensure that they do not emphasize the efficiency aspect to such an extent that children reject a method they understand in favour of a more efficient one that they do not. Research suggests that children make fewer errors when using their own methods – either mental or written.

One important aim of the National Numeracy Strategy, launched in 1999, was to ensure that children were confident with and competent at mental addition and subtraction of any two-digit numbers before they left primary school. At the time this seemed like a rather lofty aim. However, over 100 years earlier, Bidder (1856) had declared at an inaugural lecture of the Society for Civil Engineers: 'I have for many years entertained a strong conviction that mental arithmetic can be taught, as easily as, if not with greater facility than, ordinary arithmetic, and that it may be rendered conducive to more useful purposes than that of teaching by rule . . .'

References

Askew, M., Bibby, T. and Brown, M. (2001) *Raising Attainment in Primary Number Sense: From Counting to Strategy*. London: BEAM Education.

Beishuizen, M. (1997) Two types of mental arithmetic and the empty number line. Paper presented at the BSRLM conference, University of Oxford Department of Educational Studies, June.

Bidder, G.P. (1856) *Minutes of Proceedings of Civil Engineers*, vol. 15.

Bierhoff, H. (1996) *Laying the Foundations of Numeracy: A Comparison of Primary School Textbooks in Britain, Germany and Switzerland*. Discussion Paper No. 90. London: National Institute of Economic and Social Research.

Carpenter, T.P. and Moser, J.M. (1984) The acquisition of addition and subtraction concepts in grades one through three, *Journal for Research into Mathematics Education*, 15(3): 179–202.

Curtis, P. (2008) Primary pupils without basic skills highlight Labour's biggest failure, *Guardian*, 21 August, p. 4.

DCSF (Department for Children, Schools and Families) (2008) *Independent Review of Mathematics Teaching in Early Years Settings and Primary Schools* (Williams Review). Nottingham: DCSF. http://publications.teachernet.gov.uk/eOrderingDownload/Williams%20Mathematics.pdf (accessed March 2010).

DES (Department of Education and Science) (1982) *Mathematics Counts: Report of the Committee of Inquiry into the Teaching of Mathematics in Schools* (Cockcroft Report). London: HMSO. http://www.dg.dial.pipex.com/documents/docs1/cockcroft.shtml (accessed March 2010).

DfES (Department for Education and Skills) (2006) *Primary Framework for Literacy and Mathematics*. Norwich: DfES.

Ineson, G. (2007) Year 6 children: Has the British mathematics curriculum helped their mental computation? *Journal of Early Child Development and Care*, 177(5): 541–55.

Maclellan, E. (2001) Mental calculation: its place in the development of numeracy, *Westminster Studies in Education*, 24(2): 145–54.

Murphy, C. (2004) How do children come to use a taught mental calculation strategy? *Educational Studies in Mathematics*, 56: 3–18.

Ofsted (Office for Standards in Education) (2008) *Mathematics: Understanding the Score*. London: Ofsted.

Reys, R. (1984) Mental computation and estimation: past, present, and future, *The Elementary School Journal*, 84(5): 546–57.

SCAA (School Curriculum and Assessment Authority) (1997) *The Teaching and Assessment of Number at Key Stages 1–3*. Discussion Paper No. 10. London: SCAA.

Thompson, I. (2008) From counting to deriving number facts, in I. Thompson (ed.) *Teaching and Learning Early Number*, 2nd edn. Maidenhead: Open University Press.

13 The empty number line

Meindert Beishuizen (1935-2009)

Prologue

This chapter was published for the first time in 1999. It deals with the teaching and learning of mental calculation strategies in the number domain up to 100. At that time the so-called 'realistic approach' to mathematics education (RME) was introduced in the Netherlands on a large scale. In this approach, number sense and mental calculation are considered to be at the heart of the mathematics curriculum, and a substantial amount of research has been done to study the learning effects of the new curriculum. A central issue in this research as far as the number domain up to 100 is concerned, is related to the question of whether so-called sequential strategies (strategies in which the first number in a problem is taken as a whole while the second number is partitioned) should be preferred to splitting strategies (strategies in which both numbers are partitioned). In the chapter, first, the international context of the issue is described. Second, an overview is given of the arguments why sequential strategies, especially when introduced with the empty number line as a supporting model, have important advantages over splitting strategies. Third, a number of experiences are described within a research project at Leiden University. These experiences relate to an experimental empty number line programme that was put to the test in a large number of Dutch schools. As is stated in the chapter, the results of the first part of this programme were very promising. Ten years after the first publication of the chapter, the model of the empty number line has become a frequently used model in Dutch primary school mathematics education. The results that were obtained with the model (Kraemer et al. 2005), can be seen as a powerful confirmation of the most important conclusions in the chapter. Thus the relevance of the chapter has hardly diminished.

Dr Kees Buijs, Curriculum Developer and Researcher in Mathematics Education

Introduction

The empty number line was introduced in Holland not just as a new idea, but as a result of evaluation and discussion on how to improve existing practice. Reasons for this came from the experiences with new 'realistic' textbooks during the 1980s and from the outcomes of the first National Arithmetic Test in 1987. At the Freudenthal Institute a proposal for a revised early number curriculum was formulated by Treffers and De Moor (1990). Mental arithmetic had already been the focus for a long time in Dutch lower grades, given the realistic view on mathematics education in the Netherlands (Treffers and Beishuizen 1999) that teaching should begin with children's informal strategies. More emphasis was being put on the basic computation skills up to 100, and for that purpose the empty number line (ENL) was introduced as a new model.

In international research there was also the recognition that after a long period of studying the number domain under 20, mental strategies with larger numbers should be given more attention. In this area our knowledge of how children carry out number operations 'lags far behind' as Fuson (1992) put it. In Holland such research was carried out at Leiden University (Beishuizen 1993), which led to a new project with an experimental ENL programme implemented in Dutch 2nd grades (Year 3) in collaboration with the Freudenthal Institute (Klein et al. 1998). A description of the empty number line in this chapter is based on this project, which took place in several schools during the period 1992–96. But first we summarize some background arguments, because there are interesting similarities with English discussions on how to improve early number teaching. For instance, some English authors have also argued for children's informal strategies instead of the early introduction of standard vertical algorithms (for a broader discussion see Beishuizen and Anghileri 1998).

Dissatisfaction with existing models was one of the arguments for the ENL. In the 1960s and 1970s manipulatives like Dienes Multibase Arithmetic Blocks (MAB) or Unifix cubes were widely used in Dutch schools, but teachers complained about children hanging on too long to these materials and passively reading off the answer from the blocks when doing sums (Beishuizen 1993). Apart from this low level of mental activation there was the other drawback of a low modelling function. Blocks are helpful for the representation of abstract number structure, but they are weak in the representation of number operations when these become more complicated. Such a critique was voiced by other authors in the 1980s, for instance by Hart (1989) when she analysed a solution of the number problem $56 - 28$. After the removal of three from five ten-blocks ($50 - 30$), two unit-blocks are returned ($+2$) and then the blocks left on the table are counted for the answer ($2 + 20 + 6 = 28$). Hart (1989: 142) concluded that this manipulation of blocks has very little connection with the intended (written) algorithm, and 'that the gap between the two types of experience is too large'.

In Leiden, such research was done in relation to the mental strategies involved. The computation procedure described by Hart, where the tens are 'split off' in both numbers and are added or subtracted separately (50 – 20 = 30), we have given the acronym *1010*. This *partitioning* or *split* method (see Thompson, Chapter 12) proceeds mostly by adding or subtracting the units (6 – 8) as the next step. In this case that causes a conflict which correctly could be solved by putting 10 of the 30 with the 6 to make 16, finding 16 – 8 = 8 and adding this to the remaining 20 to give 28. Many children, however, solve this conflict in the procedure by the wrong 'smaller from larger' bug (6 – 8 is interpreted as '6 from 8', that is, 2, and the answer is 30 + 2 = 32). These difficulties of the 1010 partitioning method, in particular with subtraction and regrouping problems, are well known (Plunkett 1979). Nevertheless this 1010 strategy is widely used, because at first sight splitting up numbers in tens and units seems an easy procedure to children. It follows the decimal (formal) structure of our hundreds, tens and units (HTU) number system and is also elicited and reinforced by the use of arithmetic blocks (Beishuizen 1993). The difficulty of the 1010 strategy is not so much in the decomposition procedure but more in the correct recomposition of numbers (Beishuizen et al. 1997b). A less vulnerable and more efficient computation procedure (fewer steps) is the mental strategy which proceeds in a sequential way (56 – 28 = via 56 – 20 = 36, 36 – 8 = 28). We have used the acronym *N10* for this strategy because the first number is not split up but kept intact while the tens are added or subtracted through counting by tens. The N10 strategy or *jump* method is less common as a spontaneous method of children, because it is not elicited by the HTU number structure and needs some initial support by making the sequential number patterns (56, 46, 36, and so on) more noticeable.

1010 and N10

There is now a growing body of (international) research underlining the important role of these two main strategies (and mixed methods in between) for mental arithmetic with larger numbers up to 100 and beyond. Fuson has described them as the 'separate tens' (1010) and the 'sequence tens' (N10) strategies at an experts' meeting in Leiden (Beishuizen et al. 1997a). In Holland both 1010 and N10 are widely used as mental strategies, while in the USA (and in the UK) 1010 seems more common because of dominance of the HTU (place value) number structure as well as arithmetic blocks in teaching. In Holland it has been found (Beishuizen et al. 1997b) that many better pupils prefer the more efficient strategy N10, while most weaker pupils choose 1010 as the 'easier' procedure at first sight, which, however, may take them into difficulties (see above). Another conclusion has been that most pupils are rather consistent but rigid in preferring either only 1010 or only N10 as their computation procedure, with just a minority using both strategies in a flexible way: 1010 for addition and N10 for subtraction. Outcomes of the National Arithmetic Test in 1987 confirmed this lack of flexibility, and this became another argument for the introduction of the ENL: to raise pupils' level of flexibility in mental arithmetic (Treffers and De Moor 1990).

Earlier in the 1980s the Dutch dissatisfaction with blocks had led to the introduction of the hundred square as a richer model for visualizing both number relations and number operations for mental arithmetic up to 100. The abacus was introduced for illustrating better the HTU number structure and the corresponding vertical algorithms. Both models, being more abstract, had the potential function of eliciting a higher level of mental activation but, because of this same characteristic, also turned out to be more complicated for weaker children. The hundred square, when used in its mentally most activating format with empty boxes (instead of numbers), may confuse children so that they get lost when drawing arrows or jumps on it. Moreover, the increasing influence of the RME approach in mathematics teaching in our country ran counter to the pre-structured character of the hundred square, a model which leaves little room for informal and flexible strategies of children.

Consequently, Treffers and De Moor (1990) came up with the idea of the old number line in a new format: the empty number line up to 100 as a more natural and transparent model than the hundred square. The growing research into mental strategies also played a role as summarized above. First and foremost, however, the well-known argument for emphasizing mental arithmetic in the lower grades should be mentioned (Treffers 1991; Thompson 2008): dealing with whole numbers supports pupils' understanding and insight in number and number operations much more than the early introduction of vertical algorithms dealing with isolated digits. Therefore, columnwise (written) arithmetic, which was already being introduced later in the Dutch curriculum, was now postponed even further until Year 4 in the new proposal.

Another argument, already mentioned as central in the Dutch RME approach as well as in the views of some English authors, is that early mathematics teaching should start by building on children's informal (counting) strategies instead of imposing formal procedures. A further didactic RME principle is to level up informal strategies to higher (formal and efficient) procedures as well as to their flexible use. For that purpose the ENL is very well suited because, on its sequential model, counting strategies can be accepted and abbreviated towards counting in jumps of twos, fives and tens, that is, a gradual transition to the N10 strategy of counting by tens. Treffers and De Moor (1990) have sketched the development of N10 for a subtraction problem like $65 - 38$ through the following stages: (i) $65 - 10 - 10 - 10 - 5 - 3$,

(ii) 65 – 30 – 8 and (iii) 65 – 40 + 2. After procedural abbreviation on the first levels we see at the highest level a short-cut adaptation of N10 used as a compensation strategy (acronym *N10C*). Notice that the lowest level of N10 is long-winded and inefficient, as often happens in the beginning of new strategies. Is this a reason not to trust these informal strategies and to teach 'straightforward and efficient standard methods' as an alternative, as sometimes seems to be the official English viewpoint (SCAA 1996)? In the RME view it is not, and the early number curriculum should provide opportunities (learning sequences and tasks) as well as learning time for children to develop their own strategies through 'progressive mathematization' to more efficient and flexible levels. In Dutch classrooms working with the experimental ENL programme, this happened by having children draw their jumps on the ENL, by practising their recording of mental strategies on the ENL and by whole-class discussion of different problem solutions drawn on the blackboard.

In summary we have given four arguments for the ENL, which are described more extensively in Klein et al. (1998):

1   a higher level of mental activation in providing learning support;
2   a more natural and transparent model for number operations;
3   a model open to informal strategies and also providing support for children to develop more formal and efficient strategies;
4   a model enhancing the flexibility of mental strategies, in particular variations of N10.

In addition to the last argument we should add that one of the conclusions of the research into mental strategies was also (Beishuizen et al. 1997b) that to enhance flexibility in mental arithmetic Dutch pupils should learn to use both strategies N10 and 1010. For reasons given above, the didactic sequence in the experimental ENL programme is first to invite N10-like strategies. Later in the same programme (three months before the end of the 2nd grade or Year 3) 1010 is introduced, using another (not sequential) grouping model like blocks or money as learning support. An argument for this order of introduction is that children will learn the more complicated 1010 procedure more quickly, and become more proficient, if they have already acquired a conceptual and procedural knowledge base of two-digit number operations up to 100 through N10. Further experiences in Holland in 2nd and 3rd grades with revised textbooks like *Wis and Reken* (Buijs et al. 1996), integrating both N10 on the ENL and 1010 with blocks, do confirm how children indeed attain such higher levels of proficiency and flexibility.

Empty number line model

English discussions and official viewpoints about mental arithmetic are interesting but not always clear. We return to this at the end of this chapter. But before giving a description of the ENL programme, we have to clear up one misunderstanding – namely, that children doing mental arithmetic should not be allowed to use a pencil for making written notes (see Bramald 1998). This misunderstanding also surfaced at the international experts' meeting in Leiden (Beishuizen et al. 1997a), when Fuson from her American perspective said that 'students in Holland do not learn mental strategies first, because they start with a lot of written activities on the empty number line' (1992: 296). But written work on the ENL has only a secondary function: supporting or recording the strategies chosen as mental decisions in the first place. One might object that this is also true for vertical algorithms. So 'mental' versus 'written' does not seem to be a good contrast (but a commonplace one), because the real distinctions are between the different types of strategies and procedures as described above.

Figures 13.1–13.8 give an impression of the development of mental strategies in our experimental ENL programme for the 2nd grade (Year 3). A fuller description is available in Klein (1998). The sequential model is introduced at a concrete level through a 10-structured bead string up to 100 (Figure 13.1). Two-digit numbers are introduced by building on the (quantity) number concept using both an ordinal and cardinal representation. Through positioning, this knowledge is immediately practised on a corresponding number line. During the first three months a structured empty number line is used (Figures 13.1 and 13.2) before the complete empty line is introduced on which children position and mark the numbers themselves (Figure 13.3). Number operations are first practised with addition and subtraction of single-digit numbers in combination with two-digit numbers up to 100 (Figures 13.2, 13.3 and 13.4).

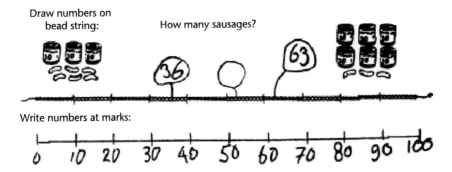

Figure 13.1   Number concept and number positioning.

Draw the sums on
the number line:

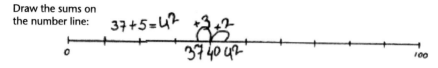

Figure 13.2   Crossing-ten on a structured empty number line.

Draw the sums on
the number line:

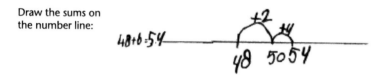

Figure 13.3   Crossing-ten on a completely empty number line.

Solve context
problems on the
number line:

Kees has 9 stamps.
He gets 28 more.
How many stamps does he have now?

Figure 13.4   Flexible solution of a context problem.

This deliberately builds on arithmetic under 20 in the 1st grade (Year 2), because counting on, splitting up in complements of ten and using number facts instead of counting need further practice for most children in order to reach a level of mental recall. Here we have to add that whole-class oral exercises and games (with speed limits) support this process of further automatization. The results of this first part of the ENL programme (from September until January) were very promising: speed tests showed a substantial increase in total number of correct answers, whereas interviews with children showed an almost complete vanishing of counting strategies by January (Klein et al. 1998).

Notice that the mental strategies for crossing-tens are quite different from the way this is done with vertical algorithms in Britain. In problems like 37 + 5 and 48 + 6 (Figures 13.2 and 13.3) the algorithm would proceed with splitting off the units and adding them up separately, which means continuing but limited practice of number bonds like 7 + 5 and 8 + 6 under 20. The sequential mental strategy involves crossing-tens quite differently by splitting up the (second) units in complements to (new) decadal tens (37 + 5 = via 37 + 3 = 40, 40 + 2 = 42; 48 + 6 = via 48 + 2 = 50, 50 + 4 = 54). By this latter strategy children practise not only procedural knowledge but also the extension of number relations and number sense up to 100.

Realistic problems

Realistic context problems play an important role in the RME approach, inviting a greater variety of 'using your head' problem-solving strategies than standard number problems which suggest mainly the application of routine computational procedures. Context problems have been part of Dutch realistic mathematics teaching for a long time, and so they are also used in our experimental programme. In this respect the (open) ENL model proved to be a good help for the representation of different problem structures. Context problems, combined with the ENL model, were used a lot to evoke more variety and flexibility in children's solution strategies and computation procedures (Figures 13.5, 13.6 and 13.7).

In particular, the 'Leiden on Sea' problem in Figure 13.7 gives an example of how children come up with various strategies for solving a new type of 'difference' problem. The weaker pupil Wilco sticks very closely to the structure of the problem by working in small steps and creating several footholds on the ENL. He does this by using the new strategy of 'adding-on to tens', for which we use the acronym *A10* (bridging to ten). The better pupil, Brit, on the

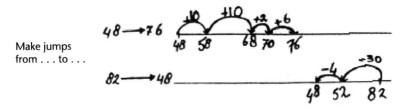

Make jumps from . . . to . . .

Figure 13.5 Sequential N10-jumps in small and large steps.

Try different solutions:

In the bus are 56 people sitting.
At the bus stop 29 people get out.
How many people remain in the bus?

Figure 13.6 Two different solutions: standard N10 (above) and N10C (below) using compensation.

Difference problem 'Leiden on Sea' in worksheet:

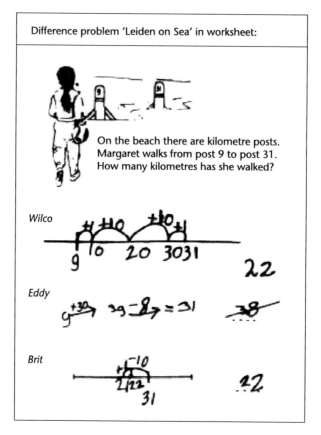

On the beach there are kilometre posts. Margaret walks from post 9 to post 31. How many kilometres has she walked?

Figure 13.7 Context problem evoking various solution strategies.

other hand, transforms the problem structure into a subtraction and uses the compensation strategy N10C for a very efficient and elegant solution (31 − 10 + 1). The pupil Eddy lies somewhere in between, solving the problem in his own way and preferring mental steps without the ENL, but his use of the N10C strategy is still inefficient and incorrect (he added 8 instead of 'minus 8'). Later, Eddy gets things right by using N10 and his own version of A10 on the April test (Figure 13.8), which illustrates his development to a higher level of understanding and flexibility (beyond the ENL). The weaker pupil Wilco still uses the support of the ENL a lot in the April test (Figure 13.8) and has developed a rather rigid preference for the N10C strategy for all kinds of problems. These examples also illustrate how the recordings on the ENL contain much information about the sources of errors and about the strategy development of children. The teachers in our experiment agreed that providing diagnostic feedback is another very helpful feature of the ENL.

Figure 13.8   Good results at different levels: ENL – support (Wilco) and mental steps (Eddy).

After practice with single-digit addition and subtraction as described above, the acquisition of number operations with two-digit numbers proceeded much more quickly than we expected. The introduction of N10 takes place as a game of jumping by tens on the ENL (November). Because the pupils are now familiar with all number positions up to 100, making jumps like 15, 25, 35, and so on (forward) and 82, 72, 62, and so on (backward) goes rather easily. This game of jumping is continued by presenting new problem types asking pupils to go from . . . to . . . (Figure 13.5). Adding constraints like the instruction to do this in three jumps or in two jumps enhances the further abbreviation and automatization of larger steps (+30, –20). These conditions, however, leave much room for individual variation in levels of abbreviation, as can be seen in Figure 13.5. Notice that no sums with two digits are presented in the beginning, but then between December and April all two-digit problem types are mastered rather rapidly. The teachers were surprised that the acquisition of the difficult sums like addition and subtraction with regrouping went much more smoothly than usual (Figure 13.6). For the pupils these problems were hardly new because they asked for a combination of N10-jumps and single-digit operations already practised a lot.

In the April test (Figure 13.8) the results on two-digit context and number problems reached a high level of procedural competency of about 80 per cent correct. This also included the more difficult subtraction with regrouping problems. These good results were confirmed on the test in June as well as on a National Arithmetic Test for the end of Grade 2 (Year 3). The last three months between April and June had mainly been used for enhancing the flexibility of strategy use by presenting many non-standard problems, and by whole-class discussions of different solutions (cf. Figure 13.7). Also the other strategy 1010 (see above) was introduced. An interesting metacognitive aspect was the introduction of labels for the strategies in a childlike style (for instance 'Jump Further' for N10C), which the children used with pleasure in their worksheets and classroom discussions.

Breakthrough of the ENL

More details about the ENL programme, about the flexibility of strategy use, and about the (good) performance of weaker pupils can be found in Klein (1998) and in Klein et al. (1998). The best proof of its success was the request of all experimental schools to continue with the ENL programme, now provided by a publisher and in use in hundreds of other Dutch schools. The breakthrough of the ENL can also be seen in the so-called second generation of realistic textbooks in Holland, published in the 1990s. For instance, in the revised textbook *Wis and Reken* (Buijs et al. 1996) the ENL model is extended throughout the 3rd grade (Year 4) for number problems up to 1000, followed by the delayed introduction of vertical algorithms until 4th grade (Year 5).

Looking back we can say that the greatest effort was invested during the first half of the 2nd grade programme, when the ENL model was introduced and when single-digit addition and subtraction were practised. In that period procedural errors due to counting and not splitting up units correctly were happening a lot but disappeared gradually. So, single-digit practice prepared the ground for two-digit operations, because they both have a similar sequential character as mental strategies. In our opinion this curriculum outline, as well as the curriculum condition of a continuous programme with only small interruptions for other subjects, contributed much to the positive transfer of learning.

Returning to English discussions we see a growing awareness of the role of mental arithmetic. Many authors offer suggestions for everyday mental activities in the expectation that children will improve by practising them. This enthusiasm is heart-warming, but in another publication (Beishuizen and Anghileri 1998) we have argued that combining new and old ideas is not going far enough. We agree with Straker (1996) that given the great variety of mental strategies it is important to decide on 'exactly which methods should be taught and in what order'. And the introduction of the ENL in Holland is an example of not only a new model but also a curriculum change for an improved approach to the development of mental strategies. Priority for the sequential argument (counting, crossing-ten, N10-jumping) and postponement of the partitioning (1010) strategy and the standard algorithm played an important role (cf. above).

Because of these strong sequential characteristics, we are afraid that the ENL model does not fit in with current English teaching practice on early number. For instance, in a small experiment with the ENL in an English mixed-age Year 3/Year 4 class (see Rousham 1997), pupils easily adopted sequential strategies like N10 and A10 and improved on problem solutions. But two months later many pupils had reverted to the standard algorithms, which illustrates that it is of little help to keep up two different systems. The latter situation is comparable to what happened in Holland in the 1970s and 1980s, when mental arithmetic was already emphasized but not adequately supported, resulting in children using a mixture of N10 and 1010 strategies with many of them being unclear and half-correct with difficult subtraction problems (Beishuizen 1993). Attempts to clear up this situation with two-digit number operations up to 100 became the focus (cf. above), not only in the Dutch RME viewpoint (Treffers and De Moor 1990) but also in the growing international research (Fuson 1992; Beishuizen et al. 1997a).

In Holland we struggled and still struggle in the same way towards more consistent reasoning and more balanced teaching in the early number curriculum (see the latest revision in the so-called TAL project 1998, under the authority of the Ministry of Education; TAL-team 1998). We hope that this chapter on the empty number line has illustrated not only the ENL model but also the background to the wider discussion and research on mental arithmetic that is taking place in our country.

References

Beishuizen, M. (1993) Mental strategies and materials or models for addition and subtraction up to 100 in Dutch second grades, *Journal for Research in Mathematics Education*, 24: 294–323.

Beishuizen, M. and Anghileri, J. (1998) Which mental strategies in the early number curriculum? A comparison of British ideas and Dutch views, *British Educational Research Journal*, 24: 519–38.

Beishuizen, M., Gravemeijer, K.P.E. and Van Lieshout, E.C.D.M. (eds) (1997a) *The Role of Contexts and Models in the Development of Mathematical Strategies and Procedures*. Utrecht: Freudenthal Institute.

Beishuizen, M., Van Putten, C.M. and Van Mulken, F. (1997b) Mental arithmetic and strategy use with indirect number problems up to one hundred. *Learning and Instruction*, 7: 87–106.

Bramald, R. (1998) Why does mental have to mean no fingers, no paper? *Equals*, 4: 5–7.

Buijs, K., Boswinkel, N., Meeuwisse, T., Moerlands, F. and Tijhuis, J. (1996) *Wis and Reken – Groep 3, 4 en 5* (*'Wis and Reken' Maths Textbook for Year 2, 3 and 4*). Baarn: Bekadidact.

Fuson, K.C. (1992) Research on whole number addition and subtraction, in D.A. Grouws (ed.) *Handbook of Research on Mathematics Teaching and Learning*. New York: Macmillan.

Hart, K. (1989) There is little connection, in P. Ernest (ed.) *Mathematics Teaching: The State of the Art*. London: Falmer Press.

Klein, A.S. (1998) *Flexibilization of Mental Arithmetic Strategies on a Different Knowledge Base: The Empty Number Line in a Realistic versus Gradual Program Design*. Utrecht: Freudenthal Institute.

Klein, A.S., Beishuizen, M. and Treffers, A. (1998) The empty number line in Dutch second grades: realistic versus gradual program design, *Journal for Research in Mathematics Education*, 29: 443–64.

Kraemer, J.M., Jansen, J., Van der Schoot, F. and Hemker, B. (2005) *Balans van het reken-Wiskundeonderwijs halverwege de basisschool 4*. Arnhem: Cito.

Plunkett, S. (1979) Decomposition and all that rot, *Mathematics in School*, 8(3): 2–5.

Rousham, L. (1997) Jumping on an empty number line, *Primary Maths and Science*, October: 6–8.

SCAA (School Curriculum and Assessment Authority) (1996) *Report on the 1995 Key Stage 2 Tests and Tasks in English, Mathematics and Science*. London: HMSO.

Straker, A. (1996) The National Numeracy Project, *Equals*, 2: 14–15.

TAL-team (1998) *Tussendoelen Annex Leerlijnen (TAL) – Hele getallen – Onderbouw – Basisschool* (*Intermediate Objectives in Learning Strands – Whole Numbers – Lower Grades – Primary School*). Utrecht: Freudenthal Institute.

Thompson, I. (ed.) (2008) *Teaching and Learning Early Number*, 2nd edn. Buckingham: Open University Press.

Treffers, A. (1991) Didactical background of a mathematics program for primary education, in L. Streefland (ed.) *Realistic Mathematics Education in Primary School*. Utrecht: Freudenthal Institute.

Treffers, A. and De Moor, E. (1990) *Proeve van een nationaal programma voor het reken-wiskunde-onderwijs op de basisschool. Deel 2: Basisvaardigheden en cijferen* (*Specimen of a National Program for Primary Mathematics Teaching. Part 2: Basic Mental Skills and Written Algorithms*). Tilburg: Zwijsen.

14 Written calculation: addition and subtraction

Ian Thompson

Introduction

For many years now, criticisms have been made of mathematics teaching that focuses on the acquisition of memorized procedures at the expense of the development of understanding and of children's own methods. Office for Standards in Education (Ofsted) reports are often critical of the overemphasis on written calculation and the underuse of mental methods: 'Other factors include gaps in earlier learning, as well as pupils' reliance on formal written methods and a reluctance to use informal or mental strategies which are sometimes more efficient' (Ofsted 2008: 21). A small-scale investigation, focusing on pupils who were at risk of not converting a Level 2 in mathematics at Key Stage 1 into a Level 4 at the end of Key Stage 2, found that these pupils preferred to use formal written methods in preference to mental methods as they believed the former were better (DfES 2007: 15).

The aim of this chapter is to look critically, and in some detail, at the 'official' approach to written calculation – specifically addition and subtraction – as set out in the *Guidance Paper: Calculation* (DCSF 2006). The underlying principle of this chapter's approach is that children should use mental methods whenever they are appropriate, whereas for calculations that they cannot do in their heads they should use an efficient written method with accuracy and with confidence.

It is interesting to note that in an earlier version of this document 'efficient written methods' were described as 'standard methods'. There is no doubt that the change in terminology in the final version was partially due to the mathematics education community's response – forcefully expressed in a *Times Educational Supplement* (*TES*) article entitled 'Outrage at return to "dark ages"' (Mansell 2006: 12) which discussed the extent to which some senior academics, numeracy consultants and practising teachers had become angry about the government's proposals that all children should be using traditional standard methods of calculation for the four basic operations by the time they left primary school. The article concluded with a response from Tim Coulson, the then director of the mathematics section of the Primary National Strategy (PNS), in which he stated categorically that his team would be addressing the concerns expressed. However, all that actually happened was that the terminology used to describe the recommended algorithms was changed from 'standard' to 'compact', 'efficient' or 'column'. No modifications whatsoever were made to the *actual* written methods: they were still the standard algorithms but with a different name (see Thompson 2007).

The *Guidance Paper – Calculation* approach to addition

This approach is divided into four stages: the empty number line; partitioning; expanded methods in columns; and column methods (originally called 'standard methods'). This progression matches the original National Numeracy Strategy (NNS) approach of counting → mental → jottings → expanded written → compact written, but unfortunately, like the NNS approach, shows a misunderstanding of the purpose of the empty number line (ENL). The Dutch, who developed the ENL, never envisaged it as a link between mental and written strategies, but rather as a tool to support mental calculation. Initially it constitutes a physical model for calculation which often later becomes a mental model (see Beishuizen, Chapter 13).

Stage 1: The empty number line

In the example below, taken from the *Guidance* (Figure 14.1), notice that only one of the two numbers to be added has been partitioned (known in Holland as the N10 strategy) (see Rousham 2003). If both numbers are partitioned (the 1010 strategy), you cannot make use of an empty number line (try it!).

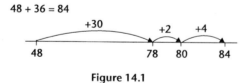

$$48 + 36 = 84$$

Figure 14.1

So, to use the ENL to support mental addition one has to keep one number fixed (usually the larger) and partition the other. Written methods, on the other hand – both expanded and compact – involve treating the ones separately from the multiples of ten (see Figures 14.7, 14.8 and 14.9 later in this chapter), which in turn means that *both* numbers have to be partitioned. This suggests that there is actually no logical progression from ENL use to expanded or contracted written methods, as they are based on conceptually different procedures. The Dutch are well aware of this, and so, after children are considered competent at mental calculation using the N10 strategy on the ENL, teachers spend some time on giving the children practice at using 'double partitioning' (the 1010 strategy) in a range of contexts, such as with money or base-ten materials, before introducing written algorithms that employ such a strategy.

Stage 2: Partitioning

At this stage children are expected to record their mental strategies horizontally using both single (N10) and double (1010) partitioning (see Figure 14.2).

$$47 + 76 = 47 + 70 + 6 = 117 + 6 = 123$$
$$47 + 76 = 40 + 70 + 7 + 6 = 110 + 13 = 123$$

Figure 14.2   Recommended horizontal layout.

Researchers often describe the two different strategies illustrated here as 'sequencing' and 'partitioning' respectively, whereas the *Guidance* describes them both by the latter name!

In a small-scale research project looking at the written calculation methods of 117 young children (Thompson 1994) it was found that 71 per cent set out their work horizontally. However, they did not generally write down the original numbers they were working with, preferring instead to record just their calculation. Rashid's calculation (Figure 14.3) illustrates the second strategy.

$$70 + 70 = 140 + 70 = 210$$

$$2 + 2 + 2 = 6$$

Figure 14.3   Rashid finding 72 + 72 + 72.

If we compare the *Guidance* layout with Rashid's, we find that there are subtle but important differences between them. One motive the authors of the *Guidance* appear to have had for recommending the format illustrated in Figure 14.2 is to try to ensure that children do not make 'incorrect' statements in their working out, even though they may have actually calculated correctly and produced the right answer. In Rashid's case (Figure 14.3) both his working out and his answer are correct, but the statement 70 + 70 = 140 + 70 is actually mathematically unsound.

Also, the layout in Figure 14.2 appears to be suggesting that children should set out their plan of attack before they execute it. The mathematical notation for the second example is really shorthand for the following: 'The problem I have to solve is 47 + 76 . . . I have partitioned both the numbers into multiples of ten and ones, and reorganized them so that I can more easily add the tens together before adding the ones . . . 40 + 70 is 110 and 7 + 6 is

13 . . . 110 and 13 is 123.' Whereas, Rashid's written marks are almost a running commentary on his thinking and calculation procedure as they happen in real time. Later discussion with Rashid suggested that his approach was more on the lines of: 'Take the 70 out of the 72 . . . Double 70 is 140 (write down 70 + 70 = 140) . . . add another 70 . . . that makes 210 (write down + 70 = 210) . . . now 2 + 2 + 2 = 6 (write this down)'. The partitioning step, where we would rewrite 72 as 70 + 2, is treated differently by many young children, who just 'take out' the tens, operate on them and then retrieve the ones later. This strategy accounts for the major difference between the layout of the children involved in the research project and that recommended in the document.

The next recommended step in this stage involves writing the partitioned numbers under one another (Figure 14.4).

$$
\begin{array}{r}
47 \\
+\,76 \\
\end{array}
\quad
\begin{array}{r}
= \quad 40 + 7 \\
70 + 6 \\
\hline
110 + 13 = 123
\end{array}
$$

Figure 14.4

However, there is no acknowledgement of the fact that this written method (jotting?) actually builds on the 1010 (double partitioning) strategy, and that none of the written strategies that follow involves the sequencing (N10) strategy that the children were developing while utilizing the empty number line in Stage 1!

Stage 3: Expanded method in columns

This stage builds on the example in Figure 14.4. We are informed that children should initially 'add the tens first' (Figure 14.5).

$$
\begin{array}{r}
47 \\
+\,76 \\
\hline
110 \\
13 \\
\hline
123
\end{array}
$$

Figure 14.5

Then, as they gain confidence, they should 'add the ones first' (Figure 14.6).

$$
\begin{array}{r}
47 \\
+\,76 \\
\hline
13 \\
110 \\
\hline
123
\end{array}
$$

Figure 14.6

A question that comes immediately to mind at this stage is: 'Why add the ones first, when all the research on mental calculation suggests that, left to their own devices, children will start from the left and add the multiples of ten first?' There is no doubt that the answer is that it is to prepare the children for right-to-left addition that is crucial for using the column method – that is, the standard algorithm.

A section linking Stages 3 and 4 in the *Guidance Paper* (DCSF 2006: 7) states that 'The expanded method leads children to the more compact method so that they understand its structure and efficiency'. My own research (Thompson and Bramald 2002) suggests that the aspect of place value underpinning mental calculation methods and informal written procedures is different from that which underpins the standard (or 'column') written algorithms: the former methods involve 'quantity value' (where 56 is interpreted as *fifty plus six*), whereas the latter procedures involve 'column value' (where 56 is interpreted as *five in the tens column and six in the ones column*). This research would appear to raise questions about the accuracy of the quotation above.

Stage 4: The column method

This stage introduces 'carrying' (Figure 14.7).

$$\begin{array}{r} 47 \\ + 76 \\ \hline 123 \\ \hline {\scriptstyle 1} \end{array}$$

Figure 14.7

The document states that 'Carry digits are recorded below the line, using the words "carry ten" or "carry one hundred", not "carry one"' (DCSF 2006: 7). This suggests that, as in earlier National Strategy recommendations, children are expected to refer to the actual value of the digits when performing this calculation: they should say *forty plus seventy equals one hundred and ten*. This is perhaps feasible when adding two-digit numbers, but becomes much more cumbersome with the addition of three-digit numbers. Figure 14.8 involves two 'carries'.

$$\begin{array}{r} 366 \\ + 458 \\ \hline 824 \\ \hline {\scriptstyle 1\ 1} \end{array}$$

Figure 14.8

Trying to refer to the actual value of the digits makes it much more difficult with numbers of this size. After saying *6 add 8 equals 14, put down the 4 and carry the 10*. We write 1 (that is, not a 10) under the 6 and the 5. The next step is to say *60 add 50 equals 110, and 10 more makes 120* – but there is the possibility of an error at this point, as the 10 to be added has been written as a 1 – albeit in the tens column. However, assuming that we perform the calculation correctly and get 120, the next problem is 'where do we write the three separate digits?' The official answer has to be: *put the 20 as a 2 next to the 4 in our answer (or 'in the tens column'); ignore the zero and put the 100 as a 1 under the 3 and the 4 while saying 'carry one hundred'*. No doubt the reader will find this procedure somewhat confusing. This is because, in terms of the discussion of place value above, we are shifting backwards and forwards between 'quantity value' and the more conceptually difficult 'column value'.

I would argue that column methods – being extremely compact – inevitably conceal much of what is actually going on in the calculation. They summarize several steps involving commutativity, associativity and distributivity, whereas, because they contain more detail, non-standard methods record the successive stages of the calculation, thereby allowing children to keep track of where they are and enabling them to ascertain more easily where they have gone wrong if the answer is incorrect. I would therefore question the wisdom of attempting to teach the column method to all primary children given that the expanded 'front-end' method of addition (Figure 14.5) is more easily understood because it builds on the 'double partitioning' (1010) method used by the majority of young children for mental calculation. Like the more difficult standard algorithm, it is also generalizable to the addition of larger numbers and decimals.

The *Guidance Paper – Calculation* approach to subtraction

The approach to subtraction is divided into three stages: using the empty number line; partitioning; and expanded layout leading to column methods.

Stage 1 Using the empty number line

The recommendations in this stage parallel those outlined for addition, and four examples – including the following – are provided (Figure 14.9).

I would argue that the *counting back* descriptor in Figure 14.9 is a misnomer. Most of the literature on early calculation methods suggests that counting back involves reciting backwards as many number names as the number you are subtracting (the subtrahend), and then giving the last number that you

Figure 14.9 $74 - 27 = 47$ worked by counting back.

said as your answer to the subtraction. An example from the original framework (DfEE 1999) supports this interpretation: '*We made six mince pies. We ate two of them. How many pies are left? (Count back two from six: 5, 4. Say together "6 take away 2 is 4")*' (Section 4: 17).

The strategy illustrated in Figure 14.9 actually involves the following procedures:

- partitioning the subtrahend;
- subtracting the multiple of ten (74 − 20 = 54);
- partitioning the ones in such a way that 50 will be reached after the next subtraction, that is, 7 = 4 + 3;
- subtracting the requisite number of ones to reach 50 (54 − 4);
- subtracting the remaining ones (50 − 3 = 47).

No counting back is involved whatsoever!

Also included in Stage 1 is a sub-section entitled 'The counting-up method' (see Thompson 2009). The strength of this procedure is that it involves adding appropriate chunks to the smaller number until you reach the larger one. The calculation can be recorded on an empty number line or in columns. This procedure allows the number of steps to be reduced as the children's mental strategies improve. In Figure 14.10 the calculation is solved in five steps. This can develop into a more compact form of recording as the children's mental calculation skills and confidence improve (see Figure 14.11 for a two-step solution). It is also possible to complete the calculation in either three or four steps.

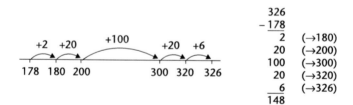

```
        326
      - 178
          2   (→180)
         20   (→200)
        100   (→300)
         20   (→320)
          6   (→326)
        148
```

Figure 14.10

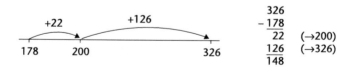

```
        326
      - 178
         22   (→200)
        126   (→326)
        148
```

Figure 14.11

It is interesting that in the original framework (DfEE 1999) children were expected to:

Understand subtraction as:

- taking away
- finding the difference between
- complementary addition.

(Section 5: 29)

However, in the new version, only the first two bullet points are mentioned; complementary addition has been dropped as a named aspect of subtraction. This is odd, given that this is precisely the strategy recommended for the *counting up* method.

Stage 2 Partition

This section seems to be a needless and irrelevant backward step. The final example in Stage 1 used the *counting up* method to solve a quite difficult calculation: 22.4 – 17.8, whereas now in Stage 2 the document is recommending using basic partitioning to calculate 74 – 27, even though we have just seen it used several times in the *six* 'counting up' examples provided in Stage 1. Also, the empty number line example used to illustrate the calculation is exactly the same that in Stage 1 (see Figure 14.9). The real purpose behind this section is, unfortunately, to emphasize that *decomposition* – the method covered in the following section – is the favoured strategy. This is confirmed by the fact that counting up, the only other written method mentioned, is consigned to Stage 1, accompanied by a note saying: 'The counting up method can be a useful alternative for children whose progress is slow' (DCSF 2006: 8).

To illustrate yet again the document's obsession with ultra-formal recording I leave you to ponder on the feasibility of teaching young children to record their subtractions in the manner represented in Figure 14.12.

$$74 - 27 = 70 + 4 - 20 - 7 = 60 + 14 - 20 - 7 = 40 + 7$$

Figure 14.12

Stage 3 Expanded layout leading to column method

As was mentioned earlier, in order to appease the 'anti-standard-algorithms' group that responded vociferously to the consultation document, the Primary National Strategy simply substituted the word 'column' for 'standard', without changing any of the actual algorithms. The main subtraction goal in this document is to have children progress inexorably towards the standard compact decomposition method. The procedure is introduced via the 'expanded method', initially using an example that requires no 'exchanging'

or 'borrowing'. We are taken through a progressive sequence that begins with
563 – 241 (Figure 14.13).

$$
\begin{array}{rcl}
500 + 60 + 3 & & 563 \\
-200 + 40 + 1 & & -241 \\
\hline
300 + 20 + 2 & \text{leading to} & 322
\end{array}
$$

Figure 14.13

This sequence then progresses to 563 – 278 (Figure 14.14).

$$
\begin{array}{cccl}
& & \overset{150}{\underset{}{}} & \\
& & 400 \quad \cancel{50} \quad 13 & \quad 4\ 15\ 13 \\
500 + 60 + 3 \quad \text{or} & 400 + 150 + 13 \quad \text{or} & \cancel{500} + \cancel{60} + \cancel{3} & \text{leading to} \quad \cancel{563} \\
-200 + 70 + 8 & -200 + 70 + 8 & -200 + 70 + 8 & \quad -278 \\
\hline
& 200 + 80 + 5 & 200 + 80 + 5 & \quad 285
\end{array}
$$

Figure 14.14

To someone who can already perform written subtraction, this progression no doubt appears perfectly logical. However, we know from research and from the combined experience of many teachers that children have great difficulty with the decomposition algorithm. Hart (1989) found that children struggled to make the anticipated connections between the manipulation of practical apparatus and their pencil and paper calculations when learning the decomposition algorithm.

One particular weakness of the recommended layout can lead to a particular type of error where children add rather than subtract one or more of the partitioned elements. For example, see Figure 14.15.

$$
\begin{array}{lcl}
\begin{array}{r}
500 + 60 + 3 \\
-200 + 40 + 1 \\
\hline
300 + 20 + 2
\end{array}
& \text{can be erroneously calculated as:} &
\begin{array}{r}
500 + 60 + 3 \\
-200 + 30 + 1 \\
\hline
300 + 90 + 4
\end{array}
\end{array}
$$

Figure 14.15

This type of error is, of course, a function of the recommended layout, which incorporates addition symbols between the separate partitions in a context where children are expected to subtract. This could be avoided by relating the layout to place value cards, where 563 looks like 500 60 3 when the three components are separated. The resulting calculation would be written as in Figure 14.16.

$$
\begin{array}{rrrlrrr}
500 & 60 & 3 & & 500 & 60 & 3 \\
-200 & 40 & 1 & & -200 & -40 & -1 \\
\hline
300 & 20 & 2 & \text{leading to} \quad 300 & 20 & 2
\end{array}
$$

Figure 14.16

Another problem with this algorithm is that children are expected to be able to make non-standard partitions, such as 73 = 60 + 13 or 563 = 400 + 150 + 13. Ross (1989) has shown that children generally find this quite difficult.

Given that a stated aim of the *Guidance Paper* (DCSF 2006) is to develop written procedures that build on children's mental strategies, it is important to point out that in the extensive literature on children's idiosyncratic mental calculation strategies there is, to my knowledge, no example of any child ever inventing decomposition. This would appear to provide important evidence that might help explain why children find decomposition so difficult. On the other hand, *counting up* (or *complementary addition*) is the only subtraction procedure with a built-in natural progression from basic mental strategy through a range of levels of jottings and informal notation to a more formal written notation.

One reason for teaching the complementary addition procedure rather than decomposition is its widespread use in real-life situations, such as giving change (hence its alternative descriptor, *shopkeeper arithmetic*); finding the difference between two given measurements; calculating elapsed time; and so on. For example, most people would solve time problems using this method: 'It's 9.40 now and my train is at 11.25. So how much time have I got? 20 minutes plus an hour plus 25 minutes . . . so that's an hour and three quarters.' Another reason is the fact that children can choose the size of the chunks that they decide to add on and the number of steps they take to complete the task. This can range from the five steps of Figure 14.10 to the two steps of Figure 14.11 (see Thompson 2010).

Conclusion[1]

The *Guidance Paper – Calculation* document needs to be interpreted with care. It is a great pity that in the early stages of its development the National Numeracy Strategy did not set up a research project to attempt to ascertain which of the wide range of written algorithms incorporated into the framework were the most 'child-friendly'.

Note

1   A more comprehensive Conclusion, covering all four basic operations can be found at the end of Chapter 16.

References

DCSF (Department for Children, Schools and Families) (2006) *Primary Framework for Literacy and Mathematics – Guidance Paper – Calculation.* http://national-strategies.standards.dcsf.gov.uk/node/47364 (accessed March 2010).

DfEE (Department for Education and Employment) (1999) *The National Numeracy Strategy Framework for Teaching Mathematics from Reception to Year 6.* London: DfEE.

DfES (Department for Education and Skills) (2007) *Keeping Up – Pupils Who Fall Behind in Key Stage 2.* London: DfES.

Hart, K.M. (1989) Place value: subtraction, in D. Johnson (ed.) *Children's Mathematical Frameworks 8–13.* London: NFER-Nelson.

Mansell, W. (2006) Outrage at return to 'dark ages', *Times Educational Supplement*, 26 May, p. 12.

Ofsted (Office for Standards in Education) (2008) *Mathematics: Understanding the Score.* London: Ofsted.

Ross, S. (1989) Parts, wholes and place value: a developmental view, *Arithmetic Teacher*, 36(6): 47–51.

Rousham, L. (2003) The empty number line: a model in search of a learning trajectory, in I. Thompson (ed.) *Enhancing Primary Mathematics Teaching.* Maidenhead: Open University Press.

Thompson, I. (1994) Young children's idiosyncratic written algorithms for addition, *Educational Studies in Mathematics*, 26(4): 323–45.

Thompson, I. (2007) The revised primary framework: an exercise in consultation? *Primary Mathematics*, 11(1): 3–5.

Thompson, I. (2009) Can we count on the early years foundation stage 'Practice guidance'? *Primary Mathematics*, 13(1): 10–13.

Thompson, I. (2010) Subtraction in Key Stage 3: which algorithm? *Mathematics in School*, 39(1): 29–31.

Thompson, I. and Bramald, R. (2002) *An Investigation of the Relationship between Young Children's Understanding of the Concept of Place Value and their Competence at Mental Addition.* Report for the Nuffield Foundation. University of Newcastle upon Tyne. www.ianthompson.pi.dsl.pipex.com (accessed March 2010).

15 Progression in the teaching of multiplication

Ian Thompson

Introduction

Take a close look at some of 9-year-old John's answers to a page of multiplications from his school maths book. See if you can work out what he is doing wrong before reading on (Figure 15.1).

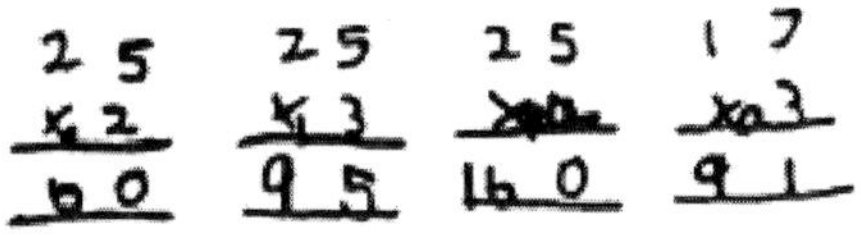

Figure 15.1 John's multiplications.

Notice that John is actually carrying out all of the correct steps involved in the execution of the standard algorithm for multiplication: it is just unfortunate that he has reversed the order of two fairly crucial steps. In each example John successfully multiplies the units digits and 'carries' the appropriate tens digit, correctly placing it under the other tens. However, in the second calculation, for example, instead of saying 'Two times three is six, plus one more makes seven', he says 'Two plus one is three and three times three is nine', which unfortunately gives him a totally erroneous solution.

John's work provides us with an excellent illustrative example of what some researchers into children's errors have found, namely, that the mistakes that children make in written calculations are generally not random, but are more often than not the result of consistently following an incorrect or faulty procedure (known in US literature as a 'bug'). (For an alternative view of children's errors see Ryan and Williams, Chapter 11.) John did not question the accuracy of any of his answers; so far as he was concerned he was correctly following the method that his teacher had taught him, and so was quite confident that his answers were correct. If John were using his own method rather than his teacher's he might well be getting the right answers.

Early stages

The expectations for the acquisition of mental multiplication facts set out in the *Primary Framework for Literacy and Mathematics* (DfES 2006) progress through the following stages:

- counting aloud at the Foundation Stage in 2s, 5s and 10s, and counting repeated groups of the same size;
- deriving multiples of 2, 5 and 10, and recalling doubles of numbers from one to ten in Year 1;
- recalling multiplication facts for the 2, 5 and 10 times tables in Year 2;
- recalling multiplication facts for the 2 to 6 and the 10 times tables in Year 3;
- recalling all the facts up to 10×10 in Year 4;
- recalling all of these facts *quickly* in Year 5.

Of course, there is more to multiplication than learning tables facts. The following examples illustrate how children can combine their increasing acquisition of multiplication facts with previously learned skills and knowledge in order to solve suitably targeted problems. The examples are taken from those used by 59 children from Year 2 (6- to 7-year-olds) and 44 from Year 3 who were involved in a small-scale research project primarily investigating addition and subtraction mental calculation strategies. The children had very little experience of work on multiplication. However, there were some children whose grasp of number seemed sufficiently developed to warrant asking them a few basic multiplication questions. Consequently, the range of strategies was quite restricted and, as might be expected, counting was very much in evidence. For example, to find, say, three lots of four, several children inevitably interpreted the problem as an addition, and counted out all three sets on their fingers, however, other children used more interesting strategies.

Kevin used doubling in an interesting way to calculate 6×6:

Something like 36 . . . six and six makes twelve . . . 24 . . . 36.

Melissa's used doubling plus counting on to find 3 lots of 4:

8 . . . 9 . . . 10 . . . 11 . . . 12.

Rebecca extended this strategy when she worked out 6×6 by first doubling six then doubling twelve and finally counting on in ones from 24 to 36.

One or two children found 4×5 by counting in fives. Some researchers call this 'step-counting'. Charlotte's response to 4×6 used step-counting combined with counting-on:

$$6 \ldots 12 \ldots 18 \ldots 19 \ldots 20 \ldots 21 \ldots 22 \ldots 23 \ldots 24.$$

Other children used a known fact combined with some form of counting. For example, Camilla used a sophisticated procedure, but made an unfortunate mistake in the process. Her solution to 6×9, a hard calculation reserved for the more able Year 3 children, went as follows:

Fifty-one . . . six tens are sixty and then I counted down nine.

Her error came from counting down 'nine' rather than 'six', but her method of calculation – compensation – was quite ingenious, given that she had never been taught such a procedure.

One of the most creative examples from the whole project came from Andrew, an obviously able 7-year-old. Asked to work out four lots of eight he explained his correct answer in the following way (you may have to read his answer more than once!):

Three sevens are 21 . . . add on all the next ones to get eight . . . you have three more units, so you get 24. Add on eight and you get . . . 24, 25, 26, 27, 28, 29, 30, 31, 32.

Ben used step-counting combined with addition to calculate $13 + 15$:

33 . . . I counted in fives after fifteen and added three on.

Ben had actually counted on one five too many using this method. It is interesting to note that children appear to make errors very rarely when using their own personal heuristics. However, an analysis of the thinking involved in Ben's solution suggests a potential source of error. He first had to recognize that fifteen was an element in his five times table and that thirteen comprised two (or perhaps just 'some') fives and a three. Once he started step-counting from fifteen in fives he also had to keep track of the number of fives he was counting. One possible reason for his error is that he was distracted by the fact that the number he had begun counting from (that is, fifteen) contained three fives, and so this made him count on three rather than two fives. The fact that several children used this strategy suggests that 'step-counting' and the more difficult 'step-counting from different starting points' are useful activities for teachers to use in interactive whole-class or small-group mental calculation sessions.

A deeper understanding of multiplication

In parallel with the learning of multiplication table facts and ways of using them to solve problems, children need to acquire a deeper knowledge of multiplication that will help them develop an awareness of modifications that they can make to the numbers in a calculation that will still give the same answer as the original numbers: what the Dutch call 'clever calculating'. This 'awareness' relates to the section entitled 'Understandings' in the model described in Chapter 12, and includes becoming aware that:

- if they know that 4 sevens are 28, then 8 sevens will be twice as many (56);
- they can find 8 sevens by doubling 7 three times (14, 28, 56)
- if they know that 6 sixes are 36, then they know that 7 sixes are 6 more (42);
- knowing how to multiply by 10 allows them to multiply easily by 20, 30, 40 . . .;
- they can find 14×4 by halving 14 and doubling 4, provided that they know 7×8 is 56;
- to multiply by 25 they can multiply by 100 and then divide by four;
- they can find 14×12 by multiplying 14 by 3, then by 2, and then by 2 again because 12 is $3 \times 2 \times 2$ (168);
- they can find 19 sevens by finding 20 sevens and then subtracting one seven (133);
- they can find 15 thirteens by adding 10 thirteens to 5 (half of 10) thirteens (195).

With reference to multiplication by 10 mentioned above, official policy, and that of probably every teacher (plus 99 per cent of mathematics educators) is to ensure that children do not learn to say that 'To multiply by ten you just add a nought (or zero)' as this can lead to bad habits where children will extrapolate from this and say that 4.5 multiplied by 10 is 4.50. However, for an iconoclastic perspective on this issue see Thompson (2003).

The *Guidance Paper* – *Calculation* approach to teaching multiplication

The recommended progression is presented as comprising six stages: mental multiplication using partitioning; the grid method; expanded short multiplication; short multiplication (by Year 4); two-digit by two-digit products (by Year 5); and three-digit by two-digit products (by Year 6).

Stage 1 Mental multiplication using partitioning

The document recommends various types of 'informal recording' for mental multiplications. (There seems to be something not quite right about 'recommended' informal recording; to me, 'informal recording' implies that children jot down anything that helps them keep track of their calculation or that offers them support during the calculation process.) However, it is suggested that children might record a mental calculation such as 14×3 in the way illustrated in Figure 15.2.

$$14 \times 3 = (10 + 4) \times 3$$
$$= (10 \times 3) + (4 \times 3) = 30 + 12 = 42$$

Figure 15.2   Recommended recording of 14×3.

I would argue that this procedure is far too formal. Typically, this approach considers the calculation from a mathematician's perspective, observing that the strategy makes use of the distributive law: a 'law' that many of us did not encounter formally until we met algebra in secondary school when we were taught to 'expand brackets' to show that $a(b + c) = ab + ac$. However, the 'recommended recording' totally ignores what we know about how children think and work. Children's jottings to support their mental calculation often, as one might expect, result in written marks that are almost a running commentary on their thinking and 'working out' as they happen in real time (see Thompson 2004). It is a fact that some children in Years 3 and 4 have an implicit understanding that multiplication is distributive over addition. For example, Thompson (1993) describes 13 young children's different informal written methods for tackling a problem that could be solved either by adding four 144s or calculating 144×4. The four children who solved the problem using multiplication all showed an implicit understanding of distributivity (see Andrew's solution in Figure 15.3).

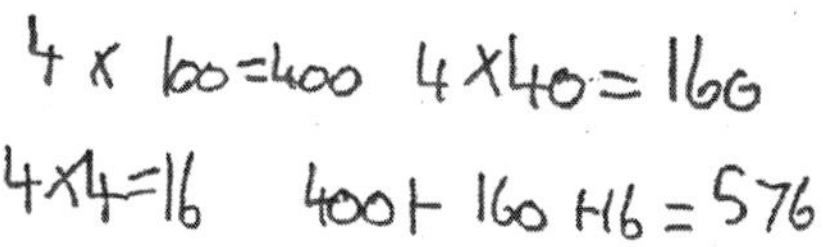

Figure 15.3   Andrew calculating 144×4.

However, I doubt whether any of the children would have been able to express their respective calculations as:

$$144 \times 4 = (100 + 40 + 4) \times 4 = (100 \times 4) + (40 \times 4) + (4 \times 4) \ldots$$

Just as young children develop an implicit awareness that addition is commutative (that is what is involved in the 'put the larger number first' strategy) without being able to articulate this verbally or on paper, older children similarly become aware of the distributivity of multiplication over addition. Expressing these laws of arithmetic formally in words or in writing is too difficult for most young children, and is a particularly redundant exercise in Stage 1, given that this section is entitled 'Mental multiplication using partitioning'.

Stage 2 The grid method

The recommended layout for using the 'grid' method – described as a 'staging post' – for the calculation 38×7 is illustrated in Figure 15.4.

×	7
30	210
8	56
	266

Figure 15.4

I have never been particularly impressed by the National Strategy's notation for the grid method, given that different publications draw the grids in different and sometimes non-user-friendly formats. For example, this notation is different from that illustrated in the *Five Day Course – Course Handbook* (DfEE 2001: 87) (Figure 15.5).

×	30	8	
7	210	56	266

Figure 15.5

The *Guidance Paper* (DCSF 2006: 13) advises us to 'place the number with the most digits in the left-hand column so that it is easier to add the partial products', as in Figure 15.4. However, what this advice really means to say is that 'this is preparing you for future work on column (standard) multiplication methods'.

An alternative to the 'grid' model is the 'area' model. However, although these two words are often used as synonyms, the recommended layouts in this section show that the two models are quite different. The grid here is just a structure built around the numbers in the calculation; it has no contextual meaning. On the other hand, the area method does. Personally, I prefer to start with squared paper – working to scale – where (in this case) the calculation would involve finding the number of squares in a 38 by 7 rect-angle. The 38 could be partitioned in various ways: 10 + 10 + 10 + 8, 20 + 10 + 8 or 30 + 8, thereby allowing children some control over the size of the smaller internal rectangles they would be working with. As the children gain con-fidence with the concepts underlying the procedure, they can progress to abbreviating by sketching rectangles that are no longer to scale (Figure 15.6). These sketches retain the partitioning and distributive aspects of the calcula-tion, and can provide a useful mental model for more formal methods intro-duced at a later stage (see Thompson 1996).

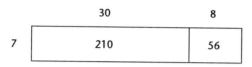

	30	8
7	210	56

Figure 15.6

Stage 3 Expanded short multiplication

The next stage (if we ignore the two unnecessary intermediate procedures that the document describes) is shown in Figure 15.7.

$$\begin{array}{r} 38 \\ \times \ \ 7 \\ \hline 210 \\ 56 \\ \hline 266 \end{array}$$

Figure 15.7

This is described as 'expanded short multiplication'. It involves operating with quantities by treating the 3 in 38 as 'thirty' and working from left to right by finding the solution to 30 × 7 first. This written strategy develops quite naturally from mental multiplication methods and from the area model (see Figures 15.6 and 15.10) – though less obviously from the recommended grid models. It partitions 38 into 30 + 8 and multiplies both parts by 7, starting with the larger partition, following the natural left-to-right way of proceeding in mental calculation (see Thompson, Chapter 12).

In order to make the arguments in the following sections a little more easy to follow, I need to provide a brief discussion of place value. It has been argued elsewhere, with detailed examples (Thompson and Bramald 2002), that the aspect of place value underpinning mental calculation methods and informal written procedures is different from that which underpins the stand-ard (or 'column') written algorithms: the former methods involve 'quantity value' (where 56 is interpreted as *fifty plus six*), whereas the latter procedures involve 'column value' (where 56 is interpreted as *five in the tens column and six in the ones column*). Unfortunately, the *Guidance Paper – Calculation* fails to acknowledge that such a difference exists.

Stage 4 Short multiplication

Here 'The recording is reduced further, with carry digits recorded below the line' (DCSF 2006: 13). We are given the impression that there is a smooth transition between the algorithms illustrated in Figures 15.7 and 15.8.

$$
\begin{array}{r}
38 \\
\times\ \ 7 \\
\hline
266 \\
\scriptstyle 5
\end{array}
$$

Figure 15.8

The following argument may appear a little abstruse, but nonetheless it is quite important from the perspective of the learner. In order to correctly perform the algorithm in Figure 15.7 we are informed that the first step in calculating 38 × 7 is 'thirty multiplied by seven', not 'three times seven', that is, working from left to right with quantities. However, for the algorithm in Figure 15.8 we are told 'The step here involves adding 210 and 50 mentally with only the 5 in the 50 recorded' (DCSF 2006: 13). What puzzles me is whether or not I am still supposed to be working from left to right. If this is the case, then surely, having mentally worked out the 210, followed by the 56, I would want to write down the 6 so that I do not forget it while I'm in the process of adding the 50 to the 210 as recommended. There seems to be little point in writing down the 5 (except that we have always done this with the standard algorithm!).

On the other hand, if I am actually calculating from right to left, then I need to work out the 8 × 7 first. In this case, would it not be more sensible to record the 50 somewhere while I am writing the 6 in the ones column and working out 30 × 7? Doing this will help me remember that I have to add 50 to the answer to 30 × 7. If I write down 5 as suggested, am I not likely to just add 5 rather than 50 to my 210? You have to remember that up to this point in the development of this approach to multiplication, no mention has been made of working with numbers in columns. All the algorithms covered so far (plus those to be found in stages 5 and 6) involve working with quantities, not digits with specific column values.

Given the user-friendliness of the procedure in Figure 15.7 and its close relation to mental multiplication and the area method, why do we need to introduce the potentially confusing algorithm for 'short multiplication' at all? Yet again, it would appear to be a throwback to the past: we have always taught children 'short multiplication' before progressing to 'long multiplication'.

Stages 5 and 6: two-digit by two-digit products and three-digit by three-digit products

As Stage 6 merely extends the recommendations in Stage 5 to more challenging calculations, I shall confine my discussion to the latter.

Here, the grid method is extended to calculations like 56×27 (Figure 15.9).

×	20	7	
50	1000	350	1350
6	120	42	162
			1512
			1

Figure 15.9

At this stage the grid layout bears some resemblance to the area method layout (Figure 15.10), but this resemblance soon disappears when the next stage is introduced (Figure 15.11).

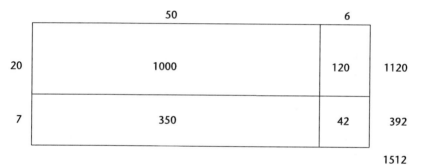

Figure 15.10   Area method layout (not to scale).

	50	6	
×	20	7	
	1000	350	1350
	120	42	162
			1512
			1

Figure 15.11

In my opinion this layout has now lost any real relationship to what educators normally refer to as the grid or area method. For example, what connection do the diagonal moves to find 6×20 and 50×7 have with the grid structure? Obviously, the aim is to prepare children for the final two algorithms in this stage (Figures 15.12 and 15.13).

```
        56
      × 27
      1000      50 × 20 = 1000
       120       6 × 20 =  120
       350      50 × 7 =  350
        42       6 × 7 =   42
      1512
       1
```

Figure 15.12

```
        56
      × 27
      1120      56 × 20
       392      56 ×  7
      1512
       1
```

Figure 15.13

The algorithm in Figure 15.12 retains the partial products calculated in the grid method shown in Figure 15.11. However, no advice is given as to how to calculate the two separate products (56 × 20 and 56 × 7) shown in Figure 15.13. I am fairly sure that the vast majority of Year 5 children would have great difficulty in working out 56 × 7 mentally. As mentioned above, Stage 6 deals with the multiplication of three-digit by two-digit numbers. The reader might like to ascertain the level of difficulty of the recommended algorithm by using this method to calculate 286 × 29 – the calculation illustrated in 'Stage 6 Three-digit by two-digit products' and aimed at Year 6 children.

In Chapter 14 I mentioned the brouhaha created when an earlier version of the *Guidance Paper* proposed that all children should be using traditional standard methods of calculation for the four basic operations by the time they left primary school. Interestingly, the original document (and the following one, given that the changes were only to the language and not the content) does not *actually* recommend what most people would recognize as the standard algorithm for long multiplication. For example, 'standard algorithm language' for the calculation 56 × 27 would be something like '6 × 7 is 42. Put down the 2 and carry the 4. Next put down a zero. 5 × 7 is 35 . . .'. As can be seen in Chapter 16, exactly the same applies to the standard long division algorithm. Perhaps some of the negative publicity could have been avoided if the document's authors had acknowledged this in the first place!

Conclusion

A general conclusion covering all four basic arithmetical operations is included in Chapter 16, 'Progression in the teaching of division'.

References

DCSF (Department for Children, Schools and Families) (2006) *Primary Framework for Literacy and Mathematics – Guidance Paper – Calculation.* http://nationalstrategies.standards.dcsf.gov.uk/node/47364 (accessed March 2010).

DfEE (Department for Education and Employment) (2001) *Developing Mathematics in Years 4, 5 and 6: The Five-Day Course – Course Handbook.* London: DfEE.

DfES (Department for Education and Skills) (2006) *Primary Framework for Literacy and Mathematics.* Norwich: DfES.

Thompson, I. (1993) Thirteen ways to solve a problem, *Mathematics Teaching,* 144: 27–30.

Thompson, I. (1996) User-friendly calculation algorithms, *Mathematics in School,* 25(5): 42–5.

Thompson, I. (2003) Putting place value in its place, *Mathematics Teaching,* 184: 14–15.

Thompson, I. (2004) To jot or not to jot, *Mathematics in School,* 33(3): 6–7.

Thompson, I. and Bramald, R. (2002) *An Investigation of the Relationship between Young Children's Understanding of the Concept of Place Value and their Competence at Mental Addition.* Report for the Nuffield Foundation. University of Newcastle upon Tyne. www.ianthompson.pi.dsl.pipex.com (accessed March 2010).

16 Progression in the teaching of division

Ian Thompson

Introduction

There is a delightful sequence in an old *Horizon* TV programme entitled 'Twice five plus the wings of a bird' where pre-school Tom is baking a dozen cakes supervised by his mother. Just as he is about to put the cakes in the oven his mother reminds him who is coming to dinner and asks how many cakes each person will be able to have. Tom says that there are 12 cakes and six people for dinner. When pushed to say how many there will be for each person he counts the cakes, saying 'You can have 1, 2, 3, 4 . . . I can have 1, 2, 3, 4 . . . Auntie can have 1, 2, 3, 4'. His mother then asks what dad, Brondy and Simon are going to say. Tom's instant reply is 'They can have nothing!' During the brief excerpt we see Tom make the discovery that 'Six and six makes 12'; he has clearly learned something about addition. However, he has some way to go yet before we can say that he has learned something about division!

Early stages

The build-up to written division in the *Primary Framework for Literacy and Mathematics* (DfES 2006) is fairly gradual (although not gradual enough for Anghileri and Beishuizen 1998). The first reference to activities that are division related appears in the 40–60+ months section of the *Practice Guidance for the Early Years Foundation Stage* (DfES 2007: 69) where we are informed that children need to 'Share objects into equal groups and count how many in each group'. The *Framework* (DfES 2006: 94) informs us that most children in Year 1 will learn to 'Solve practical problems that involve . . . sharing into equal groups'. Having also learned the doubles of numbers 1 to 10 in Year 1 children are expected to learn the corresponding halves in Year 2 and be able to 'derive and recall . . . division facts' for the 2, 5 and 10 times tables. They will also 'represent sharing and repeated subtraction (grouping) as division' and will learn to deal with calculations involving remainders.

A deeper understanding of division

Over time children need to come to appreciate the following: that sharing situations can be represented by division (how many bricks does each child get if there are 12 bricks and 4 children?); that grouping (repeated subtraction) situations can also be represented by division (how many children can get 4 bricks if there are 12 bricks?); and that division and multiplication are inverse operations ($3 \times 4 = 12$ so $12 \div 4 = 3$).

Also, in addition to knowing all the basic division facts and the knowledge described above, children need to develop a sufficient level of confidence with division so that they become aware that:

- they can find $36 \div 4$ (a quarter of 36) by halving and then halving again;
- if $12 \div 3$ is 4, then $12 \div 4$ is 3;
- if $12 \div 3$ is 4, then $24 \div 3$ is twice as many and $6 \div 3$ is half as many;
- if $12 \div 3$ is 4, then $24 \div 6$ will be the same, as will $48 \div 12$;
- $96 \div 4$ is the same as $80 \div 4$ added to $16 \div 4$;
- knowing how to divide by 10 allows them to divide easily by 20, 30, 40 . . .

The *Guidance Paper – Calculation* approach to teaching written division

In the introductory section to division on page 16 of the *Guidance Paper – Calculation* (DCSF 2006) we are informed that: 'These notes show the stages in building up to long division through Years 4 to 6 – first long division TU ÷ U, extending to HTU ÷ U, then HTU ÷ TU, and then short division HTU ÷ U.' This progression seems to me to be somewhat 'logically challenged': why cover long division before short division? Surely, if children can successfully carry out a long division calculation using a procedure that produces a correct answer, then they can use that same procedure for short division – which is likely to involve an easier calculation. However, the *actual* five-part sequence of stages set out on subsequent pages is slightly more logical (although still questionable): mental division using partition; short division of TU ÷ U; expanded method for HTU ÷ U; short division of HTU ÷ U; and then long division.

Stage 1 Mental division using partition

It is recommended that children record mental division as illustrated in Figure 16.1.

$$87 \div 3 = (60 + 27) \div 3$$
$$= (60 \div 3) + (27 \div 3)$$
$$= 20 + 9$$
$$= 29$$

Figure 16.1

I see several conceptual difficulties with this suggestion, over and above the inappropriate formality of the notation, which is, after all, supposed to be the recommended recording for a *mental* calculation. The *Guidance Paper* (DCSF 2006: 17) informs us that 'Many children can partition and multiply with confidence. But this is not the case for division'. A reason given is that the correspondence to mental multiplication methods has not been sufficiently stressed. For me, the main problem concerns the limited distributivity of division. Multiplication is both left and right distributive over addition (and subtraction), whereas division is only right distributive. This means that, because $12 = 4 + 8$, then 7×12 can be calculated as $(7 \times 4) + (7 \times 8)$, and, because $7 = 3 + 4$, then 7×12 can be calculated as $(3 \times 12) + (4 \times 12)$, that is, either number can be partitioned. However, although $84 \div 7$ is equivalent to $(70 \div 7) + (14 \div 7)$, it is not equivalent to $(84 \div 4) + (84 \div 3)$. This situation suggests many opportunities for children to make inappropriate partitions: they need to remember that only the dividend (the number being divided) and not the divisor can be partitioned. Much work will need to be done to explore this aspect of division.

The second problem with this algorithm is that children are expected to be able to make non-standard partitions, such as $73 = 60 + 13$ or $563 = 400 + 150 + 13$. Ross (1989) has shown that children generally find this difficult (this is also discussed in Chapter 14 in the context of subtraction). Also, if the wrong partition is made, the result can be somewhat 'messy' (see Figure 16.2) even though (in theory) you should still get the correct answer.

$$87 \div 3 = (50 + 37) \div 3$$
$$= (50 \div 3) + (37 \div 3)$$
$$= 16\tfrac{2}{3} + 12\tfrac{1}{3}$$
$$= 29$$

Figure 16.2

Anghileri (2001) shows the workings of a child calculating $1256 \div 6$ by finding, separately, $1000 \div 6$, $200 \div 6$, $50 \div 6$ and $6 \div 6$. These work out, respectively, to 106 R2, 21 R2, 8 R2 and 1, and are then added to give 136 R6.

This requirement for a formal approach to mental calculation is found in the official recommendations for each of the four basic operations. I have argued in other chapters that this demands that children make a 'statement of intent' and ignores the fact that research suggests that children's jottings are – inevitably – more like a 'running commentary' (see Thompson, Chapters 14 and 15). I would also argue that the level of ability of a child able to correctly partition 81 into two parts each of which is exactly divisible by three is such that they would not need to write anything down, as they would be able to complete the calculation completely in their head. A more typical approach would be to:

- scrutinize the 81 (or even 82, 83, 84 . . .) and recognize that there is a 60 in there;
- divide the 60 by 3;
- jot down 20;
- take 60 from 81 (or 82, 83, 84 . . .);
- divide 21 (or 22, 23, 24 . . .) by 3;
- jot down 7 (or 7 remainder 1, 7 remainder 2, 8 . . .);
- add the two jotted numbers (20 and 7 . . .).

Stage 2 Short division of TU ÷ U

I have written elsewhere (Thompson 2003) about different interpretations of short division – both as a concept and as an algorithm. This *Guidance Paper* (DCSF 2006: 18) states that for the calculation 81 ÷ 3 the short division method is to be recorded as in Figures 16.3 and 16.4.

$$\frac{20 + \ \ 7}{3\overline{)60 + 21}}$$

Figure 16.3

This is then to be shortened to:

$$\frac{2\ 7}{3\overline{)8^2 1}}$$

Figure 16.4

We are informed that 'The carry digit "2" represents the 2 tens that have been exchanged for 20 ones' (p. 18).

Interestingly, this is the first time that the concept of 'exchanging' has been mentioned in the entire document, despite the fact that there is a detailed section on subtraction (see Thompson, Chapter 14). Written subtraction algorithms are often based on a model that involves base-ten materials and the exchange of 'flats' for 'longs' (hundreds for tens) and 'longs' for 'ones'.

In the 1970s the language of 'exchanging' in subtraction superseded that of 'borrowing' (although mathematics educators in the USA still use the latter). The subtraction method recommended in this document, however, is based on the concept of 're-partitioning' (although the word is never actually used). Consequently, the progression from the notation in Figure 16.3 to that in Figure 16.4 involves an unacknowledged conceptual shift from partitioning to exchanging. Given the difficulties that children experience with exchanging in subtraction, even when preparatory work has been done with base-ten materials (Hart 1989), it is difficult to believe that the recommended progression in division will be any more successful.

This progression also involves a shift from the quantity value aspect of place value (80 and 1) to the column value aspect (8 tens and 1 one) discussed in more detail in Chapter 14 by Thompson. However, this particular shift is slightly more complicated, in that children have to be able to partition 81 into $60 + 21$, as illustrated in Figure 16.3, and then switch to interpreting 81 as 6 tens and 21 ones. Also, as discussed above, the partition has to be such that both parts are known to be exactly divisible by three ($70 + 11$ or $50 + 31$ would not be particularly helpful). Given the research mentioned above (Ross 1989) that children have great difficulty making non-standard partitions such as $81 = 60 + 21$, it would also be useful to know whether children find the idea of 81 being equivalent to 6 tens and 21 ones difficult.

Stage 3 'Expanded' method for HTU ÷ U

The recommended method here is the one we have come to know as 'chunking' (or 'chunking down'), where multiples of the divisor are subtracted from the number to be divided, that is, the dividend) (see Figure 16.5).

$$
\begin{array}{r}
6\overline{)196} \\
-\ 60 \quad 6 \times 10 \\
\hline
136 \\
-\ 60 \quad 6 \times 10 \\
\hline
76 \\
-\ 60 \quad 6 \times 10 \\
\hline
16 \\
-\ 12 \quad 6 \times \ 2 \\
\hline
4 \qquad\ 32 \\
\text{Answer:} \qquad 32\,\text{R}4
\end{array}
$$

Figure 16.5

Having done some preliminary work on the development of estimation strategies, children are expected to progress to the following, more succinct notation:

$$6\overline{)196}$$
$$- 180 \quad 6 \times 30$$
$$\overline{\quad 16}$$
$$- \underline{12} \quad 6 \times \underline{2}$$
$$\overline{\quad 4} \qquad 32$$

Answer: 32 R4

Figure 16.6

The way in which the procedure is presented in the document gives the impression that it comes in just two forms: you either repeatedly subtract the smallest multiple of ten of the divisor or you subtract the largest. In fact, the strength of the chunking algorithm lies in its great potential for differentiation: it allows for a range of levels of sophistication in children's confidence and understanding, in that the less confident can remove small chunks; the more confident can take away larger chunks; and the most confident can subtract the maximum-sized chunks.

Stage 4 Short division of HTU ÷ U

In addition to the issues raised above concerning the introduction of short division in Stage 2, the following question is offered: why do we need to teach a conceptually difficult strategy for dividing a three-digit number by a single-digit number when the chunking method introduced in Stage 3 for solving three-digit by two-digit divisions is much easier to understand, allows for differentiation and is probably more effective?

Stage 5 Long division

For most children long division will be introduced in Year 6. The recommended method involves estimating to find the maximum amount to subtract initially, as in Stage 3, and then continuing with the standard chunking procedure (see Figure 16.7).

$$24\ \overline{)560}$$
$$20 - 480 \quad 24 \times 20$$
$$\overline{\quad 80}$$
$$3\ \ \underline{72} \quad 24 \times 3$$
$$\overline{\quad 8}$$

Answer: 23 R8

Figure 16.7

One reason offered for the rather strange positioning of the 20 and the 3 down the left-hand side is to keep the links with 'chunking' – although I would have thought that the notation down the right-hand side, and the calculation procedure itself might already be doing that! A second reason given is that it reduces the errors that tend to occur with the positioning of the first digit of the quotient. Because the first digit of the quotient is 2 – written as 20 on both the right- and the left-hand side in Figure 16.7 – I have difficulty in understanding what this talk of 'positioning' is all about. Also, as the answer is to be written at the bottom of the procedure, the extra inclusion of the 20 and the 3 down the left-hand side seems to be adding another level of potential confusion.

$$
\begin{array}{r}
23 \\
24\overline{)560} \\
-480 \\
\hline
80 \\
-72 \\
\hline
8
\end{array}
$$

Answer: 23 R8

Figure 16.8

The document then argues that the notation illustrated in Figure 16.8 is, in effect, the standard long division method. However, the language and thinking associated with the chunking method runs something like: *I need to find out how many 24s there are in 560. I know that there are ten of them in 240 and so there are twenty of them in 480. If I take this from 560 I get 80. Two 24s are 48, so four 24s are 96 – but this is too big. 48 plus 24 is 72, and 72 from 80 leaves 8. So, the answer is 20 and 3, that's 23, remainder 8.* On the other hand, the procedure involved when using the standard long division algorithm demands a very different way of thinking and reasoning. It utilizes a different vocabulary and a different aspect of place value: it involves a shift from quantity value to column value.

The patter associated with the standard algorithm goes something like: *24 into 5 doesn't go. 24 into 56 goes twice. Two 24s are 48, so write 48 under the 56 and subtract to leave 8. Write the 2 on the top line above the 6 of 560, and bring down the zero of 560 to make 80. Three 24s are 72. Write the 72 under the 80 and the 3 on the top line above the zero of 560. Subtracting 72 from 80 leaves 8, so the answer is 23 remainder 8.* I would agree that the resulting written work looks almost exactly like that in Figure 16.8 (except that there would be no zero after 48). However, the reasoning, the place value interpretation, the concepts underpinning the procedures and the accompanying patter are very different indeed. This suggests that there is not a particularly smooth transition from the language and reasoning associated with chunking to the language of the standard algorithm.

'Chunking down' or 'chunking up'?

The educational reasons given for the teaching of this algorithm (chunking down) appear to be sound: the method does not demand that children follow a prescribed set of steps in a specific order; the least able children can find the answer by subtracting small chunks, whereas the more confident can subtract larger chunks; because the children are in control of the size of the chunk they choose to subtract, the procedure provides a level of differentiation that is not possible with the standard algorithm. The examples shown in Figure 16.9 – which progress from the least to the most compact – illustrate a range of approaches to the calculation 977 ÷ 36 using chunking.

977	977	977	977	977	977
$\dfrac{-36}{941}$ 1	$\dfrac{-72}{905}$ 2	$\dfrac{-360}{617}$ 10	$\dfrac{-360}{617}$ 10	$\dfrac{-720}{257}$ 20	$\dfrac{-720}{257}$ 20
$\dfrac{-36}{905}$ 1	$\dfrac{-72}{833}$ 2	$\dfrac{-360}{257}$ 10	$\dfrac{-360}{257}$ 10	$\dfrac{-180}{77}$ 5	$\dfrac{-252}{5}$ 7
$\dfrac{-36}{869}$ 1	$\dfrac{-72}{761}$ 2	$\dfrac{-36}{221}$ 1	$\dfrac{-180}{77}$ 5	$\dfrac{-72}{5}$ 2	27 R5
$\dfrac{-36}{833}$ 1	$\dfrac{-72}{689}$ 2	$\dfrac{-36}{185}$ 1	$\dfrac{-72}{5}$ 2	27 R5	
. . . 27 R5	. . . 27 R5	. . . 27 R5	27 R5		

Figure 16.9

The more sophisticated the strategy (that is, the larger the chunks) the fewer subtractions are needed. However, a particular problem with the argument that one of the strengths of the procedure lies in the fact that children can remove chunks of any size that they choose is that the least confident children, when subtracting small chunks, as in the first example above, actually make 27 subtractions. This, of course, provides 27 opportunities for making a subtraction error, whereas the more confident children only make two, three or four subtractions. It is also likely to be the case that those children performing many subtractions are the very children who have difficulties with that particular operation.

Given that subtraction is more difficult than addition, it would seem sensible to try to develop an algorithm for division that depends on addition and multiplication; this method is called 'chunking up' or 'complementary multiplication'. Two different ways of introducing this procedure can be found in Thompson (2005). Inevitably, some preparatory work needs to be done to develop the prerequisite skills for this procedure and to build up children's confidence and competence with calculations involving smaller numbers. These prerequisite skills are doubling, halving, multiplying by 10, accurate addition and a good sense of the relative size of numbers.

Borthwick and Harcourt-Heath (2007) analysed the answers of 995 children on four Year 5 Qualifications and Curriculum Authority test questions. They repeated the analysis two years later using the same questions with a cohort of 1068 children. On the second occasion 28 per cent of the children achieved the correct answer on the division question – an increase of 7 per cent over the previous cohort. Interestingly, the number of successful children using the 'chunking up' strategy was greater by almost 50 per cent than the number of successful children using any other strategy.

Conclusion

An Ofsted report on the teaching of calculation in primary schools (Ofsted 2002: 3) states the following: 'However, at Key Stage 2 they [teachers] often overlook the importance of linking pupils' mental strategies to the introduction of expanded and compact written method.' This belief in a natural progression from mental methods to compact (standard) algorithms permeates many National Numeracy Strategy (NNS), Primary National Strategy (PNS), Qualifications and Curriculum Development Agency (QCDA) and Her Majesty's Inspectorate (HMI) publications. However, the arguments presented in this chapter and Chapters 14 and 15 suggest that this progression is not as natural as it first appears to be, and that more thought needs to be given to – and more research carried out about – the 'seamless links' suggested in the *Guidance Paper* and elsewhere.

Moreover, there is too much emphasis in the document on advancing children to compact methods for all four basic operations as quickly as possible. For the vast majority of children it would be more useful to focus particularly on algorithms that, unlike compact algorithms, have in-built variability that allows for the important principle of differentiation. The following algorithms fit neatly into this category: front-end addition, subtraction by complementary addition, multiplication by the grid method and division by chunking ('up' or 'down') (see Thompson 1996).

Another important aspect of the discussion is that often what appears to be logically or mathematically sound is not necessarily always pedagogically sound. Many of the recommendations in the *Guidance Paper* are made from the perspective of the experienced, mathematically literate adult, without taking into account the available research findings about how children develop calculation strategies and learn written procedures. This situation obtains particularly with reference to the final step in the recommendations for each of the four basic arithmetical operations, when children have to complete the progression to the compact (that is, standard) method. In each case this step involves a major shift in the way the digits in the numbers are interpreted: a shift from treating them as quantities to treating them as digits in columns. Work needs to be done on ways of helping children to make this important step.

In a seminal article written more than 30 years ago, Plunkett (1979: 4) argued that the reasons for teaching standard algorithms were out of date then, and that their use led to *frustration, unhappiness and a deteriorating attitude to mathematics.*

Plus ça change, plus c'est la même chose!

References

Anghileri, J. (2001) Intuitive approaches, mental strategies and standard algorithms, in J. Anghileri (ed.) *Principles and Practices in Arithmetic Teaching.* Buckingham: Open University Press.

Anghileri, J. and Beishuizen, M. (1998) Counting, chunking and the division algorithm, *Mathematics in School,* 27(1): 2–4.

Borthwick, A. and Harcourt-Heath, M. (2007) Calculation strategies used by Year 5 children, *Proceedings of the British Society for Research into Learning Mathematics,* 27(1): 12–17.

DCSF (Department for Children, Schools and Families) (2006) *Primary Framework for Literacy and Mathematics – Guidance Paper – Calculation.* http://nationalstrategies.standards.dcsf.gov.uk/node/47364 (accessed March 2010).

DfES (Department for Education and Skills) (2006) *Primary Framework for Literacy and Mathematics.* Norwich: DfES.

DfES (Department for Education and Skills) (2007) *Practice Guidance for the Early Years Foundation Stage.* Nottingham: DfES.

Hart, K.M. (1989) Place value: subtraction, in D. Johnson (ed.) *Children's Mathematical Frameworks 8–13.* London: NFER-Nelson.

Ofsted (Office for Standards in Education) (2002) *Teaching of Calculation in Primary Schools.* HMI 461. http://www.ofsted.gov.uk/Ofsted-home/Publications-and-research/Browse-all-by/Education/Curriculum/Mathematics/Primary/Teaching-of-calculation-in-primary-schools (accessed March 2010).

Plunkett, S. (1979) Decomposition and all that rot, *Mathematics in School,* 8(3): 2–5.

Ross, S. (1989) Parts, wholes and place value: a developmental view, *Arithmetic Teacher,* 36(6): 47–51.

Thompson, I. (1996) User-friendly calculation algorithms, *Mathematics in School,* 25(5): 42–5. www.ianthompson.pi.dsl.pipex.com (accessed March 2010).

Thompson, I. (2003) United we stand; divided we fall, *Mathematics in School,* 32(3): 21–3. www.ianthompson.pi.dsl.pipex.com (accessed March 2010).

Thompson, I. (2005) Division by complementary multiplication, *Mathematics in School,* 34(5): 5–7. www.ianthompson.pi.dsl.pipex.com (accessed March 2010).

SECTION 5
Special needs issues

The final section of this edited collection comprises two chapters that address issues at both ends of the attainment spectrum: one is written by members of the Every Child Counts team and focuses on intervention; the other examines a range of issues pertaining to that group of children identified as the 'gifted and talented'.

In 2008, the Williams Review recommended that a new Wave 3 numeracy intervention be developed to provide one-to-one, teacher-led support for those children in Key Stage 1 who had the greatest difficulties with mathematics. The outcome of this recommendation was Numbers Count, a new numeracy intervention that was launched at the start of the school year 2008–09. Chapter 17 is written by Sylvia Dunn, Louise Matthews and Nick Dowrick, members of the Every Child Counts team that developed this intervention. The authors describe the background to and development of the Numbers Count intervention explaining how it makes use of diagnostic assessment and multi-sensory resources, and involves close liaison with the children's parents and class teachers. The results of the first cohort are discussed, and the authors argue that their findings have implications that are relevant to all classroom teachers as well as those working in one-to-one interventions.

In the final chapter, John Threlfall addresses a few questions about the concept of the 'gifted and talented', by attempting to identify the nature of the issue, and by asking who the gifted and talented children actually are, how those identified in this way appear to learn, what their specific needs might be and how we might cater for these needs. Several pages are devoted to the important issue of 'acceleration or enrichment'.

17 Numbers Count: developing a national approach to early intervention

Sylvia Dunn, Louise Matthews and Nick Dowrick

Introduction

Every year since the National Numeracy Strategy was launched in England in 1999, about 6 per cent of children have achieved below National Curriculum Level 3 in mathematics when they leave primary school; this means that about 35,000 11-year-olds have been at least four years behind national expectations every year (DCSF 2008). If children's difficulties in mathematics become entrenched, they generally persist through secondary school and into adulthood and have a serious impact on life chances. Adults with the lowest level of numeracy skills are the most likely to be unemployed or to have low incomes, to have long-term health problems including depression, and to be in prison (Gross 2009); their own children are also likely to struggle with numeracy so that problems pass from one generation to another (Moser 1999). Most of these problems are more strongly associated with low numeracy than with low literacy. So it is important that children who fall behind in mathematics are supported to 'get back on track' early in their school careers and that they develop the skills that will enable them to continue to learn mathematics effectively thereafter.

There has been growing international interest since the 1990s in the use of intensive intervention programmes to help children who have difficulties with mathematics. Dowker (2004: v) examined a variety of interventions and concluded that: 'Children's arithmetical difficulties are highly susceptible to intervention. Individualized work with children who are falling behind in arithmetic has a significant impact on their performance.' She recommended that interventions are best carried out at a very early stage in a child's mathematics education, both to correct any misconceptions that the child may have acquired and to avoid the child developing an anxiety that could impede further learning.

In England, the Primary National Strategy (DfES 2005) introduced the 'waves' model of teaching to suggest how interventions might be organized in school. This can be summarized as:

> Wave 1   'Quality first teaching' in a daily mathematics lesson for all children;
> Wave 2   Targeted small-group interventions for children who are expected to be able to catch up with their peers;
> Wave 3   More intensive, individualized or specialized support for children for whom Waves 1 and 2 are insufficient.

A variety of Wave 3 mathematics intervention programmes were used in schools throughout the country in the early 2000s (reviewed in Dowker 2004; DCSF 2008), without any one scheme predominating. In literacy, on the other hand, the Every Child a Reader initiative began to achieve remarkable success on a national scale from 2005 in tackling underachievement through the use of the Reading Recovery intervention.

In 2008, the *Independent Review of Mathematics Teaching in Early Years Settings and Primary Schools* (the Williams Review) (DCSF 2008) recommended that a new Wave 3 numeracy intervention should be developed in England to provide one-to-one, teacher-led support for children in Key Stage 1 who had the greatest difficulties with mathematics, based on the model of Every Child a Reader. Unlike Every Child a Reader, however, which was built around the long-established Reading Recovery intervention originally developed in New Zealand (Clay 2005), Williams advised that the new Every Child Counts initiative should not adopt an existing numeracy or mathematics intervention because he did not feel that any one scheme exhibited all the features essential for success. He recommended that the new intervention should make use of diagnostic assessment and multi-sensory resources, and involve full liaison with children's parents and class teachers.

The Every Child Counts team researched a large number of existing interventions, including three that were particularly commended by Williams:

- Mathematics Recovery (Wright 2008) was first developed in Australia in the 1990s, drawing on original research into mathematics learning in the USA. It was particularly successful in the north-west of England.
- Numeracy Recovery (Hackney Learning Trust, unpublished) began in London in 2002 by adapting the principles and practices of Reading Recovery to mathematics. It successfully spread to a number of authorities in the south east.
- Multi-Sensory Mathematics (Education Leeds, unpublished), was started in Leeds in 2006 as a collaboration with the publishers of

Numicon materials. Its approaches were successfully adapted in a number of other authorities.

The outcome of the Every Child Counts team's research and Williams's recommendations was Numbers Count, a new numeracy intervention that was launched at the start of the school year 2008–09. Its diagnostic assessment drew upon the Numeracy Recovery approach of a wide-ranging, confidence-building exploration of what a child already knew, and was informed by Mathematics Recovery's identification of key aspects of early number knowledge that should be assessed. A problem-based approach to teaching and learning rooted in a constructivist model of learning (Wright 2000) was adopted, as in Mathematics Recovery, and was influenced by Numeracy Recovery's emphasis on creativity and stimulus and by the Multi-Sensory Mathematics lesson structure and use of multi-sensory resources to develop children's concepts of number. Strategies for regular liaison and communication between Numbers Count teachers and children's parents and teachers, including invitations to observe Numbers Count lessons, were developed after learning from the experiences of both Mathematics Recovery and Numeracy Recovery teachers.

'Numbers Count' in action

Children as learners

The Numbers Count programme is underpinned by a belief in a social constructivist model of learning. Children are seen as active learners who seek to make sense of their world and who try to build on what they know and believe already when presented with new mathematical experiences. Reasons for adopting a social constructivist model of learning include:

- Mathematics is based on logico-mathematical reasoning. This reasoning cannot be transmitted from one person to another but has to be developed by each individual in their own mind; the importance of developing logico-mathematical reasoning is often overlooked when teaching children with difficulties. Nuñes et al. (2007) carried out a small-scale project with low-attaining Year 1 pupils which showed that teaching aimed at helping children develop these understandings can have lasting benefits on the attainment of the children involved.
- Successful learners are autonomous and can take responsibility for their own learning; children with difficulties in mathematics may have become accustomed to a passive role in learning and to reliance on the teacher or teaching assistant.

- Children's understanding develops when they can exchange viewpoints and think critically about their own ideas in relation to other people's views. Although Numbers Count is a one-to-one intervention, the teacher engages the child in dialogue which encourages them to critically examine their own beliefs about mathematics. One outcome of the intervention is that children are seen to participate more readily in discussions within the classroom.

A key principle of Numbers Count is that children learn mathematics through solving problems. This does not mean that they should be constantly completing mathematics puzzles or word problems but that they are given tasks that are, for them, challenging and require them to think in reaching a solution. Activities should be pitched just beyond what the child can already do comfortably. This principle also underpins other successful intervention initiatives such as Mathematics Recovery and Reading Recovery.

Diagnostic assessment

The key to the success of Numbers Count is the personalized teaching programme, delivered by a highly skilled teacher. No two children have the same skills, strengths, needs and ways of seeing the mathematical world. In order to meet the unique needs of each child, the individualized teaching programme can only be designed after a detailed assessment of each child's mathematics learning. Diagnostic assessment to inform teaching is a critical ingredient of the intervention. Wright (2008) argues that a detailed assessment of children's current knowledge and strategies is an essential first step in the development of a successful early mathematics intervention programme. The Numbers Count entry assessment phase includes a comprehensive diagnostic assessment that lasts for approximately seven days. It has two purposes:

1 To help the teacher to find out more about the children: to enable the teacher to find out more about *what* the children can do and *how* they do it; to find out which aspects of mathematics they are competent with; to find out which aspects of mathematics they are confident with and willing to 'have a go' with; to find out about what helps them to learn and what equipment, models and images they are familiar and competent with; to listen to the mathematical language they use, and how they explain their thinking and the reasons for choices made; and to find out more about their attitudes to mathematics.
2 To help the children to make a positive start to the intervention: to provide immediate success for them; to help the children to 'know what they know', so that they can be helped to build on this know-

ledge and understanding; to establish good relationships and expectations and a safe learning environment where the children are confident to take risks with learning; to settle the children into the programme, familiarizing them with the environment, the teacher and the resources; and to establish that the sessions will be enjoyable and fun.

The diagnostic assessment is designed to enable teachers to develop an in-depth analysis of the child's mathematical understanding. It provides opportunities for exploration of how the children make sense of the mathematical world and how they have constructed mathematical meaning. During this series of lessons the teacher deliberately avoids teaching any new skills or concepts and stays with what the child already knows how to do. This is similar to the Reading Recovery intervention, in which 'Roaming around the known' is used by the teacher to establish what the child can do well and how the child responds to different tasks. As Clay (2005: 33) argues: 'The most important reason for "Roaming around the known" is that it requires the teacher to stop teaching from her preconceived ideas. She has to work in ways that will suit each child, working with what he is able to do.'

The teacher has to learn to listen carefully to the child, to suppress the need to start teaching when misconceptions are displayed and above all, not to jump in when the child is thinking – even if, like many teachers, she is a 'compulsive silence breaker'! The teacher has to begin the diagnostic phase with the underlying belief that the child is trying to make sense of the world and to create meaning from experiences. If you begin with the assumption that the child does not construct knowledge but simply absorbs (or fails to absorb) it from others, then you are unlikely to realize that what seems deficient and possibly bizarre, nevertheless serves some useful function for the child, and may even result from sensible thought (Ginsburg 1997). For example, when one child was using toy cars to make pairs of numbers with a total of four, he partitioned the four cars into two sets, one containing one car and one containing three cars. When asked how many cars he had altogether he said 'thirteen'. One may conclude from this that the child knew nothing about addition or was guessing. Further investigation revealed that the child was trying to apply a sensible strategy from a previous encounter with partitioning where a 1 and a 3 came together to make 13.

It is important during the diagnostic phase to investigate children's answers to problems and ways of thinking in order to see how the problem makes sense to the child. Otherwise, according to Ginsburg (1997: 118), you will 'miss what is of value in what the child says and the child is unlikely to say much of value'. One strategy that has proved extremely successful for diagnostic assessment is the use of the puppet as a 'third person in the room'. This seems to enable the child to reveal more about their thinking and the strategies they are using. One child had already demonstrated that he could orally count back accurately from 15 to 1, but when asked to count back from 20 he consistently responded with 20, 90, 80, 70, 60, 50, 40, 30, 12, 11, 10, 9, 8, 7, 6, 5, 4, 3, 2, 1. A puppet was used to make some counting errors for the child to identify and correct. To establish that the child understood the task a simple sequence was used initially.

Puppet:	I'm going to count forwards in ones from 3.
Child:	OK.
Puppet:	3, 4, 5, 6, 8, 9 . . .
Child:	STOP you did it wrong! (Interrupting confidently)
Puppet:	What did I do?
Child:	You missed out seven!
Puppet:	Can you show me how to do it?
Child:	3, 4, 5, 6, 7, 8, 9, 10
Puppet:	I'm going to count backwards from fifty in tens.
Child:	That will be too hard for you.
Puppet:	50, 40, 30, 12, 11, 10, 9
Child:	Stop (Interrupting hesitantly)
Puppet:	Why did you make me stop?
Child:	Because he went from 30 to 20 to 19, err . . . 9.
Teacher:	What should come after 30?
Child:	40.
Teacher:	When you're going backwards.
Child:	12.
Teacher:	12?
Child:	No, 20.
Teacher:	You do it for him then.
Child:	50, 40, 30, 20, 10, 0
Puppet:	You are really good at counting.
Child:	You mix up 20 and 12 and I sometimes do that.
Puppet:	Can you count backwards in ones from 20?
Child:	Yes 20, 90, 80, 70, 60, 50, 40, 30, 12, 11, 10, 9, 8, 7, 6, 5, 4, 3, 2, 1. I think that's right or I might have done it again.

By drawing attention to the errors of the puppet, the child had the opportunity to think about his own counting errors and to verbalize them without having his own errors highlighted by the teacher. The teacher could still ask questions to probe the child's understanding and was able to find out more about the child's knowledge and understanding of counting. The child could correct the puppet when it was a counting sequence that he was confident with, but he was more hesitant in the counting back in tens from 50.

Multi-sensory teaching

Numbers Count is an intervention in which the adult and the child establish a 'co-construction' of meanings through scaffolding children's learning, using carefully planned interaction and appropriate resources. The Numbers Count teacher establishes which types of resources would most effectively support each individual child in constructing knowledge and understanding of mathematics and then considers the types of structured adult interaction that would accelerate development. Children in the programme almost invariably need to develop a concept of number. It is actually quite difficult to define a concept for 'five' and it is (mercifully) not necessary that we define 'five' in order for children to develop a useful understanding of what adults refer to when they use the word (Wing 2006). For example:

- we can count to five;
- we can give a child five sweets;
- we can point to a pattern on a domino;
- we can introduce a structured image for five;
- we can tell a child he is five;
- we can sing about five speckled frogs.

We can also talk about and show 'one less than six' and 'one more than four' and 2 + 3. In these and infinitely more varied ways we can keep offering children experiences that will link with each other in their mind.

Through common language and through increasingly powerful numerical insights children will construct a concept image of 'five'. The concept image is something non-verbal associated in our mind with concept name. It can be a visual representation or a collection of impressions or experiences and will vary between individuals (Vinner 1992). Numbers Count uses structured imagery including Numicon to develop concept images. Numicon is a form of apparatus that lends itself to multi-sensory teaching, integrating the auditory, visual and kinaesthetic modalities. The shapes represent numbers in a series of structured patterns.

This resource enables children to see relationships between numbers and to see numbers as objects, not just the end of a count. If a child only experiences numbers through counting, then he knows that the last number word used tells him how many things he has counted, that is, he sees numbers as adjectives (describing the set) but not as nouns. Gray (2008) explores this further by referring to numbers as processes and concepts and by developing the notion of the 'procept'. He states that children who are stuck on count-all strategies for addition are stuck on seeing the process embedded in each symbol but that children who count-on are treating the first number as an object (or concept) and the second number as a process, that is, seeing numbers as procepts. Children cannot begin to develop counting-on strategies until they develop secure number concepts and this development can be enhanced through the use of structured imagery, which helps children to develop concept images.

Thompson (2008: 99) also explores the complexity of counting-on by describing it as the cardinal/ordinal switch followed by the ordinal/cardinal switch: 'the cardinal number 5 in 5 + 6 is transformed into an ordinal number so that the count can be continued to 11, then the ordinal number 11 is converted back to a cardinal quantity to give the answer'. It appears that a child, who can only see numbers as ordinal, cannot be expected to master the complex strategy of counting-on until he can see numbers as cardinal. The use of structured apparatus can support children in developing cardinality as they develop concept images of the numbers and start to see them as wholes.

As in all teaching, the success depends on how resources are used not just on the resources themselves. Coltman et al. (2002) used the notion of scaffolding and working within the child's 'zone of proximal development' in a study that showed how structured adult intervention increased the effectiveness of learning and the development of secure and transferable concepts. Even though they acknowledged the importance of free play, they stated that children alone cannot discover all the important knowledge through manipulation of resources; they learned more effectively through carefully structured joint activity with experienced others. The Numbers Count teacher's role in developing understanding of mathematics is to plan these activities to help the child to build up connections between new experiences and previous learning. Learning without making connections can be referred to as rote learning or learning without understanding. Children need to build up a complex network of connections between language, symbols, concrete materials and pictures (Haylock and Cockburn 2008) in order to understand a mathematical concept (see Delaney, Chapter 5).

Partnership with parents and carers

Developing a partnership with the child's parents and carers is essential in enabling the child to make progress while they are on the Numbers Count programme and in helping them to continue to learn in the future. This can, however, be difficult for teachers to achieve as the parents and carers of these children include many seen by the schools involved as hard to reach. Parents are welcomed into Numbers Count lessons and home–school books are used to encourage dialogue between the parent and the teacher (see Winter, Chapter 9). Children are given games and other activities to take home to play with their parents and siblings. The purpose of these is to encourage parents to talk to their children about what they are doing in mathematics and to enable them to enjoy sharing games with them, not to turn parents into teachers. The activities sent home are personalized both to the child and to the family so that they are more likely to be used at home. One Numbers Count teacher found that the child's mother only really had time to play with the child when she was bathing her. She devised a waterproof game to practise number bonds that was sent home and used successfully with the child.

Outcomes in the first year of Numbers Count

In its first year (2008–09), 2621 Year 2 children took part in Numbers Count, supported by 207 teachers in 27 local authorities across England. They were chosen by their schools because they had the lowest mathematical achievement in their class: their number ages were an average of 11 months behind their chronological ages when they began Numbers Count (see Table 17.1).

This means that in only their second year of formal schooling they had already fallen about a year behind their classmates. Their teachers predicted that, without specialist help, the children would soon fall even further behind and none of them would meet the national target of National Curriculum Level 2 in mathematics at the end of Key Stage 1.

The children received an average of 40 individual, half-hour Numbers Count lessons in a term, including their initial diagnostic assessments. They took standardized numeracy tests on entry and exit to the programme, and follow-up tests three months and six months later. Table 17.1 indicates that their number ages had caught up with their chronological ages by the time they exited from the programme. In other words, 20 hours of one-to-one support in one term not only stopped the lowest-achieving children from falling further behind but also enabled them to make 14 months of progress and to catch up with their classmates. Not only this, but they also continued to make good progress through their normal class lessons in the months after exiting Numbers Count, so that in their follow-up tests their number ages had moved

Table 17.1 Number ages and chronological ages

	Programme entry	Programme exit	3-month follow-up	6-month follow-up
Number age	70.0	83.5	86.4	87.9
Chronological age	80.6	83.5	85.3	86.7
Number age – chronological age	−10.6	0	+1.1	+1.2

All ages shown in months.

over a month ahead of their chronological ages. This progress was reflected in the Key Stage 1 assessments at the end of Year 2: 72 per cent of the children who had completed a Numbers Count programme were assessed as achieving National Curriculum Level 2 in mathematics, despite having been originally predicted to achieve no more than Level 1.

Children's confidence and attitudes towards mathematics also improved significantly. In an attitude survey specifically designed for Numbers Count, 89 per cent of the children were judged by their teachers and parents to have grown more confident in mathematics by the end of the programme, with the biggest gain coming in children's willingness to take part in whole-class lessons and to put their hands up to answer questions. The changes are best described by the children, their parents and teachers themselves:

> They'll probably be easy for me.
> (A, who hardly dared speak to her Numbers Count teacher at first)

> Let's do maths for two hours.
> (B, who had said he hated mathematics when he entered Numbers Count)

> I can't believe how much C has developed. She really enjoys school now. She never seemed to talk before and now she is so excited when she talks about her day in school.
> (C's mother)

> D has developed in his confidence. He used to be very shy and is now expressing himself clearly. He is alert and can say how much money I give him for his pocket money (I can't cheat him out of that any more!). His concentration has improved vastly. He used to sit at the back of his class and didn't want to join in and now he wants to put his hand up and be the first. His younger brother is working with him and is learning from him.
> (D's father)

> E used to physically hide behind other children so she wouldn't have to answer questions in class. Now she puts her hand up.
> (E's teacher)

> F's mam used to have to bring her to school in her pyjamas. But since Numbers Count she gets out of bed to go to school happily.
> (F's head teacher)

Implications and conclusions

The experiences of those working in the Numbers Count programme in its first year have confirmed Dowker's finding that numerical difficulties are 'highly susceptible to intervention' (Dowker 2004), and have shown that children can make dramatic progress in both attainment and attitude in a short time with appropriate intervention. The programme also has implications that are relevant to classroom teachers as well as those working in one-to-one intervention. The first of these is that time spent on assessing children's ways of thinking and working in mathematics is vital in enabling the teacher to scaffold children's learning most effectively. A teacher working with a class of up to 30 children will clearly not be able to spend lengthy periods of time working one to one assessing all the children in depth, and this level of assessment is probably unnecessary for the majority of children. What teachers can do, however, is encourage children to talk to them about mathematics, and to *listen* to them, not in order to identify 'wrong' answers and put them right, but to enter more fully into the children's minds so that they can build on the children's strengths (see Ryan and Williams, Chapter 11).

A second issue for teachers is to consider the extent to which children who are perceived as successful at mathematics may be learning procedures without developing matching mathematical understanding. This can lead to children experiencing difficulties in mathematics later as each procedure has to be memorized individually because they cannot make conceptual links with what they have learned already. Before they begin a Numbers Count programme, children have often learned some facts and procedures but are not able to use these as they lack a real understanding. For example, one child was able to identify odd and even numbers accurately as long as he could see the number line used in every classroom in the school. On this even numbers were red and odd numbers were blue; he could not identify any numbers as odd or even when this was out of sight. Another child identified odd numbers as 'the ones you whisper'. In both cases the child had no concept of why numbers were odd or even but had simply learned a strategy for giving correct answers. Using resources which enable children to construct an image of what makes a number odd or even rather than focusing on ways of helping children remember them simply as a sequence would have helped these children to develop understanding as well as a limited strategy for responding to questions.

Lessons from Numbers Count should not be seen as relevant only to teachers and teaching assistants working with very low attaining children. Feedback from Numbers Count teachers and head teachers is that it is relevant to *all* children.

References

Clay, M. (2005) *Literacy Lessons Designed for Individuals. Part One: Why? When? and How?* Auckland: Heinemann.

Coltman, P., Petyaeva, D. and Anghileri, J. (2002) Scaffolding learning through meaningful tasks and adult interaction, *Early Years*, 22(1): 39–49.

DCSF (Department for Children, Schools and Families) (2008) *Independent Review of Mathematics Teaching in Early Years Settings and Primary Schools* (Williams Review). Nottingham: DCSF. http://publications.teachernet.gov.uk/eOrderingDownload/Williams%20Mathematics.pdf (accessed March 2010).

DfES (Department for Education and Skills) (2005) *Supporting Children with Gaps in their Mathematical Understanding*. London: DfES.

Dowker, A. (2004) *What Works for Children with Mathematical Difficulties?* London: DfES.

Ginsburg, H.P. (1997) *Entering the Child's Mind: The Clinical Interview in Psychological Research and Practice*. Cambridge: Cambridge University Press.

Gray, E. (2008) Compressing the counting process: strength from the flexible interpretation of symbols, in I. Thompson (ed.) *Teaching and Learning Early Number*, 2nd edn. Maidenhead: Open University Press.

Gross, J. (2009) *The Long Term Costs of Numeracy Difficulties*. London: Every Child a Chance Trust.

Haylock, D. and Cockburn, A. (2008) *Understanding Mathematics for Young Children*, 2nd edn. London: Sage Publications.

Moser, C. (1999) *Improving Literacy and Numeracy – a Fresh Start: The Report of the Working Group Chaired by Sir Claus Moser*. London: DfES.

Nuñes, T., Bryant, P., Evans, D. et al. (2007) The contribution of logical reasoning to the learning of mathematics in primary school, *British Journal of Developmental Psychology*, 25(1): 147–66.

Thompson, I. (2008) From counting to deriving number facts, in I. Thompson (ed.) *Teaching and Learning Early Number*, 2nd edn. Maidenhead: Open University Press.

Vinner, S. (1992) The role of definitions in the teaching and learning of mathematics, in D. Tall (ed.) *Advanced Mathematical Thinking*, Dordrecht: Kluwer Academic.

Wing, T. (2006) *Numicon: A Clear Image for Mathematics*. Newhaven: Numicon.

Wright, R.J. (2000) Professional development in recovery education, in L. Steffe and P. Thompson (eds) *Radical Constructivism in Action: Building on the Pioneering Work of Ernst Von Glasersfeld*. New York: Routledge Falmer.

Wright, R.J. (2008) Interview-based assessment of early number knowledge, in I. Thompson (ed.) *Teaching and Learning Early Number*, 2nd edn. Maidenhead: Open University Press.

18 The 'gifted and talented'

John Threlfall

Introduction

In this chapter I address five questions about children who are 'gifted and talented' mathematically: the nature of the issue; who these gifted and talented children actually are; how those identified in this way appear to learn; what their specific needs might be; and how we might cater for these needs.

1 What is the issue?

All primary teachers will be able to think of at least one example of a child who has stood out as mathematically 'gifted' – the 4-year-old who is found rummaging in a basket of nursery 'wellies', looking at the sizes on their soles to find a matching pair that will fit them; the 7-year-old who spontaneously extends an activity to find 'numbers that add to 10' into mixed numbers that involve fractions; the 11-year-old who toys with ideas of infinity when dividing using a calculator; and so on.

It is often asserted that the needs of such children are not well met by the usual provision for mathematics in the classroom (Koshy et al. 2009). Anecdotally, many primary teachers in the formal stages following the Foundation Stage admit from time to time to feeling guilty about children in their class who they feel have not been 'stretched' as much as they should have been. For example, they may feel that they tend to give just occupying activities to the children who finish work early, rather than activities that form part of a properly structured provision shaped to their individual needs.

In policy terms, as well as the invocation to meet all students' needs, there is often reference to the importance to the future of the country of a good supply of creative scientists, engineers and mathematicians (Koshy et al. 2009) and the value to the school of having the best students meet their potential in terms of achievements. In the English context, the policy overtones are evident in the gifted and talented section of the Department for Children, Schools and Families standards site (DCSF 2009). However, in this chapter I focus on the classroom issue – what is the best way to meet the needs of the children who are most talented in mathematics?

This is partly an organizational issue – is it better to identify a group of children and give them extra provision in withdrawal groups, where the identified children are taken out of their classes, or is it better to deal with them in the whole class context, through 'differentiation'? It is easier in some ways to deal with a small group of children taken out of their class, and this may boost their self-esteem, but if they feel singled out and isolated from their friends, then otherwise excellent activities will not lead to the hoped-for benefits.

The alternative, differentiation in the whole-class context, can sometimes be achieved by giving the same mathematics starting point to everyone, and, through differentiated responses to it, meet the needs of all (see Ollerton, Chapter 6). Piggott (2004: 9) claims that many of the resources on the NRICH website (www.nrich.maths.org), which is one of the most extensive sources of activities for gifted mathematics students, can be used in this way, as they have 'something to offer pupils of nearly all abilities'. She calls them 'low threshold–high ceiling' tasks.

More often, however, differentiation for the gifted is achieved by giving them different activities to do that are felt to be more suited to their needs. A particular approach related to this is 'compacting' – in which the gifted spend less time on basic curriculum coverage in order to have time to do additional, more challenging, activities.

The other aspect of the issue of how to meet the needs of the most able in mathematics concerns what kind of mathematical provision to offer. Is it better to keep gifted and talented children working on the standard mathematics curriculum, and allow them to move ahead of their peers to do the work that is normally done by older students (usually called 'acceleration') or is it better to give them challenging activities that remain related to the curriculum for that age group, for example, more problem solving, or exploration of relationships to deepen understanding (usually called 'enrichment')?

2 Who are the gifted and talented?

Students who are gifted and talented in mathematics are fairly readily identifiable in the abstract, but it is not so easy to identify exactly who should be included in such a group in any particular class. What criteria should be used? Should it be about performance or potential? Should test scores be used, for example, NFER tests, national assessment (SATs) results, and so on, or should children be selected because of a perceived insightfulness, skill in mathematical problem solving or feel for mathematical pattern? Koshy (2003) suggests that teachers might use a fluid and iterative approach based on observing children's mathematical behaviour, using indicators such as speed of reasoning, flexibility of thinking, ability to generalize, ability to work with abstract ideas and to recognize and use the mathematical structure of problems.

There are different possible criteria, and this poses an issue for selection. There may be some obvious candidates who score well on all points, but there will be others who seem by some considerations to be appropriate, but be excluded by others. As Koshy et al. (2009) report, primary teachers are reluctant to use the label 'gifted' for children who do not perform well in tests, but doing well in tests may just reflect reasonable levels of ability supported by hard work and focused teaching (after all, that is how standards are expected to continue to rise, not by creating a greater number of gifted children).

There is some evidence for the validity of selecting on the basis of potential rather than looking always at achievement. For example, in a project reported in Koshy et al. (2009) teachers selected students based on criteria developed from the qualities identified by Krutetskii (1976) as typical of students who are very able in mathematics. And although it was found that many of these students were not among those who had performed well in formal tests, and were not initially as fast or fluent with numbers as many people would expect able students to be, they then justified their selection (and the criteria) by becoming fluent quickly within the project.

However, the procedure of identifying children first, and looking second for suitable provision for them is not necessarily the best one, as it may be difficult to find criteria that will identify a sufficiently homogenous group to make a particular kind of special provision appropriate to meeting their needs. An alternative approach is to decide first what additional provision will be made, and then select children who would benefit from it. Very different groups might be formed, depending, for example, on whether an 'acceleration' or 'enrichment' approach is to be used. An extension of this approach is to offer the additional provision to a wide range of children and see who responds well to it.

Whatever procedures are used, though, the process is inevitably based on a number of assumptions, and so it is sensible to keep under review both the different provision being offered and the membership of the group receiving it.

3 What are the students who are 'gifted and talented' like, as learners?

From the comparative studies of children reviewed in Steiner and Carr (2003) and the work of Shore and Kanevsky (1993), it seems that gifted learners – in any subject – differ from their peers by:

- having a broader and more interconnected knowledge base;
- being quicker at solving problems, while spending more time planning;
- being more efficient at representing and categorizing problems;
- having more elaborated procedural knowledge;
- being more flexible in their use of strategies;
- preferring complex, challenging problems;
- being more sophisticated in their meta-cognition, including self regulation.

In mathematics in particular, Krutetskii (1976: 332–40) identified a number of elements of advanced mathematical thinking, through an extensive study of students of different abilities in Soviet Russia. Only some of these are said to be identifiable among primary age children, chiefly:

- the inclination to look for relationships between elements of a problem;
- a tendency to generalize from the particular case to a general rule;
- a willingness to be flexible in adopting different ways to approach problems.

Krutetskii (1976: 331) characterizes these traits as the 'embryonic forms' of more advanced abilities – leading later to the ability to curtail reasoning, to having a 'mathematical memory' of generalized forms, and striving for economy and rationality in solutions. He also believes that what is shown at this age 'largely depends on the conditions of instruction'. However, this is not to say that the qualities are *created* by instruction, more that there are lines of development, progress through which is significantly affected by instruction. This is a perspective on what Shore and Kanevsky (1993: 134) call the 'developmental controversy' – whether the abilities of the most able are 'merely precocity' or 'reflect fundamental differences in thinking processes'. Freeman (1998) observes that how the gifted are taught should be profoundly affected by the answer to this question.

The students who are characterized as gifted and talented in mathematics are often successful in mathematical tasks that are usually seen as more appropriate for older students. The question is whether that is essentially all they are doing – acting mathematically ahead of their age. There are different views about this, but evidence is hard to come by. In a rare example, Threlfall and Hargreaves (2008) report a study in which the same problems were given to 9-year-old children identified by their teachers as gifted in mathematics and to average ability (middle set) 13-year-old students, and found that the same methods and approaches were used by each sample.

According to Ericsson et al. (2007), there is no evidence for innate differences, and all actual differences in achievement can be accounted for by greater practice, and so should be called 'expertise' rather than 'giftedness'. Each of the observed differences between the 'gifted' and the 'average' – as highlighted in the bullet point lists above – can also be said to be characteristics of expertise. For example, making more reference to what they already know when solving problems, rather than just using what is presented as information, is symptomatic of those who are thought of as experts (Ericsson et al. 2007) as well as those described as gifted. If this is correct, the gifted are different from their peers not because of a special internal 'giftedness' quality but because they are precocious.

That is not to say that innate elements have no part to play, because, as Koshy et al. (2009) observe, there may be inborn characteristics that are favourable to the development of mathematical abilities, propensities which, for example, might be manifested in primary age children as an interest in numbers and a pleasure in playing with shapes, which in effect make them want to practise more. This then could lead to a relatively spontaneous or easy acquisition of mathematics that for other students is a hard-won product of instruction (and which some never learn).

Another way in which the gifted seem to be fundamentally different from their peers is in attitudes, since they tend to be more persistent, curious, precise, motivated, rigorous and interested in mathematics than other children, who are, by and large, relatively passive in classroom mathematics. However, the passivity of the majority can be thought to arise from their experience of mathematics lessons in which children are only expected to understand what is explained to them, or through practice to master a reasonable number of the skills that have been demonstrated to them. When the classroom is changed, with different kinds of activities and different expectations from the teachers, many more children become active and enthusiastic (Fielker 1997; Piggott 2004) – suggesting that attitudes are not reliable signs of giftedness. Indeed, as Watson (2001) has shown, with the appropriate teaching, even children of supposed lower ability can be found to look for relationships, generalize and show flexibility in thinking – that is, can manifest the qualities and skills associated with giftedness. The difference may be that the gifted show these qualities *despite* teaching and, critically, show them in relation to more advanced mathematical ideas.

4 What are their needs?

Needs are most poignant (and most easily specified) when there are observable consequences of not meeting them, and to that extent the need not to be bored can seem to be a paramount need that the gifted and talented have – and it is common for provision for the gifted and talented to be a kind of

entertainment, in which a succession of novel tasks and activities are provided that seem designed to ensure that they are never bored again. Even when
provision has other purposes, however, the gifted do need a stimulating
environment, where there is always more to turn to. When needs are less
demonstrative, they are harder to specify, and it is often left at the general level
of gifted children needing more stretch and challenge, or needing a broad
mathematical provision that helps in realizing their potential.

One way to become more specific about needs is to talk in terms of
opportunities to develop those aspects of experience that are characteristic of
giftedness. For example, there is extensive reference to problem solving in
how the gifted are described, so more opportunity for problem solving would
seem a candidate to be a specific need. Similarly, one can recognize in gifted
children the ability to handle mathematics that is advanced for their age, so it
can be argued that there is a need for the most able to be exposed to more
advanced mathematics.

One can also refer to the different mathematical processes that gifted
children manifest – which can be listed for example by elaborating on the basis
of professional experience the traits identified by Krutetskii (1976). Gifted
primary age children are, relatively speaking, noticeably more:

- systematic;
- conceptually clear;
- inclined to explore and investigate rather than just accept what
  is given;
- able to connect different areas of mathematics (not just deal with
  mathematics in compartments);
- able to relate mathematics to reality (and vice versa);
- able to tolerate uncertainty;
- strong in their mathematical reasoning;
- aware of their own thinking (meta-cognition);
- able to explain or justify their thinking;
- autonomous in their decision making;
- insightful about underlying mathematical structures;
- able to create an approach to fit the circumstances;
- fluent in mathematical skills (such as calculation);
- persistent in carrying through to completion;
- flexible in approach;
- able to generalize from given examples and make conjectures about
  relationships.

It can then be argued that children who are gifted in mathematics need to be
given opportunities to practise and develop each of these aspects of mathematical experience: to be given tasks in which they can be (or have to be) system-

atic; to be given more advanced explanations, so that they can further develop their conceptual clarity; to be allowed to explore and investigate rather than just expected to complete closed exercises; and so on.

5 How do we cater for their needs?

Whether the teaching provision to meet their needs is attempted in a withdrawal group or through in-class work, the mathematics experience offered to the children who are gifted in mathematics is very varied, the sharpest difference being between 'acceleration' and 'enrichment'.

Acceleration and enrichment

The issue of acceleration versus enrichment is a key one to the question of how to meet the needs of the children who are gifted in mathematics. Acceleration means moving the identified children on to the next set of work, as they learn what is provided, in effect giving them (progressively) work that is usually given to older pupils. Acceleration challenges children in a direct way, by giving them mathematics to learn that is usually considered too advanced for children of that age. Through acceleration it is not unknown for gifted children at the primary school to be doing GCSE mathematics – but more often it is just work that is a few years 'ahead'.

Enrichment challenges gifted children in another way, by giving them work that has more 'depth' or 'breadth' than usual provision, perhaps using more demanding examples, setting problems, representing familiar mathematics in an unusual way, doing mathematics that crosses different areas of familiar content, or exploring corners of mathematics that there is usually not time for (see Ollerton, Chapter 6). Enrichment is focused more on realizing the potential of gifted children to be advanced for their age in terms of mathematical processes. In terms of mathematical content, enrichment activities are usually at the same level as those activities being completed by other children of that age.

Acceleration or enrichment – which is better?

Any review of mathematics educators' views, whether taken from their writings or in person, would find an overwhelming majority supporting enrichment over acceleration. Fielker (1997: 9) for example writes: 'They do not learn more about mathematics this way. What they do is merely learn the same mathematics sooner.' Yet, acceleration remains the preferred approach in many schools, and some of the primary teachers in the study of Koshy et al. (2009) are reported to have adopted that approach. What are the apparent advantages and disadvantages of each?

The benefits of acceleration
- Children are readily stretched – you can always find material that is at the leading edge of what they can do.
- Resources are readily available (for example, the texts used by older students).
- Children can have a good sense of progress.
- Children enhance their self-esteem through success and being ahead.

In terms of meeting the needs of children who are gifted in mathematics, acceleration does give a form of stretch and challenge and can be said to help in realizing children's potential (especially if that is viewed in terms of measured achievements). Acceleration also certainly exposes children to more advanced mathematics, as well as getting some opportunities for concepts to be clarified and to practise and develop fluency.

The risks of acceleration
- If the textbooks for older students are used (which is the most convenient way to accelerate) the work can be too formal for the children, but creating more suitable material is very time consuming.
- If students just learn the new mathematics in the way in which it is taught to older students, which is mostly through learning procedures and practising, a narrow understanding of mathematics is allowed to persevere.
- If students are always moving on to the next thing, they remain dependent on teaching, and may lose interest in mathematics.
- Being good at mathematics becomes what mathematics means. In so far as mathematics contributes to children's sense of identity, it tends to be only in terms of success.
- The higher-level mathematics can be unfamiliar to the teacher, who either has to learn it or pass responsibility for teaching over to a book.
- Once acceleration has been started, students will have done next year's syllabus before they get to it, reducing the options for the next teacher.
- Responding to different degrees of giftedness by different amounts of acceleration would lead to an individualized programme for every child who is ahead, which is not sustainable, but flattening out the acceleration could lead to unfulfilled potential.

In terms of needs, acceleration seems to be limited in its capacity to be broad and stimulating, or to offer opportunities for genuine problem solving, including the chance to operate systematically, apply reasoning, be autonomous, generalize, and so on.

The risks of enrichment
- Because it is broadening and deepening the content of the ordinary curriculum, gifted children in an enrichment programme may not acquire a sense of progress in mathematics, or a feeling for the cumulative nature of the subject.
- If the enrichment programme is interesting, students may lose the ability to learn through practice, undermining their fluency in 'basic' skills.
- Enrichment activities can also challenge the teacher's own mathematical understanding, and the source books rarely give adequate support.
- Children may not show what they are capable of in the national assessments.

In terms of needs, enrichment seems to threaten the realization of potential (viewed as achievement), and limit children's exposure to more advanced mathematics.

The benefits of enrichment
- The activities are interesting.
- The deeper understanding of mathematics that results is a better foundation for subsequent learning.
- Children develop a realistic sense of self in mathematics, related to interest as much as success.
- Children engage with and enjoy mathematics as a subject in which reasoning is important.

In terms of needs, enrichment can offer a stimulating environment with plenty of stretch and challenge, and can help in realizing children's potential when that is viewed in terms of mathematical process. Enrichment also gives opportunities for children to be systematic, to receive conceptual explanations, to explore and investigate, and so on.

Koshy et al. (2009: 222) report that in their study of primary aged children, in which both acceleration and enrichment approaches were used, the enrichment activities were preferable: 'pupils responded, in most cases, to open-ended investigational tasks with greater motivation than they did to mathematical exercises and tasks selected from mathematics text books designed for older age groups'. And yet there are benefits to acceleration that are not replicated by enrichment. Is it possible to have both?

Acceleration **through** *enrichment – how to have both*
When acceleration is done through the commonly shallow activities of textbooks, it can be too fast, in the sense of moving children on to higher and

higher levels where all that is learned is what to do, creating dependency on exposition by others. This risks replicating the potentially alienating experience that exists for many students in the normal progression of the curriculum.

An alternative is to address more advanced mathematics in the context of enrichment activities. Often children make choices in tasks that extend them into new curriculum areas (for example 'numbers that add to 10' into fractions). This can be encouraged by the use of open-ended enrichment tasks, since: 'if motivated by an investigative task, children tended to seek knowledge and skills required from higher levels on the mathematics curriculum without being prompted to do so' (Koshy et al. 2009: 222).

By exploiting this, enrichment tasks can involve a kind of acceleration as well. As Koshy (2003) reports, when students are involved in complex in-depth exploratory mathematical activity, they often learn more advanced mathematical concepts from a higher level in the curriculum, either because the higher-level concepts are implicit in the students' own structuring of the mathematical objects in the activity, or because they find they need higher-level mathematics to do what they are attempting to do.

Can enrichment activities be used to meet specific needs?

Gifted children benefit from enrichment activities as opportunities to develop mathematics process skills. Considering such tasks in relation to the processes they require is also outlining the opportunities they contain, and therefore the needs they might meet. For example, the following task can be an opportunity to be systematic (in trying out different options if the first attempt is not successful) and in persistence.

Add brackets to this number sentence to make it correct.
$$5 + 5 \times 5 + 5 \div 5 + 5 - 5 = 5$$

Similarly, the next short activity involves meta-cognition, flexibility and the ability to explain or justify one's thinking.

Explain in words how to decide what two numbers are, if you know both their highest common factor and their lowest common multiple.

These connections make it possible to design a programme for gifted children that can address their specific needs in terms of mathematical process skills, by offering enrichment activities selected because they contain the appropriate opportunities.

Making these connections is not difficult to do, and almost all published enrichment activities can serve these process-oriented specific needs of children who are gifted in mathematics, because they all involve processes that are relatively advanced for children of that age. Extension activity ideas suitable for the primary school can be found in books (Fielker 1997; QCA 2005) and on the Internet (for example, http://nrich.maths.org/public/; http://www.shodor.org/interactivate/activities/) (both accessed March 2010). They can also be invented fairly readily by the teacher, since, as Fielker (1997) shows, enrichment activities can be close to everyday activities – for example:

- inverting a familiar problem – if a cuboid has a volume of 60 cubic units, what might its dimensions be;
- asking not for a single solution, but how many solutions there are – how many different parallelograms can be made from the seven tangram pieces (Fielker 1997);
- asking 'what if' – the diagonals of a regular hexagon divide the shape into six triangles, but what if the hexagon is not regular;
- asking for an explanation or justification of a familiar fact – why is the sum of two odd numbers always an even number, but the product of two odd numbers always an odd number?
- using one fact to find others – what follows from the fact that $24 \times 11 = 264$? (for example, $24 \times 22 = 528$).

Conclusion – the challenge to the teacher

There are no easy answers to the question of the best way to meet the needs of the children in the primary school who are gifted and talented in mathematics. Identification of the group, characterizing their needs, deciding whether to operate wholly within the class or to have some withdrawal group activity, deciding whether to take an acceleration or an enrichment approach, are all complex and controversial matters, with little consensus about them in the profession.

There is, therefore, little doubt that catering for the needs of the gifted and talented in mathematics is not easy for primary teachers, and it is particularly challenging for those teachers who are not comfortable with mathematics. For example, teachers can sometimes find themselves stretched by the demands of the enrichment approach, which requires flexibility in their own mathematical thinking and reasoning in order to keep up with what the children are doing. Handling the emotions of children who are facing mathematical challenges they cannot easily solve is also demanding, especially when the teacher is having to deal with their own feelings about the challenge of the problem. As a result, less confident teachers may be tempted to approach the issue by using the acceleration approach, just because there is a textbook to use that takes over some of the teaching. However, the awkward questions are still asked by children, who still look to the teacher to be an authority. Because of this, teaching mathematics to the gifted and talented often requires teachers to develop their own mathematics subject knowledge, and to cultivate their enthusiasm for mathematics.

On the other hand, working with the gifted does have the benefit that they can and do work independently for a good deal of the time; are often pleased to be asked to work something out for themselves rather than always turning to the teacher for an answer (especially helpful when the teacher is not sure of what the answer is); and respond well to discussion contexts to compare different solutions to a problem and discuss which one is best. As a result, the gifted and talented generate a lot of new knowledge themselves, with the teacher looking on (and often learning from it). And the enthusiasm of these children for mathematics is infectious.

References

DCSF (Department for Children, Schools and Families) (2009) Gifted and Talented section of the Standards site. http://www.nationalstrategies.standards.dcsf. gov.uk/giftedandtalented/ (accessed March 2010).

Ericsson, K.A., Roring, R.W. and Nandagopal, K. (2007) Giftedness and evidence for reproducibly superior performance: an account based on the expert performance framework, *High Ability Studies*, 18(1): 3–56.

Fielker, D. (1997) *Extending Mathematical Ability through Interactive Whole Class Teaching*. London: Hodder and Stoughton.

Freeman, J. (1998) *Educating the Very Able: Current International Research*. Norwich: HMSO/Ofsted.

Koshy, V. (2003) Nurturing mathematical promise, in I. Thompson (ed.) *Enhancing Primary Mathematics Teaching*. Maidenhead: Open University Press.

Koshy, V., Ernest, P. and Casey, R. (2009) Mathematically gifted and talented learners: theory and practice, *International Journal of Mathematical Education in Science and Technology*, 40(2): 213–28.

Krutetskii, V.A. (1976) *The Psychology of Mathematical Abilities in Schoolchildren*. Chicago, IL: University of Chicago Press.

Piggott, J. (2004) Developing a framework for mathematics enrichment. Paper presented at the 10th International Congress on Mathematical Education, Copenhagen, Denmark, 4–11 July. (Conference proceedings TSG 18, session 6.)

Qualification and Curriculum Authority (QCA) (2005) *Mathsinsight²*. London: NFER-Nelson.

Shore, B.M. and Kanevsky, L.S. (1993) Thinking processes: being and becoming gifted, in K.A. Heller, F.J. Monks and A.H. Passow (eds) *International Handbook of Research and Development of Giftedness and Talent*. Oxford: Pergamon Press.

Steiner, H.H. and Carr, M. (2003) Cognitive development in gifted children: towards a more precise understanding of emerging differences in intelligence, *Educational Psychology Review*, 15(3): 215–46.

Threlfall, J. and Hargreaves, M. (2008) The problem-solving methods of mathematically gifted and older average-attaining students, *High Ability Studies*, 19(1): 83–98.

Watson, A. (2001) Low attainers exhibiting higher-order mathematical thinking, *Support for Learning*, 16(4): 179–83.

Index

Related books from Open University Press

Purchase from www.openup.co.uk or order through your local bookseller

Primary Mathematics
TEACHING FOR UNDERSTANDING

Patrick Barmby, Lynn Bilsborough, Dr. Tony Harries and Steve Higgins

> One feature of this book that sets it apart from others is the care that is taken to clarify the authors' interpretation of the phrase 'teaching for understanding'. Each component of this interpretation – connections, representations, reasoning, communication and misconceptions – is then successfully incorporated as a theme in the subsequent chapters that develop important mathematical topics.
>
> Ian Thompson, Visiting Professor at Edge Hill University and Northumbria University, UK

This important book aims to support and develop teachers' understanding of the key primary mathematics topics. It takes an innovative approach by defining exactly what is meant by 'understanding' and uses this model to examine and explain various mathematical topics.

The authors emphasize the importance of the different representations that can be used for mathematical concepts and inform the reasoning process. By focusing on understanding, the book also draws attention to common misconceptions that teachers may encounter in the classroom.

Key features:

- Specific focus on 'understanding' to offer new insights in to how to teach the topics
- Case studies to demonstrate how to communicate mathematical topics in the classroom
- End of chapter questions to stimulate discussion

The authors integrate research and theory throughout, to highlight core issues. This theoretical background is also linked directly to classroom practice and informs suggestions for how topics can be communicated in the classroom. This offers valuable guidance to trainee teachers on how to teach the topics and presents experienced teachers with the opportunity to develop their subject and pedagogical knowledge.

Contents
Introduction – Using Numbers – Addition and Subtraction – Multiplying and dividing numbers – Fractions – Decimals – Representing patterns of numbers – Understanding Shapes – Measurement – Data handling – Problem Solving – References

2009   232pp
978–0–335–22926–0 (Paperback)   978–0–335–22925–3 (Hardback)

CHILDREN'S MATHEMATICS 4–15
LEARNING FROM ERRORS AND MISCONCEPTIONS

Julie Ryan and Julian Williams

The mistakes children make in mathematics are usually not just 'mistakes' – they are often intelligent generalizations from previous learning. Following several decades of academic study of such mistakes, the phrase 'errors and misconceptions' has recently entered the vocabulary of mathematics teacher education and has become prominent in the curriculum for initial teacher education.

The popular view of children's errors and misconceptions is that they should be corrected as soon as possible. The authors contest this, perceiving them as potential windows into children's mathematics. Errors may diagnose significant ways of thinking and stages in learning that highlight important opportunities for new learning.

This book uses extensive, original data from the authors' own research on children's performance, errors and misconceptions across the mathematics curriculum. It progressively develops concepts for teachers to use in organizing their understanding and knowledge of children's mathematics, offers practical guidance for classroom teaching and concludes with theoretical accounts of learning and teaching.

Children's Mathematics 4–15 is a groundbreaking book, which transforms research on diagnostic errors into knowledge for teaching, teacher education and research on teaching. It is essential reading for teachers, students on undergraduate teacher training courses and graduate and PGCE mathematics teacher trainees, as well as teacher educators and researchers.

Contents
Acknowledgements – Introduction – Learning from errors and misconceptions – Children's mathematical discussions – Developing number – Shape, space and measurement – From number to algebra – Data-handling, graphicacy, probability and statistics – Pre-service teachers' mathematics subject matter knowledge – Learning and teaching mathematics: towards a theory of pedagogy – Appendix 1: Common errors and misconceptions – Appendix 2: Discussion prompt sheets – Glossary – References – Index.

2007   264pp
978–0–335–22042–7 (Paperback)   978–0–335–22043–4 (Hardback)

ICT AND PRIMARY MATHEMATICS

Jenni Way and Toni Beardon

Current digital technologies have the potential to enhance primary children's mathematical learning. Calculators and computers can be used as tools in mathematics to perform routine processes or to explore mathematical ideas.

Graphic and programmable calculators and computers with open–ended software can also immerse children in exciting, creative and productive learning environments. The internet allows children to venture into the enormous world of mathematics beyond the classroom.

This book provides teachers with insights into how other teachers and researchers have discovered ways to create powerful learning experiences for children. Each chapter helps the reader to understand why certain teaching approaches with technology are more effective than others, as well as providing many practical ideas for activities and projects for children with various ability levels and learning styles.

Contents
Digital technologies + mathematics education = powerful learning environments – It's not calculators but how they're used . . . – Spreadsheets with everything – Learning technologies, learning styles and learning mathematics – Teaching the computer – Expanding horizons: the potential of the Internet to enhance learning – Classroom technologies as tools not toys: a teacher's perspective on making it work in the classroom – ICT as a tool for learning – where are we going? – Index

2003   184pp
978–0–335– 21030–5 (Paperback)   978–0–335– 21031–2 (Hardback)